The Quest for Mea

The Quest for Meaning

Narratives of Teaching, Learning and the Arts

Mary Beattie (Author/Editor)
University of Toronto/Ontario Institute for Studies in Education, Canada

SENSE PUBLISHERS
ROTTERDAM/BOSTON/TAIPEI

A C.I.P. record for this book is available from the Library of Congress.

ISBN 978-94-6091-035-7 (paperback)
ISBN 978-94-6091-036-4 (hardback)
ISBN 978-94-6091-037-1 (e-book)

Published by: Sense Publishers,
P.O. Box 21858, 3001 AW
Rotterdam, The Netherlands
http://www.sensepublishers.com

Printed on acid-free paper

'The Angel that presided o'er my birth'

The Angel that presided o'er my birth
Said, "Little creature, form'd of Joy and Mirth,
"Go love without the help of any Thing on Earth."
-William Blake

DEDICATION

This book is for J.D.B., my husband and my anam cara.

ACKNOWLEDGEMENTS: A WORD OF THANKS

This book has been two decades in the making. Along the way, I have received encouragement, support and inspiration from many wonderful students, colleagues and research participants in Canada and the United States, Australia and Iceland, and in the United Kingdom and Europe. My ideas have been stimulated and nourished by all the conversations and discussions, and by the work we have done together.

I am especially grateful to my former students whose work is presented throughout the chapters of the book. I owe a deep debt of gratitude to these individuals who have collaborated with me tirelessly through the various drafts, and who have consistently shown the depth of their scholarship and soulfulness, and their commitment to the book. It is their narratives that make the book sing. I want to express a special thanks to those who also provided thoughtful responses to the drafts of my chapters from their valuable perspectives as writers, scholars and former participants in my classes. In addition, I want to thank Nancy Dawe, Laura Hegge and Robert Lompart for permission to include their work in my chapters. I want to express my deep gratitude to Winifred Hunsburger and Bob Phillips. In addition to these individuals' other contributions to the book, Winifred also co-ordinated the references, and Bob created the original artwork on the front cover.

My understandings of the connections between the arts, education, and research are continually expanded in the context of my relationships with colleagues, friends, and my current research participants, who inspire and support my ongoing explorations. I wish to express my deep gratitude to my long-time friend, Art Young for the many conversations about literature, poetry and music we have had since we first met as Masters students of English Literature. I also want to thank Art for his invaluable professional editing and proofreading expertise. I owe much gratitude to my sister, Geraldine East who loves the arts as much as I do, and who has stimulated my thinking throughout the years. Also, to Annie Blampied, Sheila Cook, Diana Cooper, Christine Crombie, Dorothy Cameron, Virginia Dawson, Nancy Desjardins, Darrell Dobson, Thomas Fleming, Laura Hegge, Lesley Holland, David Hunt, Hafdis Ingvarsdottir, Lilja Jonsdottir, Robert London, Tom Malloy, Joan Medina, Carol Munro, Philip Thatcher, Brenda Tvrdy, Lee Willingham, and Alan Wilson, I say a heartfelt thank you.

I am grateful to Peter de Liefde and the people at Sense Publishers for providing the valuable support to make this book a reality, and for their innovative approach to academic publishing. I would also like to express my sincere gratitude to Tom Barone, University of Arizona; Helen Christenson, University of Regina, Robyn Cusworth, University of Sydney, and Jack Miller, University of Toronto/Ontario Institute for Studies in Education, who agreed to read the final manuscript and to write a response.

ACKNOWLEDGEMENTS: A WORD OF THANKS

My husband Jim has provided support for this book in his usual generous, thoughtful and loving way. He dealt with the challenges of preparing the final manuscript, and shared my enthusiasm for the book since its inception. His contributions infuse every page.

Mary Beattie
University of Toronto/Ontario Institute for Studies in Education,
Toronto, Canada.
June, 2009.

TABLE OF CONTENTS

ACKNOWLEDGEMENTS: A WORD OF THANKS ix

Part One: Choosing a Story to Live By: Connecting the Past, Present and Future of Our Lives

Prologue: *Mary Beattie* 3

Chapter 1: The Ongoing Quest for Meaning: Only Connect: *Mary Beattie* 11

Chapter 2: A Narrative, Arts-Based Pedagogy: Connecting the Personal, Professional and Scholarly: *Mary Beattie* 29

Part Two: The Dialogue with the Self: Connecting Insight and Imagination

Chapter 3: Beginning with Myself: The Power of Music: A Reflection, Renewal and Transformation by Michelle Pereira: *Michelle Pereira* 75

Chapter 4: Dancing through Life, One Story at a Time: *Melanie Markin*..93

Chapter 5: The Power of Stories: Tracing the Creative Thread and Healing the Self Whole: *Carly Stasko* 107

Chapter 6: Being Seen: *Bob Phillips* 119

Part Three: The Dialogue with Others: Hearing New Voices, Perspectives and Interpretations

Chapter 7: Between the Laments and the Lullabies*: Angélique Davies* 137

Chapter 8: Autobiography as Genesis: Linking the Student, Writer and Teacher in us all: *Carol Lipszyc* 149

Chapter 9: One Lens: The Role of the Arts: Beginning with Myself: *Catherine Dowling*..161

Chapter 10: Learning from my Experiences: The Role of the Arts: *Masayuki Hachiya* 173

Part Four: The Dialogue Between the Dialogues: Creating a New Narrative through Interaction and Integration

Chapter 11: A Recursive Path: *Winifred Hunsburger* 187

Chapter 12: The Artful Body: A Narrative of an Embodied Relationship with the Arts: *Rae Johnson*..............................199

Chapter 13: Voices: *Benjamin Bolden*..215

Chapter 14: Hearing My Voice While Listening to the Choir: *Carole Richardson*..233

Author Biographies 251

Epilogue: *Mary Beattie* 257

Appendix 1 259

Appendix 2 261

References 265

PART ONE: CHOOSING A STORY TO LIVE BY: CONNECTING THE PAST, PRESENT AND FUTURE OF OUR LIVES

Prologue: *Mary Beattie*

- Chapter 1: The Ongoing Quest for Meaning: Only Connect: *Mary Beattie*
- Chapter 2: A Narrative, Arts-Based Pedagogy: Connecting the Personal, Professional and Scholarly: *Mary Beattie*

MARY BEATTIE

PROLOGUE

I am a part of all that I have met;
Yet all experience is an arch wherethrough,
Gleams that untravelled world whose margin fades
Forever and forever when I move.
(Tennyson, 1972, *Ulysses, p. 645)*

This book is both an ending and a beginning: an ending in that it makes significant connections between my lifelong interests in the arts and education ; a beginning in that it provides an account of a pedagogy which is focussed on helping students to gain awareness of how their lives have been created in the past, on choosing how they will be influenced and conditioned in the present, and on creating more connected, integrated, meaningful narratives for their future lives. It is also focussed on helping students to learn about narrative, arts-based approaches to research. In this approach to pedagogy, students are encouraged to take full advantage of the learning relationships and collaborative learning community which are an integral part of this approach. They explore the meanings which they ascribe to their lived experiences, examine the stories which they are living out in their lives, and create new narratives for their future lives.

As a child growing up in a small village in the west of Ireland in the 50's, I loved the stories, the music and the songs that surrounded me in my everyday life. This early love affair led me to further studies in literature and music, a career in teaching and in narrative, arts-based research. The origins of this book lie in my explorations of the extent to which this early love of stories and the arts has shaped my ways of knowing and being. It is also grounded in my efforts to make better connections between the arts and education, and to use the transformative and uniting power of the arts to develop a collaborative pedagogy for graduate and undergraduate education.

The interconnected experiences, dialogues and assignments of a narrative, arts-based pedagogy provide students with a unique framework for inquiry, for the creation and re-creation of knowledge and for the creation of new narratives. This relational and collaborative approach to pedagogy is grounded in the understanding that one of our most human characteristics is that we are story-telling, meaning-seeking beings, who make sense of our experiences through narrative ways of thinking. Through inquiry, dialogue and interaction, we engage in the exploration of the stories that have formed us, in the stories beneath the surface of those stories, and learn to create and re-create new narratives for our lives. This process of

M. Beattie (Author/Ed.), The Quest for Meaning: Narratives of Teaching, Learning and the Arts, 3–9.

creating and recreating our identities is one of continuous exploration, and of reconstructing and re-forming the existing patterns of our lives into new configurations in the light of new insights, understandings and of the ever-changing circumstances around us.

One way or another, in our personal and professional lives and in our educational contexts, we all live by the stories we have inherited from our families, societies, and cultures, and those other stories that consciously or unconsciously, we have picked up along the way. These stories have made us who we are. They are what we use to interpret and understand our experiences, and to imagine and plan our future lives. As we live our daily lives, we make decisions and choices by interpreting them in the context of the past we have experienced and the future we imagine. When we explore the stories that have formed us, we learn how they have shaped our ways of thinking, and our ways of knowing and being. We also learn that we can choose the stories we live out in our lives, we can be the authors of our own destinies, and can create future narratives which will enable us to lead more connected, integrated and meaningful lives. When we change the stories by which we live, we can change our lives.

Approaches to graduate and undergraduate education do not often acknowledge the centrality of stories, of creativity and imagination, or the importance of helping students to make meaningful connections between the personal, professional and scholarly aspects of their lives. In a narrative, arts-based approach to pedagogy, the importance of these is acknowledged and fostered through inquiry, dialogue, interaction and integration. In Chapter Two, *A Narrative, Arts-Based Pedagogy: Making Connections Between the Personal, Professional and Scholarly,* I provide an account of this pedagogy in the context of a particular course in graduate education, *Research and Inquiry in the Arts,* which I have taught for over a decade at the University of Toronto/Ontario Institute for Studies in Education (OISE). Within this inquiry-based approach to learning, students learn to think narratively, to explore the meanings they ascribe to their lived experiences, and to conduct narrative, arts-based research. As they do so, they gain new insights into how their understandings have been created through the dialogues they have with themselves, and within relationships with others where "lives meet lives", and in which they:

> ...interact and inform one another, influencing and changing one another in the process as the energies of each are harnessed in the service of the other, and new possibilities, relations and forms are created. (Beattie, 1995a, p.143)

Students develop an appreciation for how the solitary, collaborative and integrative processes of the dialogues which are an integral aspect of this pedagogy enable them to:

> ...tell stories of their lived experiences, past and present, and to learn to tell and re-tell, enact and re-enact the stories through which each individual is made and re-made, told and re-told. (Eisner, in Beattie, 1995a, p. ix)

They conduct self directed narrative inquiries into the meaning of the stories that formed them, into their learning experiences in the arts, and explore the ways in which the various art forms have been a source of inspiration, clarity and meaning-making in their lives. Within the framework provided by the three kinds of dialogue of the course—the dialogue with the self, the dialogue with others, and the dialogue between the dialogues—students explore the central concerns that give their lives unity and purpose, and create and recreate not only their knowledge and understandings, but also create and re-create themselves. As they gain new insights into the ways in which the different forms of thinking they have experienced through the arts have allowed them to create different forms of meaning, they also begin to appreciate the distinctive ways in which the arts have enabled them to think, feel, see, and imagine new ways of knowing and being. When they gain fuller understandings of how the stories they are living out in their lives have been shaped and conditioned by their prior experiences, this enables them to better understand how they can create new narratives for their future lives in which they can live in more connected, integrated and meaningful ways. Drawing on an expanded conception of "interacting narratives" which also encompasses "the literary, aesthetic, ecological, and secular-spiritual forms which individuals choose for their influencing and conditioning effects" (Beattie, 2001-ongoing), students learn how to take increased ownership of their learning, and to plan and direct the course of their development as whole human beings. They learn to:

> Create contexts for contemplation and creativity in their lives, for the creation and re-creation of new knowledge, and for the continuous creation and re-creation of the self. (Beattie, 2001-ongoing)

It is only when students take full ownership for their learning that they bring themselves wholeheartedly to the inquiry process, to the reconstruction of what they know, and to the creation of the stories for their future lives. It is only when they bring their imaginations, intuition, and creativity as well as their intellects to the real questions of their lives, that they discover the joys and satisfactions as well as the challenges of making new and more meaningful connections between the personal, professional and scholarly aspects of those lives. When they bring the whole of their humanity (including the awareness of their distinctive ways of knowing) to their scholarly work and future research, students learn that they have choices in how they can represent their meanings, and can do so in ways that are personally satisfying, and which also have the potential to provide others with experiences in which to deepen their understandings and to construct new meanings.

Throughout the chapters of the book, the various authors provide accounts of their unique inquiries and quests for coherence, connectedness, and meaning in their lives. Their narratives show the extent to which the creation of a personally meaningful life is a distinctly individual process which is grounded in each individual's past, and in his or her imagined future. Written in their own distinctive language and voices, the narratives show the ways in which the solitary and collaborative dialogues have provided a framework for exploring the complexities of their learning in the context of graduate education, for addressing some of the significant questions in their lives, and for making new connections between the personal, professional and scholarly aspects of their lives. They also show how a pedagogy which acknowledges the centrality of stories, and recognizes the interconnectedness of all aspects of their humanity, has helped them to come to new understandings of themselves, and of the professional practices, and research methods and forms which will foster new kinds of meaning-making, and new ways of living and being for themselves and others.

The narratives are grouped according to how the different kinds of dialogue which are an integral aspect of a narrative and arts-based pedagogy, have provided a framework in which these authors have come to understand their processes of learning, unlearning and re-learning, and of where they have come from, what they care about, and of what they might become. In each of the sections of the book, the narratives show how the solitary, collaborative and interactive frameworks provided by the dialogues have created contexts for contemplation and reflection, for the interaction of narratives, and for integration, synthesis, and creation. They also illustrate how they have enabled these learners to determine what is significant and meaningful in their lives, to explore the influence of the past, present and imagined future on their interpretation of current realities and events, and to work on the reconciliation of opposites and on the discordant qualities of their lives. In their own voices and language, the authors of these narratives describe their meaning-making processes and the development of their truths and understandings in ways that are not possible in the expository prose of traditional research reports. In doing so, they provide us with insights into the values and impulses that animate their lives, and which illuminate the unique ways in which each individual has engaged in inquiry and in the creation of a new narrative for his or her future life. As a result, their narratives deepen our comprehension, and they advance our understandings.

The Origins of the Book

The book began over two decades ago in a strongly felt desire to create a pedagogy for graduate and undergraduate education where students would willingly engage in their own self directed inquiries, in collaborative relationships, in dialogue, and in making increasingly more significant connections between the various aspects of their lives. This desire now finds fruition in the chapter entitled, *A Narrative, Arts-Based Pedagogy; Making Connections between the Personal, Professional and Scholarly.* The chapter began with the informal documentation of my ongoing efforts to create this kind of pedagogy by making more significant connections between education and the arts, and by designing a range of activities and assignments which would focus on the development of the whole person. I kept track of my efforts through reflective writing, and in the description and interpretation of the difficulties as well as the successes of creating the kinds of relationships and dialogues where students would document the details of interacting with their own inner lives, their interactions with each other, and the integration of their understandings in a written narrative. My understandings developed through my intermittent but unremitting attempts to draw my emergent understandings together into a coherent whole. The chapter as it appears now has gone through numerous cycles of writing and rewriting over the years. As it began to take shape, I realized that I needed to dig deeper by exploring the stories beneath the surface of the stories in a chapter which would precede it. In the later stages of the writing of these two chapters, I invited the other authors in the book to respond to them, and to give me feedback from their unique perspectives as writer/readers, and also as former students of the course I was writing about.

The original versions of the narratives in the book were written in the context of a narrative and arts-based approach to pedagogy which I have described here as it is enacted in the context of one of the graduate courses I teach, *Research and Inquiry in the Arts.* As the idea for the book took hold, I made a note of those narratives written in the context of this course, where an individual's quest for meaning was also concerned with a quest for quality in narrative, arts-based research. Over the years, I invited the authors of these narratives to collaborate with me in the additional cycles of writing, responding, and rewriting necessary to produce the narratives for this book. This work also included writing a new introduction, the addition of an afterword, and the elimination of the review of the literature and the methodology sections of the original narratives that had been written for the course. Some authors chose to represent their original narratives in entirely new ways, and others stayed close to the format of the original versions they wrote in the course. The process of writing the chapters gave these authors the opportunity to reflect back on the cycles of their inquiry and on the importance of writing and rewriting as part of that inquiry. The collaborative relationships we had established in the context of the course allowed us to carry on from where we had left off, sometimes many years earlier, to journey together again, and to acknowledge once more:

> ...the ambiguity of journeying backwards in order to move forwards, and to know that all our beginnings hold within them the seeds of their endings, which in themselves hold the seeds of new beginnings. (Beattie, 1995a, p. 1)

I have included the questions which guided the various cycles of our individual inquiries, and the writing and rewriting of all the narratives in the book, in Appendix 1. The components of the course and the core readings are outlined in Appendix 2.

The Purpose of the Book: Connecting Teaching, Learning, and the Arts.

The importance of literature, stories, poetry, music, art and creativity in our lives has long been recognized by philosophers, poets and novelists who have told us that we can create the kinds of stories for our current and future lives that allow us to be and become the persons we want to be. Oscar Wilde once explained, that "the important thing about art is not what you get out of it, but what you become because of it", D. H. Lawrence said, "It is the way our sympathy flows and recoils that directs the flow of our lives", and the German poet, Goethe, tells us that "we are shaped and fashioned by what we love."

The Irish poet, Seamus Heaney (1988) explains it this way:

> Here is the great paradox of poetry and the imaginative arts in general. Faced with the brutality of the historical onslaught, they are practically useless. Yet they verify our singularity, they strike and stake out the ore of self which lies at the base of every individuated life. In one sense the efficacy of poetry is nil—no lyric has ever stopped a tank. In another sense, it is unlimited. It is like the writing in sand in the face of which accusers and accused are left speechless and renewed......Poetry, like the writing is arbitrary and marks time in every possible sense of that phrase........Poetry is more a threshold than a path, one constantly approached and constantly departed from, at which reader and writer undergo in their different ways the experience of being at the same time summoned and released. (Heaney, 1988, p. 107/108)

In today's world, contemporary neuroscientists working with the concept of brain plasticity, explain that we can change the structure of our brains and can also choose the ways in which we want to be changed and transformed, by the strategic choice of our activities, experiences, thoughts and interactions. (Doidge, 2007). These neuroscientists also tell us that the brain changes its very structure with each different activity it performs, and that it perfects its circuits so that it is better suited to the task at hand. Therefore, the choices we make in our personal, professional and scholarly lives cannot be underestimated, as these choices affect not only the structure and function of our brains, but the development of our skills, sensibilities, ways of knowing and being, and our development as whole human beings.

> The idea that the brain can change its own structure and function through thought and activity is, I believe, the most important alteration in our view of the brain since we first sketched out its basic anatomy and the workings of its basic component, the neuron. Like all revolutions this one will have profound effects...The neuroplastic revolution has implications for, among other things, our understanding of how love, sex, grief, relationships, learning, addictions, culture, technology, and psychotherapies change our brains. All of the humanities, social sciences, and physical sciences, insofar as they deal with human nature, are affected, as are all forms of training. All of these disciplines will have to come to terms with the fact of the self-changing brain and with the realization that the architecture of the brain differs from one person to the next and that it changes in the course of our individual lives. (Doidge, 2007, p. xx)

The creation of this book has been a labour of love in many ways. It has enabled me to confer order on my thoughts about a pedagogy which I believe can help learners to develop their voices, to recognize that they have choices regarding how they think and in what they do, and to take ownership and authority for the creation of narratives for their future lives where they can live with increased integrity, congruence and authenticity. I have struggled with the difficulties of doing this with each new group of students, and the stories of the failed attempts and disappointments would provide the material for another book. I have also struggled with describing this way of being in a teaching-learning relationship, and especially the ways of creating a collaborative relationship with each student, and a learning community where students learn from and with each other as well as from and with me. The difficulties linger, as it is almost impossible to describe these ways of being present in relationships with students, and of creating a community where all individuals can be present to each other. In the presence of a teacher and colleagues who are successfully present as co-researchers and soul friends, students will feel the warmth and care in every action and word that will allow them to be themselves without artifice, to show themselves as they really are, to be vulnerable and unafraid, and to open themselves to all the opportunities to learn, unlearn and re-learn through the interaction of their narratives.

In the processes of writing and rewriting the narratives for the book, the collaborative relationships I had with these students were re-established from where we had left them in the context of the formal education setting. As a teacher, I found it both encouraging and inspiring to see how the initial inquiry in which these students had engaged in the context of the course, and the habits of reflection, interpretation and continuous meaning-making they had learned in their graduate studies programme, had stayed with them. I also found it inspiring to see how the subsequent cycles of writing, feedback and rewriting for the book chapters had helped them to reconstruct their visions, and to adapt, redefine and respond to the changing circumstances of their lives in personally meaningful and satisfying ways. These processes allowed me to see with greater confidence how this approach to pedagogy provides educators in graduate and undergraduate programmes with ways to engage their own students in these kinds of experiences, interactions, and assignments in their own educational settings, to improvise and play with them, and to adapt them according to their own unique situations.

This book is one that I would have found valuable as a new professor in education, and as a graduate and undergraduate student who has always needed stories to understand the complexities, the wonders and the mysteries of life, of learning and teaching, and of learning to do research. My hope is that the different voices you hear throughout the book, will encourage you to fall in love with your own questions, and to engage in your own quest for meaning with imagination, courage and creativity. Your search for greater clarity, cohesiveness and integration will involve you in changes in your knowledge and understandings, and in the inevitable movement towards the ever shifting horizons of a destination that is undefined and only gradually emergent. I hope that you will find inspiration, hope and support in our attempts to compose lives that are personally meaningful to us, and which describe our attempts to refocus, redefine and to improvise as our circumstances have changed. I hope that you will create a narrative for your future life which in the words of the poet Seamus Heaney, will make your 'hopes and history rhyme'.

MARY BEATTIE

1. THE ONGOING QUEST FOR MEANING: ONLY CONNECT

SOUL TIME

Sometime in your lifetime
take a walk along a sandy shore
when the waves are high
and the tide is rolling in.

As the sea tries to claim you,
let your blood pulse to the ocean beat.

Let it take you down
into the warm
and waiting arms
of your lonely, welcoming soul.

(M. B. 2009)

In this chapter, I tell the stories that lie under the surface of the story of the development of a narrative, arts-based orientation to pedagogy. In this approach to pedagogy, it is important that we all tell and re-tell the stories of ourselves, and acknowledge that each telling is a temporal one which will be re-told in the light of new insights and understandings. For teachers and students alike, this process of creating a life is an ongoing, creative, never-ending quest, where we make new connections through dialogue with ourselves and others, and through the processes of integration and re-creation, where we continually transform what we know, and transform ourselves.

I have outlined the principal features of this pedagogy before I journey back through the cycles of stories which show how it has been developed through my own ongoing inquiry and quest for meaning. I believe that this approach to pedagogy is distinctive in that it provides students with a unique framework for inquiry, for receiving feedback from a variety of others, and for integrating what they know in the creation of a narrative. It also provides students with a range of experiences and relationships within which they learn to come to research narratively, to conduct self-study research, and to do narrative, arts-based research with others. This narrative, arts-based pedagogy has five distinctive features:

M. Beattie (Author/Ed.), The Quest for Meaning: Narratives of Teaching, Learning and the Arts, 11–28.

- It is grounded in inquiry, dialogue, self-study research and the writing of an educational narrative, through which students not only create and re-create what they know, but also create and re-create themselves.
- Collaborative relationships and a supportive learning community are vitally important aspects to this approach to learning and teaching.
- Teachers and students are committed to staying connected to the source of their creativity, intuition and inspiration as well as to their intellectual lives.
- The interconnectedness of the past, present and future of individuals' lives is recognized, as is the interconnectedness of all aspects of their being—intellectual, social, physical, emotional, aesthetic, moral, spiritual.
- Education is understood as the process of becoming more human and of making increasingly more sophisticated meanings and connections—between all aspects of the self, between self and others, between the personal, professional and scholarly dimensions of one's life, between self and society, and between the self and the universe.

Staying Close to the Source of Creativity and Inspiration

As I was writing the chapter on this narrative, arts-based approach to pedagogy for this book, I was invited to give a talk to a group of educators on this orientation to teaching and learning in graduate and undergraduate education. I wanted to begin my talk with a statement about how important it is for teachers at all levels of education to be connected to the source of their creativity and imaginations as well as to their intellectual lives, and to be involved in the ongoing development of all aspects of themselves as human beings. In doing so, I was keen to emphasize how critical it is for teachers to be engaged in ongoing inquiry, to be connected to what they love, to appreciate and value the questions that emerge in their personal and professional lives, and to do in their own lives what they expect and hope that students will do in theirs. I wanted to show how strongly I believe that for teachers and students alike, staying close to our creativity and imagination allows us to plumb the depths of our experience, enables us to stay in touch with the desires that animate and move us, and helps us to continually find our way home to ourselves. In preparation for this talk, I wrote an early version of the lines at the beginning of this chapter and I began by reading these lines aloud.

Reading the rough and unfinished draft of the poem to the group allowed me to introduce my talk about a pedagogy which is centrally focused on helping students to explore the landscape of their inner lives, to make connections between the inner and external dimensions of their lives, and to create more meaningful, connected stories for their future lives. I explained that it had come about as a result of the quiet observation of my inner feelings and images, and my persistence in staying connected to the source of my creativity—my spirit, soul, energy, or what Bernard Shaw calls my 'life force'. As the words and lines began to cohere, I felt as if I had managed to get a firm hold on the lifeline that connects me to that place inside where images and feelings are alive and vibrant. The joy of having made something stayed with me all week, and I felt that I had brought some of my inner music out into the external world. Continuing to play with the lines, I was able to remember the rhythm of the waves in my blood, recall the sensual quality of the solitary time I had experienced, and inhabit the wonderful feeling of coming home to myself. It was several weeks later that I became more fully aware of the connection between the image of the ocean and the landscape of the inner life, both with their unfathomable depths, allurements and fears, and to recognize my attraction to the capacity of both to engulf and overwhelm and also to energize, delight and inspire.

I explained to the group that in a narrative and arts-based approach to pedagogy, continuous inquiry and a creative engagement with life is as relevant and necessary for teachers as it is for students. Imagination and creativity are essential to the ongoing development of our abilities to create images of the possible that help us to see the actual in new ways, and to create something beyond it. The development of our powers of observation, interpretation and meaning-making, and the strengthening of the bonds between the senses, the imagination, intuition and intellect, are important aspects of developing ourselves as whole human beings. Through continuous inquiry and a strong connection to the source of our creativity, we can engage in the explorations that take us into the past that still flows all around us, and in making connections between this living past, and the new ideas, new impressions, and new experiences which we have in the present. These processes allow us to acknowledge our uniqueness as whole human beings, and the interconnectedness of our intellects, emotions, morals, creativity, values, purposes and passions. For teachers and for students, the acknowledgement of all these aspects of our humanity in our learning communities allows us to keep our individual questions and preoccupations, our hopes and our dreams, vibrant and alive. It allows us to recognize them as valuable and integral aspects of our learning and teaching, of our personal, professional and scholarly selves, and of the processes of constructing and re-constructing the narratives for our future lives.

Connecting Education and the Arts: Exploring our Stories

> Literature is the domain where story belongs. In good literature a story is always working on several levels at once; it holds within it a suggestiveness of the other stories that it is not; it has an irony and ambivalence about its own identity and posture and immunizes itself against take-over by any definitive reading or interpretation. From this perspective, it seems that much of what passes for story in contemporary spirituality and psychology is more reminiscent of tabloid pastiche than real story. Even the pre-literate tradition of oral culture had complex tapestries of story that left the most subtle openings into the resonance fields of myth and mystery.
>
> A human life is the most complex narrative of all; it has many layers of events which embrace outside behaviour and actions, the inner stream of the mind, the underworld of the unconscious, the soul, fantasy, dream and imagination. There is no account of a life which can ever mirror or tell all of this. When telling her story all a person can offer is a sample of this

> complexity. The best stories suggest what they cannot name or describe. They deepen respect for the mystery of events through which identity unfolds... Since story is now widely used in psychology, spirituality and sociology, a deepening of the mystery of what a story is would serve to illuminate the beauty that dwells deep in the individual life. As the Jewish writer and human rights campaigner Elie Wiesel once said, God created man because he loves stories. (O'Donohue, 2003, pp. 137/138).

In a narrative, arts-based approach to pedagogy, the centrality of story and the arts is acknowledged. Through literature, stories and the various art forms, I have been reminded continually of the wholeness of my life, the interconnectedness of its various aspects, and of my connectedness to others and to all things. The arts show us that in all human lives, in nature, in organic systems and in the universe, things are not fragmented and separate, but interconnected and whole. They show us that our intellects are not separate from our emotions, imaginations, our bodies, or our self-image; they enable us to see the corners of our lives illuminated, and to gain access to the conscious and unconscious aspects of our beings. The various art forms allow us to inhabit the feeling of what it is like to be human in any time and place, and to experience things vicariously. They provide us with experiences within which we gain insights into the secret places and the mysteries of the lives of others, as well as our own, to imagine lives that are different to ours, and to make connections to those who are different to ourselves. They teach us to acknowledge that our understandings, values, and ways of knowing and being are not universally shared, to respect and value others' ways of knowing and being, to feel compassion and empathy towards them, and to understand them as they understand themselves.

Through my experiences in the arts, I have learned that it is only when we bring our whole selves, our feelings as well as our thoughts, to our experiences and interactions, that we gain the insights, and make the kinds of meanings which enable us to develop as whole human beings. We need to engage all aspects of ourselves in our efforts to become more wide awake to the various dimensions of ourselves as human beings, to the processes of making connections between ourselves and others, and between ourselves and that which is larger than ourselves. Through my experiences in the arts, I have learned significant lessons about some of the ways in which to inhabit my life with greater integrity, coherence and authenticity, interact with others in ways where I can be true to them and also to myself, and in which I can make new understandings and meanings.

The desire to develop a pedagogy wth strong connections between the arts and education led me to design ways to use the arts to illustrate the ways in which all human beings lead storied lives, and in which they tell stories of those lives to themselves and to others. Narrative and arts-based research texts have helped me to illustrate the ways in which inquirers have studied their own and others' experience in systematic ways, and have written narratives that show the meanings that they ascribe to their experiences and their lives. Self study research and narrative inquiry allow us to study our own experience by exploring the stories we tell and the stories under the surface of those stories, to create new understandings and new knowledge with which to create stories for our future lives. They allow us to use arts-based ways of researching and writing our narratives, of integrating the meanings we ascribe to our lived experiences, and of furnishing ourselves with the various choices and possibilities available to us. Our stories are all we have as we deal with the complexities, the changing circumstances and surprising turns that our lives take; they are what we use to create new stories for our future lives. As Caroline Heilbrun (1988) explains:

> We can only retell and live by the stories we have read or heard. We live our lives through texts. They may be read, or chanted, or experienced electronically, or come to us, like the murmurings of our mothers, telling us what conventions demand. Whatever their form or medium, these stories have formed us: they are what we must use to make new fictions, new narratives. (Heilbrun, 1988, p. 37)

Our stories are all we have as we engage in our quests for meaning, and in the creation and re-creation of our identities throughout our lives. In her inspiring book, *Composing a Life*, Mary Catherine Bateson (1989) explains that the creation of an identity and a meaningful life is a process of ongoing self-invention. She explains:

> ...we are engaged in the day-to-day process of self-invention—not discovery, for what we search for does not exist until we find it—both the past and the future are raw material, shaped and reshaped by each individual. (p. 28)

Using a framework of comparative biography for her inquiry into the processes of creating a life, she studied individuals who have complex lives, and whose energies are not narrowly focussed towards a single goal, but are continually refocussed and redefined. Bateson explains that the real challenge in creating a personally meaningful life comes from the realization of multiple alternatives, and the invention of new models, given that there are no singular models, but only resources for creative imaginations. For Bateson, certainty is not a goal. She emphasizes the acceptance of ambiguity and uncertainty in the ongoing, unpredictable, shifting processes of learning, unlearning and relearning. She also suggests that the central task of education is to teach us to be creative, adaptable and open to possibilities, to meet difference and diversity with respect, and to allow them to challenge our assumptions, values and beliefs, so that we can adapt and modify what we know, and expand our visions of who we might become, and of what might be.

> Composing a life involves an openness to possibilities and the capacity to put them together in a way that is structurally sound...there is a possibility that the real winners in a rapidly changing world will be those who are open to alternatives and able to respect and value those who are different. These winners will not require that others become losers. The change goes on, and surely the central task of education today is not to confirm what is but to equip young men and women to meet that change and to imagine what could be, recognizing the value in what they encounter and steadily working it into their lives and visions. (Bateson, 1989, p. 74)

Bateson explains that the process of composing a life is a creative, improvisational, and life-long process which involves continuous adaptation, interaction and response, the identification of multiple alternatives, and of imagining new ways of doing and being.

> Because we are engaged in the day by day process of self-invention-not discovery, for what we search for does not exist until we find it—both the past and the future are raw material, shaped and reshaped by each individual....a continual reimagining of the future and reinterpretation of the past to give meaning to the present, remembering best those events that prefigured what followed, forgetting those that proved to have no meaning within the narrative.(pp. 28–30)

Exploring the Stories Beneath the Surface of the Stories: Creating the Connections

The story of how I came to be the teacher I am has its origins in my love of the arts, of learning, and of teaching. My work as a narrative, arts-based researcher and teacher has allowed me to acknowledge the importance of story, personal experience, creativity, context, historicity, interpretation, inquiry, interaction, integration, relationships, connectedness, temporality, and of the aesthetic and spiritual in everyday life. I have used narrative as a philosophical foundation in which to understand the meanings of the phenomena I have studied, and have also used narrative methods to represent the findings of the research. In this work, I have used story, poetry, accounts of practice, portraits, and dialogue to evoke individuals' lived experiences of learning, unlearning and re-learning, and to reveal the qualities and complexities of teaching and learning in ways that would not be possible with the expository prose of standard research reports.

My decision to become a teacher at the end of my schooling was quite straightforward, as I had wanted to be a teacher for as long as I could remember. When I envisioned myself as a teacher, I had an image of a life being spent among young people, where I would have literature and music in my daily life, and a lifetime of opportunities to help my students in the way that my best teachers had helped me. The exploration of the origins of that image and of the influences of story, music and literature in my life takes me back to a childhood in the west of Ireland, where I was surrounded by an everyday culture that was rich in music and story. I was also surrounded by a rugged limestone landscape of great natural beauty, and by the timeless stories of the people who had inhabited that place. My childhood's chief storytellers were my parents, teachers, relatives and friends, and my early abilities were nurtured at home and in school. I delighted in the great variety of stories around me—Celtic and Norse myths and legends, stories of Vikings and fairies, ghosts and saints, of ancient Greece and Rome, and especially the stories that were told in poems and songs. Literature was never mentioned, but stories and poetry and music were everywhere, in English, and in the Gaelic language which had its own distinctive beauty, music and rhythms.

Looking back I now understand that it was through my experiences with stories and song that I learned about myself and the world around me, and created an identity where I understood myself as a 'maker of things'. Stories, poetry and song had the power to transport me imaginatively to new worlds, to open up new realities and new possibilities, and to nurture my desire for a creative engagement with life. They allowed me to better understand my own experiences and those of others, by helping me to step outside my own perspective and ways of knowing, to feel what others feel, and to imagine what it is like to be someone other than myself. They also taught me to be attentive to the language, the patterns, and rhythms that provide insights into the hidden worlds of others, and to learn to listen and to hear.

At an early age, I learned the importance of paying close attention to sound and tone, of noticing the patterns and meanings above and below the words, and of listening into the spaces and the silences. I am consciously aware of continuing to keep my ear tuned to the different voices and sounds around me, to the various kinds of language we use across the disciplines, and to the development of my abilities to understand things from the perspectives of others.

I have come to recognize that it is from literature and the arts, and especially from Celtic myths and legends, that I inherited the idea of a world where all things are interconnected, and where divinity is in our everyday experiences and interactions if only we can be aware of it. In this way of understanding the meaning of things, there is no separation of the visible and the invisible, of the past, present and future, the mind, body and spirit, of humans from nature, or of a people from the places they inhabit, and the stories and the cultures they inherit. The Irish philosopher poet, John O'Donohue (1997) explained in his book, *Anam Cara*, that the wisdom of the Celtic imagination was neither discursive nor systematic. It did not contain the dualism which separates the visible from the invisible, time from eternity, the human from the divine. The Celts found divinity all around them, in the rivers and hills, the sea and sky and in every kind of animal. As O'Donohue explained, it is a vibrant legacy of mystical wisdom that is unique in the western world.

In my everyday life, I recognize the need to stay closely connected to nature, and to literature, poetry and music, knowing that they provide me with ways to stay connected to myself. They allow me to recognize that the power of life comes from within, as time after time my spirit plunges into the unknown and returns renewed. Tennyson explained this longing for a creative engagement with life to me when I first read his poem *Ulysses,* many years ago. He explained this felt longing for creativity and imagination as well as for intellectual engagement, as the desire to "drink life to the lees", to "roam with a hungry heart", and for the "grey spirit" of his soul:

> .....yearning in desire
> To follow knowledge like a sinking star,
> Beyond the utmost bound of human thought.
> (Tennyson, 1972, Ulysses, p. 645)

I have recognized the attraction of poetry, stories, music and literature for as long as I can remember. At an earlier time in my life I tried to explain the meaning of this attraction, the reason for its continuity in my life, and explained:

> My choice of literature to read is often connected to the questions I am dealing with in my life, and it is here that I not only find the answers to my questions, but where I also find the seeds of new questions. (Beattie, 1995a, p. 14)

The attraction continues for all these reasons, and also because my experiences in the arts help me to consider the story that I am living out in my life and work, and to ask the questions about what it serves, as well as what it is. The love of the quest and of the questions continues, and experiences in the arts allow me to explore the gaps between the story I tell, and the one I observe myself living, and in making the connections between these. They also provide me with the kinds of experiences that only an aesthetic and creative engagement with life can bring.

Education as a Process of Becoming More Human

It is from literature, poetry and the arts that I learned that education is a process of becoming more human. Through the arts I have been allowed to understand the learning, unlearning and re-learning experiences of others, to see inside their minds, and to see how they have given meaning to their experiences and their lives. I have been allowed to see how they have learned (or not learned) from their lived experiences, and have developed (or not developed) themselves as whole human beings. Through the various arts, I have gained insights into how individuals have addressed the significant questions of their lives, have adapted and modified what they know, learned to respond to unforeseen situations, and to imagine the persons they might become. They have shown me the details of individuals' quests for meaning, connectedness and coherence in their lives, how they make connections between the intellectual, emotional, social, moral, spiritual, physical and aesthetic aspects of themselves, and between the truths and authenticity of their inner worlds and their actions and work in the external world. As we read about the lives of others, we can choose to make connections to the mythology of our own lives, can ask questions about how we have created the persons that we are, and can consider the meaning of the stories we are enacting in our own daily lives. As we learn how we have been shaped and directed not only by the narratives we have inherited—cultural, gendered, familial, linguistic—we also learn that we can choose those narratives by which we wish to be influenced and conditioned, and can create the conditions for our own future learning and becoming.

The development of my understandings of teaching and learning over the years, owes much to the ongoing inspiration provided by literature and the arts, and to my efforts to make more significant connections between the arts and education in my life. "Only connect..." says E. M. Forester in the often quoted words which appear underneath the title of his novel, *Howard's End,* where he writes about the complexity of human affairs, and the values and impulses that animate peoples' lives. In the middle of the novel, the character Margaret Wilcox speaks these words and those that follow to her husband Henry. Refusing to acknowledge the disconnections between his espoused moral values and his actions, Henry is unconcerned with his double standards and hypocrisy. Margaret hopes that eventually he will recognize the consequences of living a fragmented life and will connect his thoughts and actions, and his mind, heart and soul. She says:

> It did not seem so difficult. She need trouble him with no gift of her own. She would only point out the salvation that was latent in his own soul, and in the soul of every man. "Only connect"! That was the whole of her sermon. Only connect the prose and the passion, and both will be exalted, and human love will be seen at its height. Live in fragments no longer. Only connect, and the beast and the monk, robbed of the isolation that is life to either, will die. Nor was the message difficult to give. It need not take the form of a good "talking". By quiet indications the bridge would be built and span their lives with beauty. (Forester, 1910, pp. 174–175)

For Forester, it is only when we make connections between the various dimensions of ourselves, that we can become more human. The characters in the novel who can make connections, provide the support for redemption for those characters who fail to develop their humanity because they lead fragmented lives, and lack guiding principles by which to live. Forester makes it clear that if only we could make the necessary connections in our lives, and between ideas, people, cultural groups, different value systems, different ways of knowing and being...the world would be a very different and better place in which to live for us all.

The process of becoming more human is a process of making new connections, and of creating and re-creating a more connected and integrated narrative for our future lives. These cyclical processes involve us in exploring what lies beneath the surface of the stories we enact in our lives, examining the disconnections as well as the connections, and in searching for ways in which to make better connections between the guiding principles which we espouse, and the personal actions and professional practices which we observe in our daily lives. However, it is only when we engage in the creative act of giving form to the disparate threads of our lives, and weave them into temporal, coherent and integrated wholes, that we transform what we know, and can use it to transform ourselves.

I draw here from writing first published in 2001 (Beattie, 2008/2001), to show how my efforts to draw the seeming disconnected threads of my life together helped me to make new connections between the arts and education in my life, and also helped me to use what I knew then to develop my understandings of a narrative, arts-based approach to pedagogy.

> Narrative ways of thinking, knowing and representing have been with us for a long time, and narrative as a form of communication has been with us since the beginning of language. Reaching back to a preliterate oral culture, our ancestors told stories to make sense of the mysteries of their worlds, to pass cultural knowledge on from one generation to another, and to communicate societal norms, values and shared understanding. Narrative is more than a

> communication system; it is a mode of thought. It is only in this century that narrative has been recognized and acknowledged as a way of thinking and as a fundamental way that individuals structure their experience and make sense of their worlds. As Bruner (1986) explains, we construct ourselves through narrative and make sense of our lives by telling stories of those lives. Bruner makes the distinction between paradigmatic modes of knowing and narrative modes of knowing. The former seeks truth; the latter seeks verisimilitude, or observations with the ring of truth. These modes of thinking are used for different purposes. They provide us with different ways of making sense of the world and of responding to the different phenomena in the world—animate and inanimate. Our stories provide us with the conceptual structures that enable us to store and retrieve knowledge we have created; they are the structures within which we understand our lives and plan our future lives....... Hardy (1968) describes narrative as a fundamental aspect of our lives and as a "primary act of mind." Rosen (1986) explains that the narrative forms we master provide us with genres for thinking with and ways to engage in the "eternal rummaging in the past" (p. 226), and in the "daring, scandalous rehearsal of scripts for the future" (p. 237) (Beattie, 1995a, p. 41).

Making Connections Between the Personal, the Professional and the Scholarly

In the context of my efforts to develop new practices which would support a narrative, arts-based pedagogy, I explored ways of creating an experiential activity at the beginning of each class which would make connections between the arts and education, between individuals' inner and external lives, and between all the members of the learning community. This led to the development of a practice I called a "centering activity", in which we engage in short, aesthetic, experiential activities at the beginning of each class in order to strengthen the mind, body, spirit connection, to connect us to the sources of our energy and creativity, and to the interconnected life of our senses, imaginations, intuitions, and intellects. The purpose of these activities is also to connect us to each other, to emphasize the connections to the larger cycles and patterns of our own and others' lives, and to those of the natural world and the universe. These shared experiences can help us to slow down, to temporarily separate ourselves from the busy, bustling worlds from which we come, and to prepare us for the work we will do together in the class.

When I meet each new group of students, I present the first of these activities and invite them to present the centering activities in the remaining classes. I explain to students that their choices can draw on their own backgrounds and expertise and on the richness and diverse ways of knowing of the arts and humanities. Their choices can serve to remind us that art is an experience, and that down through the ages, poets, philosophers and artists of all kinds have given us the kinds of aesthetic experiences that help us to deal with the great questions of existence, of what it means to learn, to explore, to fail, to succeed, and to develop as whole human beings. Their choices can range from the reading of a few lines of a poem like the one at the beginning of this chapter, listening to an excerpt from a short story or to a piece of music, contemplating a painting, artefact, or web-site, engaging in guided imagery, drawing, or in a yoga, dance or movement exercise. These activities should help us to become fully present and attentive to ourselves and to each other, and also help us to co-create a learning environment that is collegial and collaborative rather than competitive, and that is creative and supportive rather than critical and judgmental. They should also provide us with opportunities to breathe, to feel, and to make ourselves available for the various kinds of dialogue we will have during the class; the solitary and collaborative explorations of the patterns that connect in our lives, and the interactions that can lead us to new levels of connectedness, coherence and integration.

Some students are initially surprised at the nature of this invitation in an academic environment. However, they soon learn to value the opportunity to participate in these activities which allow us to establish relationships of trust, respect and shared expertise so that we can share ideas, perspectives, and understandings. They quickly come to recognize the benefits of a participatory environment that will provide them with support as they negotiate the uneven, circuitous and uncharted territory of exploring the inherited stories, myths and legends of their lives. Students also learn to appreciate the private spaces created by some of these activities, and to connect them to the solitary dialogues they have in the context of the reflective writing. Some of these students' voices can be heard later in this chapter, and throughout the following chapters as they tell from their own perspectives how the various solitary and collaborative activities and dialogues of the course have helped them to explore the ways in which they have learned, unlearned and re-learned throughout their lives.

As the course progresses, many students develop an appreciation for the extent to which the centering activities help to build the kinds of relationships and community that provide a context for dealing with the challenges of graduate studies, the complexities of real learning, and working at the edges of their understanding and meaning-making. They assist in the process of helping individuals to position their studies in graduate education within the larger context of their lives, and in using their inquiries to address questions such as, Who am I, Why am I here, What is it that defines my humanity, What is the purpose of my life, and What does it serve? These experiential, arts-based activities also help students to more fully understand the ways in which to establish deeper kinds of relationships with themselves and their colleagues, to explore the issues of identity, and the concept of a relational self where the self is given shape and meaning in the context of relations with others. They promote the creation of the close, supportive relationships between and among students and the teacher, which are critically important to enabling them to redefine their understandings of identity, and to create new understandings of identity as that which is formed not only in isolation, but also in relation with others and in social contexts through interacting narratives.

The centering activities and the relationships they foster provide students with a variety of opportunities for making new connections, and they provide practical ways of answering Dewey's (1938) call to recover the continuity of aesthetic experience with the normal processes of living, and of doing so in the context of graduate studies. In the words of the poet Goethe, “A person can find no better retreat from the world than art, and a person can find no stronger link with the world than art.”

Learning About Relationships: Wide Awake in the Kindergarten

Throughout my teaching career, I have learned that good teachers are centrally concerned with students’ learning because they have the learner’s interests at heart. I have also observed the extent to which good teacher-student relationships promote students’ ability to learn and grow. In my view, good teachers work to create the kinds of relationships and learning communities where students can make connections between their inner lives and their external actions, can establish relationships with their colleagues, significant texts and the teacher, and can learn to make meaningful connections between the personal, professional and scholarly aspects of their lives. Good teachers develop their pedagogical practices out of the desire to help students to identify their own purposes and passions, to help them to fall in love with their own questions, and to continually re-create what they know as they create and re-create new narratives for their future lives. Good teachers work to develop their abilities to stimulate students’ curiosity and creativity, their imaginations, intuitions, and intellects, and to awaken each individual to the possibilities of his or her own life.

This kind of teaching requires not only a deep understanding and passion for the subject matter, for developing a wide array of pedagogical strategies that will stimulate and inspire students’ learning, but also a deep understanding of students themselves, and of the ways they learn. It can never be understood as a set of skills, strategies or gimmicks, and it cannot be prescribed, translated into formulae or generalized. For teachers, it is crucially important to know who we are and why we are here, for as Parker Palmer (1998) explains: “We teach who we are” (p. 2). In this view, our professional development is connected to our commitment to the ongoing development of ourselves as whole human beings, to keeping our desires and purposes alive, and to the connections between this and our work with students. Here, professional learning is a life-long journey of self development, of developing the ability to be present in relationships with students, of creating contexts for authentic dialogue and interaction, and of developing the abilities to create learning communities where individuals re-form and transform their understandings and themselves.

> Good teachers possess a capacity for connectedness. They are able to weave a web of connections among themselves, their subjects and their students, so that students can learn to weave a world for themselves.......the connections made by teachers are not held in their methods but in their hearts—meaning “heart” in its true sense as the place where intellect and emotion and spirit will converge in the human self. (Palmer, 1988, p. 11)

As I have continued to dig under the surface of the pedagogical story that I tell and enact in my current life, I have searched for those significant experiences which have shaped my understandings of the meaning of good teaching, and which I use to interpret and judge my own teaching and that of others. One of my earliest memories of school provides me with an image of learning and teaching that tells me of important lessons that have stayed with me throughout my career as a teacher. The image is of a kindergarten class in a small rural school, which was home to four classes of children, and which I experienced as a joyful, friendly and stimulating place to be. The Junior Room as it was called, felt like a place where things that mattered took place among people who mattered. My favourite time of the school day was reading class. Here, my kindergarten group would move to the desks at the front of the room. Each of us would take a turn to sit by the open turf fire beside our teacher, Mrs. Loftus, and to read to her, while the rest of the group listened. In my memory, the classroom was filled with the warmth of her presence, with stories and songs, and with the rich smokey smell of the turf fire. I have a vivid memory of what it felt like to sit beside her, almost drowning in her soft brown eyes when I looked into them, as they were like deep and limitless pools of love and caring for children. I remember feeling the warmth of her presence beside me, the warmth of the fire on my back, and the way she gently helped me to say any new words that I hadn't seen before. I loved the stories, and I loved that I was able to say them out loud.

It was only after I had been teaching adolescents for a number of years that I came to realize the extent to which these early experiences influenced my understanding of learning and of good teaching. It was then that I began to recognize the origins of my desire to create a classroom like this, and to re-create the environment of connectedness, curiosity, trust, caring, and joy that I had felt in this place. I wanted my classroom to be filled with stories, music, literature, and the arts too, so that my students could benefit from them as I did. I wanted my students to have the stories that would help them to explore the questions that intrigued them and which would also help them to deal with the challenges, inconsistencies and mysteries of their adolescent lives.

As a teacher of English to secondary school students, I had all the students in my classes write their autobiographies at the end of a unit called, *Who Am I?* Students collected the data for this assignment by exploring the significant experiences in their lives, and by engaging their parents in conversations about their early childhood experiences that were beyond the reach of their memories. They shared all these stories, read the literature, poetry and stories of the unit that would help them to imagine lives other than their own, role-played these lives, and expanded their understandings of themselves through the writing of their autobiographies. Working to recreate the kind of learning community I had experienced myself, I also saw the value of students' participation in the content of the curriculum, and I encouraged them to bring their own songs, stories and poetry into the classroom. These students who came from such a rich array of cultures and societies, provided a wealth of opportunities for us all to access ideas from different worlds, and to imagine the new and varied possibilities available to us.

My later work was as a curriculum and staff development consultant with teachers in the same multicultural school board in the east side of Toronto, which is ascribed to be one the most multicultural cities in the world. In this work with teachers, we encouraged students to bring in to the classrooms, the stories from their diverse backgrounds, their unique cultures and histories. Hearing these stories had the effect of greatly expanding all our horizons;they helped us to understand each other, and to develop not only our self-knowledge, but our intercultural knowledge and understandings. In my collaborative research with one of these teachers, Anne, we created a unit on mythology that began with the myths and legends from the vast array of students' own countries and cultures. Many of these stories had been handed down orally, and students documented them through taped conversations with their grandparents, relatives and parents. In sharing these stories in the classroom setting, these students came to new understandings of each others' lives, heard the sounds and rhythms of the many languages they spoke other than English, and had their eyes opened to the rich cultural knowledge and heritages to which they had access. This work with Anne developed into the site of my doctoral research.

In this research, (Beattie, 1995a) and in the representation of its insights and understandings, I used a narrative and arts-based orientation to the collection of data, to the representation of the qualities and complexities of professional development, and of our co-created understandings and knowledge-making. I used story, poetry, dialogue and accounts of practice to evoke Anne's lived experience of change, the reconstruction of her professional knowledge, and her identity, and in the description of the details of classroom life. In this research, I also drew extensively on the work of another exemplary teacher, a teacher and researcher I encountered in the context of my graduate studies, (Hunt, 1987) and from whose writings and professional practice I learned so much about the "reflexivity, responsiveness, and reciprocality of a mutually adaptive interpersonal relationship" (Beattie, 1995a, p.121).

I had completed this doctoral research and thesis writing, and had been teaching for many years when I went to visit Mrs. Loftus, my kindergarten teacher, during one of my trips to Ireland to see family and friends. I told her about the influence of her teaching on my work as a teacher and researcher, and of my fond memories of life in the Junior Room. I also told her how we all knew how much she cared about us, as she had treated each one of us as if we were very special persons in her life, even when she met us in the village outside of school time. She talked about her love of teaching, and the happy memories she had of her long teaching career. I could see that she was visibly moved to hear me talk about her influences on my work, and to hear that her former pupils remembered her in this way. As I left she gave me a gift of a white Irish linen tablecloth that she said would remind me of her. Inside the package was a small card that I still keep beside me on my writing desk. On it she had written:

KILFENORA, JULY, 1989

Good luck, Good health
God bless you, and guide
you on your way.
May all your hopes come true.
....
With love and best wishes
from your former teacher in the Junior Room, Kilfenora.

Creating Relationships: The Teacher as Soul Friend

My understanding of the nature of a good teacher-student relationship developed through my ongoing reflections on my practice, interactions with colleagues and with texts, and in conversations with a wide range of colleagues and friends. It was also expanded and inspired by the work of John O'Donohue (1997), whose book, *Anam Cara,* brought the Gaelic term for friendship into our everyday language and thought. In Gaelic, *anam* means soul, and *cara* means friend. O'Donohue explains that the Celtic understanding of this kind of anam cara friendship was where you felt a sense of affection, of intimacy and of recognition. In the presence of your soul friend, you could be your real self without fear or artifice. Your soul friend would accept you as you are, and would always have your best interests at heart. With your soul friend you would feel a sense of belonging, a level of trust that would allow you to reveal the intimacies of your life, and feel the support you needed to be present to your own life, and to inhabit and enact it with clarity, honesty, and authenticity.

Reflecting on this in an educational context, I came to new understandings of how within these Celtic soul friend relationships, teachers and students could be present in each other's lives in ways that recognize the uniqueness of each individual's journey through life. As soul friends to each other, we can, through our presence and ways of being as well as in our actions and words, support and enrich each other's attempts to inquire into the meaning of things, to recognize and develop our unique attributes and capacities, and to find expression for them in the external world. I became increasingly aware of the extent to which these kinds of student-teacher relationships could affect students' abilities to learn, and I worked to enact this kind of relationship with my students in the graduate and teacher education settings, in spite of the difficulties of doing so.

In my doctoral research with Anne (Beattie, 1995a), I had explored the kinds of learning that can take place within close relationships of trust, respect and intimacy, where individuals collaborate to transform each other's understandings, and the stories they tell and enact. This understanding of relationships was expanded in the context of my current (Beattie, 2001–2007), and still ongoing research, when I came to new levels of recognition of the importance of the internal relationships that individuals have with themselves, as well as the relationships they have with external others. I came to a fuller appreciation of the significance of the solitary dialogues that individuals have with their inner selves, as well as the significance of the dialogues they have in relationships with others. These new insights gave me a strong desire to develop practices which would encourage students and research participants to explore the stories they tell and enact in their lives, and to recognize that they have choices in how they tell, retell, enact and re-enact those stories in their lives. This research explores the ways in which individuals with longstanding practices in the arts and in secular-spiritual practices, do this in their lives. These research participants use their chosen narratives (music, literature, visual art, mindfulness-meditation, nature...) to provide them with contemplative contexts in which to explore the landscapes of their inner lives, and to create the new narratives which enable them to achieve their inner purposes in the external world by working with and for others. Through the interaction of their chosen narratives and their life narratives, these educators create new connections between what they create internally, and what they enact in the external world. In the telling, re-telling, enacting and re-enacting of their stories, they transform what they know and can do, and continually transform themselves. (Beattie, 2001-2007)

Developing a Narrative, Arts-Based Pedagogy: Inquiry, Interaction and Integration

In the next chapter, I drawing on the specifics of one of the graduate courses I teach, *Research and Inquiry in the Arts*, to outline the ways in which I work to enact a narrative, arts-based approach to pedagogy. I explain how this approach enables students to explore the stories they are enacting in their lives, and to study the ways in which their consciousness and thought processes have been shaped by the stories they have inherited and by those other stories they have picked up along the way. In this class, students also focus on the significance of the arts in shaping their ways of knowing and being, in influencing their work in professional settings, and in directing their future scholarship as qualitative researchers. In the design of the course, I have found it useful to work with the juxtaposition of the image of myself as "maker" which I had in my early childhood —a music maker, a storyteller, a maker of my own meanings—and the image of the learner as consumer of knowledge, which I also encountered during my journey through other educational settings which emphasized a hierarchical and disembodied view of learning. Working with the tension between these oppositional views, I have explored ways to encourage students to think of themselves as embodied makers, to use their studies to create professional and scholarly lives that are intellectually stimulating and personally meaningful, and to create work that makes a contribution to knowledge, to society, and to their own development as human beings. My efforts are not always successful, and all students do not engage in the work of the course to the same extent. Over the years, I have learned to deal with the inevitable disappointments and frustrations which arise as opportunities for reflection and learning, and as a reminder to accept these unwelcome failures as a necessary part of my own quest for meaning.

This course is open to Masters and Doctoral level students, some of whom take it as the first of the eight or ten courses required for a Master of Arts or Master of Education degree. Others take it as the final course of an eight course requirement towards a Doctorate [PH.D or ED.D.] Most students taking the course choose it because they are intending to use some form of qualitative research methods for their graduate research, and others choose it because they intend to base their future research very solidly in narrative and arts-based philosophical perspectives and methodologies. All these students have unique dispositions, gifts and expertise, and it is understood that they interpret their learning experiences in graduate education in the context of their past lives and their hopes for their future destinies. Many have strong personal and/or professional backgrounds in the arts and have taught in one or more of the arts. Some of these students are practicing artists and some are teachers of the arts.

The course has a traditional structure of twelve meetings of three hours each, a package of required readings, two formal written assignments, and required class attendance and participation. Assessment is based on the two formal written assignments, an educational narrative and a qualitative research proposal, three oral presentations, and class participation. All the activities of the course are designed to provide students with opportunities to engage in the three kinds of interdependent dialogues that will aid them in the processes of inquiry, incubation, interaction and integration. The documentation of the details of these dialogues will help them to generate the materials for the two formal written assignments of the course in ways that are both scholarly and personally meaningful. The course passes through the following phases:

- Introduction to the course and to the principles of a narrative, arts-based, and holistic orientation to research and pedagogy.
- Introduction to the selected readings, overview of qualitative educational research, and of narrative, arts-based, and holistic approaches to teaching, learning and educational research.
- Explanation of the two formal written assignments of the course—an educational narrative, a research proposal for a qualitative study, and three oral presentations.
- Initiation of partnerships, small groups, and explanation of the importance of attentive listening, respectful constructive feedback, and each individual's role in the co-creation of collaborative relationships and a collaborative learning community.
- Introduction to examples of qualitative, narrative, arts-based, holistic, Masters and Doctoral theses, and explanation of the requirements of presenting one chosen example to the class, and of leading the follow-up discussion.
- Explanation of the processes of learning to do hands-on narrative research with colleagues: writing field notes, narrative interviewing, providing constructive feedback to oral presentations, providing oral and written feedback to the close-to-final drafts of the written assignments for the course.
- Ongoing discussion of qualitative, narrative, arts-based, holistic approaches to educational research through the readings, theses presentations, discussion of research proposals.

- Ongoing discussion of the kinds of knowledge created through the arts, and the connections between this and the personal, professional and scholarly in students' lives.
- Ongoing exploration of the links between the students' existing knowledge, skills and sensibilities, and the design of a qualitative, narrative, arts-based research proposal.
- Ongoing discussion of making increasingly significant connections between the personal, professional and scholarly in students' lives.

MARY BEATTIE

2. A NARRATIVE, ARTS-BASED PEDAGOGY: CONNECTING THE PERSONAL, PROFESSIONAL AND SCHOLARLY

COMING HOME

One time, I knew for sure
That I could find my way.
I saw six dolphins surfing through a wave
Heading towards me
Wetsuits glistening in the sun.

'Just cruising through', they said
To tell you that we have your number, and your name
Your state of longing and belonging
And the crazy dream of home.

(M.B. 2009)

This chapter is about a pedagogy that is centrally concerned with helping students to engage in their personal quests for meaning through the exploration of the stories in their lives, and on helping them to create new stories for their current and future lives. It is also focussed on providing them with hands-on experience in doing qualitative, narrative, arts-based research, and on preparing them for doing this kind of research with others. Based solidly in the principles of a narrative, arts-based orientation to research, this pedagogy draws on Dewey's (1938) conception of education as "the reconstruction of experience", and Bruner's (1986) explanation of narrative as a mode of thought. It is inspired by the work of Elliot Eisner (2002, 1991) who, in his groundbreaking book, *Arts and the Creation of Mind, (2002),* describes how various forms of thinking are evoked, developed and refined through the arts, and in which he makes persuasive arguments about the transformative power of art to change not only minds but also to change lives.

In this approach to pedagogy, collaborative relationships and a supportive learning community are vitally important aspects of a context where students recreate what they know, and recreate themselves through the processes of self-directed inquiry, dialogue, self-study research, and the writing of a narrative. This approach to teaching and learning is responsive to the uniqueness of individuals' lives, to difference and diversity, and to different ways of knowing. It is also grounded in the understanding that the ways in which learners perceive the realities

M. Beattie (Author/Ed.), The Quest for Meaning: Narratives of Teaching, Learning and the Arts, 29–71.

of their learning situations are grounded in the stories that have formed them, and that resonate in their beings. It is understood that it is these stories that they use to interpret their experiences, to create new meanings and understandings, and to create the stories for their current and future lives.

In this approach to teaching and learning, students learn to think narratively, and to use their inquiries, the dialogues, the oral presentations, and the writing of the narrative, to learn narrative ways of thinking, of interacting with others, and of meaning- making. The concepts of "interacting narratives" (Beattie, 1995a, 2001-ongoing), provide them with useful frameworks in which to explore the ways in which their lives have been created in the past, to choose how they will be influenced and conditioned in the present, and to create more connected, integrated, and meaningful stories for their future lives. As they learn to conduct narrative self-study research and to do narrative, arts-based research with others, they engage in:

- the search for patterns beneath the surface of events and actions,
- the search for the meanings that individuals ascribe to their experiences, from their own perspectives
- the attitude that acknowledges that events and people all have a history—a past, present and future
- the habits of mind which consider multiple possible interpretations of an event or experience from many different perspectives

The writing of the narrative is an important and integral part of students' inquiries and meaning-making. Through the processes of writing, receiving feedback, and rewriting, students identify the significant themes in their lives; work to reconcile opposites or discordant qualities, integrate the disparate aspects of themselves, and use what they know to create a narrative for their future lives. These processes allow them to identify their images and metaphors, to use them to access the language of their inner lives and to create meaning-making accounts of their life histories. By connecting to the past through their memories and feelings, and to the future through their imaginations, the cyclical processes of the writing provide them with opportunities to make significant new connections between them, and to be guided into new levels of consciousness. To create is to transform, and these processes of creating and re-creating their meanings can be transformative for the writer. The narratives, when they are well written and have aesthetic qualities, can allow others to imagine new possibilities and alternative ways of being and living, and they can also be transformative for the reader. When these narratives allow readers to enter the worlds they describe, to see what they see, understand as they do, and to expand their own knowledge and understandings, they provide opportunities for their authors to, (in Seamus Heaney's words) be here for good in both senses of the word.

In the development of this pedagogical approach, I have drawn support from Gadamer's (1975) expansion of the concept of interpretation beyond the meaning of the text to the meaning of the individual's life, of the world and one's place in it, and to the meaning of understanding itself. This work has also been valuable in helping students to understand the meaning of narrative ways of knowing and being, and of learning to enact them in their personal, professional and scholarly lives. It has helped me to model the kinds of responses and feedback to their work which will encourage them to explore the ways in which they have interpreted their experiences, to see that they have come to each interpretive event from somewhere, and to understand that we are all conditioned by the narratives we have encountered in our societies, cultures, and personal experiences. This work has also been valuable in helping me to explain that through their ongoing quests for meaning, and the process of creating a narrative for their lives, students can gain increased understandings and mastery over the composition of their lives, and can develop the adaptive, creative and improvisational abilities to continually create and re-create new narratives for their lives.

Falling in Love with the Quest: Engaging the Heart, the Spirit and the Mind

As each individual's learning journey is a unique, lifelong quest for meaning, the development of a love for the quest, for the questions themselves, and for making connections between the parts and the whole, is a major aspect of this approach to pedagogy. Students learn that it is only when they engage fully in their inquiries—with their hearts and spirits as well as their intellects— that what they learn will really matter to them in the context of their whole lives. They learn that this process will engage their imaginations, intuitions, emotions, and creativity, as well as their intellects. When they have feelings of exhaustion at the end of a class, it is because they have used all aspects of themselves in the processes of their learning—(the intellectual, social, moral, physical, spiritual, and aesthetic). As this orientation to learning is both participatory and interactive, all students are expected to focus not only on theier own learning, but also to collaborate in the co-creation of the environment where they can learn from and with each other, and in which each individual can draw on the rich body of existing knowledge that their colleagues bring to the setting.

The pedagogical practices of the course are designed to encourage students to draw on their experienced knowledge, and to use story, poetry, music, movement, metaphor, imagery and symbols to explore the stories by which they live, to capture the meanings of their experiences, and to create new stories for their future lives. They are also designed to teach them how to come to their inquiries narratively, to learn to present the results of their self-study research narratively, and to learn how to conduct narrative, arts-based, holistic research with their future research participants. The assignments are interconnected and designed to foster and support students' self-directed inquiries, the making of connections, and the integration of understandings.

In the first of these written assignments, students write narratives which provide an account of their self-study research. In the final assignment, they write a research proposal that outlines the components of a qualitative, narrative, arts-based inquiry with future research participants of their choosing. Within the research and writing partnerships they create with colleagues, students learn how to do this self-study research, and to conduct narrative, arts-based research with others which focus on the meanings which these individuals ascribe to the stories which they are living out in their lives, from their own unique perspectives.

Narrative Inquiry: The Study of Experience

We live storied lives. We make sense of our experiences by telling stories about our lives which serve to help us understand ourselves, and to communicate these understandings to others. In one way or another, we all try to make sense of our lived experiences by telling stories of them, and as we live our lives, we make our decisions and choices by interpreting them in the context of the past we have experienced and the future that we imagine. Therefore, as the philosopher MacIntyre (1984) explains:

> What is better or worse for X depends upon the character of that intelligible narrative which provides X's life with its unity. (p. 225)

Reminding us that we all use narrative in our daily lives, Barbara Hardy (1975) says that "in order to really live, we make up stories about ourselves and others, about the personal as well as the social past and future."

> We not only think in narrative, we also dream in narrative, daydream in narrative, remember, anticipate, hope, despair, believe, doubt, plan, revise, criticize, construct, gossip, learn, hate and love by narrative. (p. 5)

The philosophical concern with life as narrative involves the ongoing reflection on lived experience that allows individuals to identify what has significance and meaning to them personally, and of weaving those threads into the new and evolving story of their own becoming. Narrative inquiry provides us with a way to study experience, our own and that of others in systematic ways, to interpret and integrate our understandings, and to represent our meanings by writing narratives. In narrative self-study research, we study the meaning of our own experience, collect the data through the processes of inquiry, reflection, dialogue, story, and conversation, and engage in the systematic interpretation, integration and representation of the meanings through the writing and rewriting of our narratives. Through these processes, we identify those themes, experiential threads, patterns and narrative unities which run through our lived experiences, create new understandings of how they relate to our present and future directions, and weave them into new temporal wholes.

In a narrative approach to teaching, learning and research, it is understood that an individual's knowledge is embodied, and that it can be observed as is enacted in practical everyday situations. The process of creating and recreating knowledge is a process where something new is made, and this process of making changes not only what is known but also changes the knower. This view of knowledge is grounded in Polanyi's (1958) conception of knowledge as a personal knowledge in which the knower is inseparable from what is known, and it is always the achievement of persons. Here, individuals' actions and practices are understood as knowledge in action. This knowledge is held in personal and practical modes rather than in theoretical modes, it is subject to change, to reconstruction, and to progression; it is not fixed, immutable, objective and unchanging. Through reflection and inquiry, the knowledge held, and the meanings which individuals ascribe to their experiences and actions, can be explored and reconstructed. As they become increasingly aware of the nature and qualities of what they know, individuals can learn to use what they know to learn what they need to know, and can consciously plan the development of their personal, practical knowledge. As Polanyi explained:

> In the act of reflection we cause our personal wisdom and experience to interact with the objective realm of knowledge to produce personal knowledge which transcends the disjunctive between 'subjective' and 'objective'. (Polanyi, 1958, p. 300)

Drawing on Polanyi's work, and on the work of Johnson (1987) the concept of practical knowledge was developed in the work of Elbaz' (1983) where she described the content, orientation and structure of a teacher's practical knowledge defined in its own terms rather than in terms derived from theory. Elbaz developed the notion that practical knowledge is not just cognitive knowledge, content knowledge or structure knowledge, but that it arises, in Johnson's (1987) terms:

> out of our bodily experiences and provide[s] patterns that are meaningful to us and that influence our reasoning (p. 1)

In the context of their work in narrative inquiry, Connelly and Clandinin (1988) expanded on Elbaz' work and developed the concept of personal practical knowledge which they defined as an individual's:

> ..particular way of reconstructing the past and intentions for the future to deal with the exigencies of a present situation. (Connelly and Clandinin,1988, p. 25)

Thus, the process of doing narrative self-study research is a process of exploring our uniquely personalized ways of knowing as they are enacted in our actions, our practices, and in the stories we are living out in our daily lives. In doing this kind of research with others, collaborative relationships and shared interpretations and meaning-making are central aspects of the ways in which narrative researchers work with participants to study the meaning of these individuals' uniquely personalized concrete ways of knowing and being, from the individuals' own perspectives. These processes involve shared explorations, interpretations, and ongoing meaning-making prior to the documentation of the shared inquiry by the researcher. Research participants receive copies of transcribed interviews and are invited to discuss, clarify, and expand the interim meanings expressed there. They are also invited to comment on the interim narratives that researchers write, to collaborate in clarifying and furthering the interpretations and meaning-making, and in the co-creation of knowledge.

In narrative self-study research, we identify our own themes and look for the supporting evidence in the data we have collected, also noting the ways in which the themes overlap and intersect with each other, making connections between them and continually relating the parts to the whole. In doing this kind of qualitative research with others, this process of identifying the themes is a shared process which allows us to collaborate in structuring the analysis of the data, in the interpretation, and in the representation of its meanings. The process of identifying the significant themes in the data is outlined by Connelly and Clandinin (2000), and also by Eisner (1991) who explains:

> Themes are the dominant features of the situation or identity. In a sense, a theme is like a pervasive quality. Pervasive qualities tend to permeate and unify situations and objects...A qualitative study of a classroom, teacher or school can yield multiple themes. These themes are distillations of what has been encountered. In a sense they provide a summary of the essential features. They also provide clues or cues to the perceptions of other situations like the situation from which the themes were extracted. (Eisner, 1991, p. 104)

This process of identifying the major themes and the central concerns which give individuals' lives their unity and purpose, is supported by the concept of narrative unity which is defined by MacIntyre (1984) as:

> a concept of a self whose unity resides in the unity of a narrative which links birth to life to death as narrative [links]beginning to middle to end. (p. 205)

Building on MacIntyre's work, Connelly and Clandinin (1988) explain that in narrative inquiry research, narrative unity describes that:

> ... continuum within a person's experience [that] renders life experiences meaningful through the unity they achieve for the person...It is a meaning-giving account, an interpretation, of our history and, as such, provides us with a way of understanding our experiential knowledge. Within each of us there are a number of narrative unities, [they] emerge from our past, bring about certain practices in the present, and guide us towards certain practices in the future. (Connelly and Clandinin, 1988, p. 75)

The narratives we create for our lives are always temporal, and in narrative thinking, temporality is a central feature. All events are understood as having a past, a present (that we are experiencing), and an implied future. As our lives unfold, and circumstances change, the temporal meanings we have made must also change. The significance of an event or experience must change when it belongs to a different whole. Thus, when events in our lives take surprising turns, we must learn to see and understand the past in a different light, and to re-imagine the future that we have foreseen. In other words, when the future we imagined cannot be enacted as we had planned, we are also required to change the past from which it has come, and to weave these different parts into a new and always temporal whole. In this way, our identities are always under construction, and as human beings we are always works-in-progress and always in the process of becoming. Through the ongoing creation and recreation of our narratives we continually engage in this creative act of imagining who we can become, and of enacting this in the ways in which we live out our lives. When we do this, we keep coming home to ourselves.

One of the central aspects of an education is in enabling learners to develop the abilities to adapt, improvise, modify, create and re-create what they know and to create and re-create themselves on an ongoing basis. In this way, individuals enrich their abilities to assimilate new experience, to expand their ways of knowing and being, and to adapt to their ever-changing life situations. Polkinghorne (1988), in his influential book, *Narrative Knowing and the Human Sciences*, explained it in this way:

> We achieve our present identities and self concept through the use of narrative configurations, and make our existence into a whole by understanding it as an expression of a single unfolding and developing story. We are in the middle of our stories and cannot be sure how they will end; we constantly have to revise the plot as new events are added to our lives. Self, then, is neither a static thing nor a substance, but a configuring of personal events into a historical unity which includes not only what has been but also anticipation of what will be. (p. 150)

Making Connections Between the Personal, the Professional and the Scholarly

Approaches to graduate education, and to the education of future academics do not often include a focus on the personal, aesthetic, emotional, and spiritual dimensions of students' lives, or the exploration of the connections between their inner purposes, professional practices and future research. Graduate programmes do not acknowledge the centrality of stories in students' lives, and they can often be centered on the behaviourist identification of knowledge and skills which separate the knower from the known. In all graduate programmes, students undertake a range of learning experiences designed to help them to learn what they need to know in order to conduct a piece of original research. This includes:

- acquiring a good working knowledge of the existing literature in the field, and in related fields,
- determining what is already known about a subject and what needs to be known
- the identification and articulation of a research topic and research questions
- acquiring knowledge of the different research methodologies, and choosing a method that is appropriate to the research questions
- understanding the criteria for work that is high quality in the chosen field.
- developing a strong conceptual framework for the research
- making strong connections between the research questions, the theoretical framework, the chosen method, and other existing research studies

Students are required to create an interconnected research proposal for their future research where they chart a personal course through the existing literature, identify a significant research question to explore, create an appropriate conceptual framework, and determine a suitable methodology for the study they propose to undertake. In a narrative, arts-based pedagogy, students do all this in a context where it is acknowledged that the learning they do is not accomplished by disembodied intellects, but by people whose minds are connected to their bodies, their feelings, their hearts and their spirits. Here, students are encouraged to bring their personal purposes and passions to the research endeavour, and to create course assignments and research proposals that are scholarly, rigorous, and challenging, and also personally and socially meaningful. They are encouraged to use the activities and assignments of the course to make connections to the source of their creativity and inspiration, and between their work in learning about research, and the larger purposes and goals which animate their lives and which provide it with personal meaning.

In this approach, it is recognized that although students, like their teachers, live in a world where things are logical, rational, and technological, as human beings we also live in a world of the imagination. We need poetry, myth, metaphor, story, music, art and nature to nurture all aspects of ourselves. We knew this as children, and as adults, at certain levels of our consciousness, we all know that we need a balance between the rational and the intuitive, the intellectual and imaginative, the linear and strategic, and the literal and the metaphorical in our lives. Students are encouraged to acknowledge this and to use their educational experiences to nurture all aspects of their humanity, to reconnect to the wellsprings of their beings and to the life force that animates them. They are also encouraged to collaborate in the co-creation of pedagogical practices which will stimulate their own and others' curiosity, creativity, and imagination, and will draw on the rich body of personal and professional knowledge which they and their colleagues bring to the academic context. It is expected that as the course progresses, students will become increasingly more willing to share what they know with each other, to collaborate in the shared meaning-making which will allow them to do together what any one individual could not do alone, and to help each other to make connections between their personal purposes and their future research.

The principles of a narrative, arts-based approach to research provide the conceptual framework for this orientation to teaching and learning. Many students are appreciative of a pedagogical approach that takes them seriously enough to expect that they will want to understand the epistemological principles on which their educational experiences are based, and which help them to understand how the experiences and assignments of the course are grounded in a solid and well-established body of knowledge, to which they can contribute when they conduct their own research. Students learn that:

> The main claim for the use of narrative in educational research is that humans are storytelling organisms who, individually and socially, lead storied lives. Thus the study of narrative is the study of the ways humans experience the world. This general notion translates into the view that education is the construction and reconstruction of personal and social stories: teachers and learners are storytellers and characters in their own and others' stories. (Connelly and Clandinin, 1990, p. 2)

They also learn that narrative inquiry, arts-based research, and self-study research are now well established in the mainstream of educational research, and as the course progresses many students value the opportunities to conduct hands-on research, and to practice the processes of collecting, analysing, interpreting and representing data before they have to do this in the context of their thesis research with participants. The collaborative relationships and the supportive learning community of the course provide them with frameworks in which they receive constructive responses and feedback to their ideas, perspectives, and evolving understandings from a variety of others. This ongoing feedback can help them to adapt and modify their understandings and to expand their knowledge, ways of knowing and being.

Students learn to differentiate between paradigmatic and narrative ways of knowing, to understand that they are used for different purposes, provide us with different ways of making sense in the world, and of responding to the different phenomena in the world—animate and inanimate (Bruner 1986). They also learn to distinguish between different kinds of research, and to consider the range of possibilities available to them in their future research. As they come to new understandings of the ways in which they have learned what they know, they also begin to consider the ways in which knowledge has been defined, to explore the relationship between the knower and the known, and to redefine what counts as knowledge, and as research. As they do so, they come to more fully understand the processes involved in doing narrative, arts-based research, and to understand what it means to do this kind of collaborative research with others. As Polanyi explains:

> into every act of knowing, there enters a tacit and passionate contribution of the person knowing what is being known, and this coefficient is no mere imperfection, but a necessary component of all knowledge (p. 312)..[and]..In the act of reflection we cause our personal wisdom and experience to interact with the objective realm of knowledge to produce personal knowledge which transcends the disjunctive between 'subjective' and 'objective'. (Polanyi, 1958, p. 300)

As the course progresses, students learn to be present in their interactions with their colleagues and in the activities of the course, not only as graduate students but also as beginning narrative, arts-based researchers. They learn to practice narrative ways of knowing, to develop their listening skills, and to expand their existing understandings by listening to others who have different societal, gendered, cultural, and disciplinary ways of knowing from their own. As they develop their abilities to hear what is being expressed from the perspective of the speaker rather than from their own perspective, these students are preparing themselves for the work they will do when they interview each other for the course assignments and provide responses to each others' oral presentations. They are also developing their abilities to do narrative, arts-based research with their future research participants.

Narrative Inquiry, Arts-Based Research, and Holistic Education

The conceptual framework for this approach to pedagogy is solidly grounded in Dewey's (1934, 1938), philosophy of experience and of art as experience, of Bruner's (1986) conception of narrative as a mode of thought, and in the work of contemporary researchers such as Connelly and Clandinin (1988, 2000), Barone (1993, 2001), Bruner, (1986), Buber, (1965), Greene (1995), Gilligan, (1982) MacMurray, (1961), Miller, J. (2000, 2007), Miller, R. (1990/1997), McEwan and Egan, (1995), Noddings (2003), O'Donohue, (1997), Palmer, (1988), Polkinghorne (1988) Schon, (1987), Taylor, (1989), Van Maanen, (1997), Witherall & Noddings, (1991), and others. A pedagogy whose features are more artistic than scientific also draws on Elliot Eisner's (1976, 1991a, 1991b,2002,) pioneering work in qualitative research, which presents the view that scientific inquiry is one kind of research, that research is not a kind of science, and that research [and teaching] can be arts-based as well as science based. It also draws on Eisner's work in educational criticism, which was a forerunner of arts-based inquiry, and in which the educational critic perceives and appreciates the significant qualities of educational settings, events and materials and presents them through the expressive and evocative language of the art critic. This approach to pedagogy is also supported by the research of growing numbers of educational researchers, who within the past two decades, have taken up Eisner's call to explore approaches to research whose features are more artistic than scientific. It owes much to the narrative and arts-based movement in research that has taken place over the past three decades, for as Eisner (2000) explains:

> Perhaps the most significant development that has taken place in the American educational research community is the exploration of alternative assumptions about the nature of knowledge, the forms of legitimate inquiry, and the modes of representation that can be employed to display what has been learned. These developments are consistent with growth in pluralism of many kinds; cultural, gender, racial, epistemological and procedural. (Eisner, 2000, p. 252)

It was in the context of my graduate studies in English literature that I first encountered a theoretical approach to narrative. Later on in graduate studies in education, I discovered narrative inquiry research in the work of Michael Connelly and Jean Clandinin (1990, 2000) who were pioneers in this line of research in education. The rise of narrative inquiry in the field of educational research began with the work of the reconceptualist movement inspired by William Pinar, (1980, 1975), and Madeline Grumet (1987), which was preceded by the prominence of literary theory in the intellectual world, Hardy, (1968), Kermode, (1967), Ricoeur, (1984, 1985, 1988), Rosen, (1986), Scholes and Kellog, (1966). Narrative has long been regarded as an intellectual resource in the arts, and the origins and history of narrative inquiry can be traced back to Aristotle's *Poetics* and Augustine's *Confessions*. The use of narrative in fields other than literary theory and education is on the rise, and narrative and story are now well-established in a number of fields such as history, sociology, the philosophy of history, therapy, psychology, medicine and theology, as a way in which we make sense of our lives, and construct our meanings by telling and retelling, enacting and re-enacting the stories of those lives.

In the line of narrative research in education pioneered by Connelly and Clandinin (1988, 2000), I encountered a distinctive form of narrative inquiry where narrative is understood as both phenomenon and method. Here, I found a strong philosophical framework and research methodology for my own research over the past two decades, where I have also drawn extensively on Dewey's (1938) conception of experiential learning, Eisner's (1991a), and Barone and Eisner's (1988) principles of doing qualitative, aesthetic, arts-based research, Connelly and Clandinin's (1988) concept of personal practical knowledge, MacIntyre's (1981) concept of narrative unities, Gadamer's (1975) hermeneutic cycle, Polkinghorne's (1988) work on narrative ways of knowing and Carr's (1986) work on time, history and narrative.

The literature on holistic education, also contributes to the conceptual framework for this approach to pedagogy as it focusses on the importance of relationships, on the making of connections, and on the education of the whole person. (Miller, J. 2000, 2007; Miller, R. 1997/1990). The basic principles of holistic education are balance, inclusion and connection, which require a movement away from a fragmented approach to curriculum towards an approach that seeks to make connections at every level of learning by integrating the intellectual, intuitive, and imaginative, and by creating relationships among existing entities. As Miller, J. (2000) says:

> The focus of holistic education is on relationships: the relationship between linear thinking and intuition, the relationship between mind and body, the relationship among various domains of knowledge, the relationship between the individual and community, the relationship to the earth, and our relationship to our souls. (Miller, J. 2000, p. 13)

Miller (2000) also explains that the concept of inclusiveness in holistic education is concerned with enacting a transformational approach to teaching. This approach views the learner as a whole human being, and the person and the curriculum as connected. The concept of balance is based on the concepts of the Tao, of the yin/yang, and on the suggestion that at all levels of the universe there are complementary forces and energies which need to be recognized and nurtured in the classroom. Miller (2000) explains that traditional education has focused primarily on the yang energies such as rationality and individual competition, and has often neglected the intuitive, imaginative, interpersonal, relational and cooperative approaches to teaching and learning. In his inspiring book, *Educating for Wisdom and Compassion,* Miller, J. (2006) provides an overview of holistic education, and a valuable resource which provides practices by which we can break down the boundaries between ourselves and what we are contemplating, and can understand ourselves as whole human beings for whom the development of wisdom, compassion, care and love enables us to become more increasingly more human. In, *The Contemplative Practitioner,* Miller, J. (1994) explains how through contemplation, which is 'based on the notion of a deeply interconnected reality as described in subatomic physics and ecology [there is] an is an opportunity to restore a balance between the part and the whole'.(p. vii) He says:

> Simply put, reflection is still rooted in a dualistic view of reality in that there is a subject that reflects an object. If we stay with a dualistic view of reality, we ultimately end up with a fragmented and compartmentalized approach to life. Yes, there is a need for analysis and reflection, but there is also a need for synthesis and contemplation. Contemplation is characterized by a merging of the subject and object. As I contemplate a sunset or a flower, separateness disappears and for a moment I can become the object I contemplate. Duality disappears... It is through contemplation that we can see, or envision, the whole. (Miller, J, 1994, p. vii)

A narrative, arts-based approach to graduate and undergraduate pedagogy draws on the long-established humanistic traditions, where the quest for wholeness and meaning in individuals' lives has been documented in the work of poets, philosophers and artists, and in the interconnected ways of knowing and being that I encountered there, before I came in contact with them in the work of educational research. The need to educate the imagination and the feelings as well as the intellect at all levels of education, is not well understood, yet it is literature and the arts that enable us to imagine and picture situations other than our own, to learn to be empathetic, compassionate, and respectful towards others, and to adapt, improvise, and create our own lives, our societies and our global world. An education that neglects literature and the arts, neglects the richness and diversity of the ways that we have been shown the various dimensions of human existence and human awareness; the ways in which the myths and legends of the past influence our present actions, the interconnectedness of all aspects of ourselves as human beings, and our interconnectedness to all things in the universe. Dewey (1934) understood the profound importance of art and of aesthetic experiences in education, and in individuals' efforts to create lives which are authentic, which have integrity and are connected to that which is larger than ourselves.

> A work of art elicits and accentuates this quality of being a whole, and of belonging to the larger, all-inclusive whole which is the universe in which we all live. This fact, I think is the explanation of that feeling of exquisite intelligibility and clarity we have in the presence of an object that is experienced with aesthetic intensity. It explains also the religious feeling that accompanies intense aesthetic perception. We are, as it were, introduced into a world beyond this world which is nevertheless the deeper reality of the world in which we live in our ordinary experiences. We are carried out beyond ourselves to find ourselves. I can see no psychological ground for such properties of an experience save that, somehow, the work of art operates to deepen and raise to great clarity that sense of an enveloping undefined whole that accompanies every normal experience. This whole is then felt as an expansion of ourselves...Where egotism is not made the measure of reality and value, we are citizens of this vast world beyond ourselves, and any intense realization of its presence with and in us brings a peculiarly satisfying sense of unity in itself and of ourselves. (p. 195)

Writing in 1805, William Wordsworth explained it in the First Book of *The Prelude* when he says:

> Dust as we are, the immortal spirit grows
> Like harmony in music, there is a dark
> Inscrutable workmanship that reconciles
> Discordant elements, makes them cling together
> In one society. (Wordsworth, 1979, p. 47)

Doing Narrative, Arts-Based Research in Graduate and Undergraduate Classrooms.

Graduate and undergraduate faculty have a wealth of support for enacting a narrative, arts-based pedagogy in their classrooms, for engaging students in self-study, in helping them to write their educational narratives, and teaching them how to do this kind of research with others. Many contemporary researchers in the fields of narrative and arts-based research have written about the processes, criteria and qualitative features of these approaches to research. For example, in their book *Narrative Inquiry*, (2000), Jean Clandinin and Michael Connelly trace the origins of narrative inquiry in the social sciences, provide a wealth of examples, and a wide range of narrative methods. They outline the processes of doing narrative inquiry and the criteria for good narrative research and say:

> We wrote about good narrative as having an *explanatory, invitational quality*, as having *authenticity*, as having *adequacy and plausibility*. (p. 185)

In the field of self-study research, Bullough and Pinnegar (2001) provide a framework and a set of guidelines for those engaged in self-study research, and for determining the qualities of good research-based, autobiographical writing. These researchers draw their insights from literary conventions, and they present them in the article entitled, *Guidelines for Quality in Autobiographical forms of Self-Study Research.* The recent text, *Self-Study Research Methodologies for Teacher Education,* by Lassonde, Galman &Kosnik (2009) provides a range of research methodologies for doing self-study research, and further resources are provided by the chapters in *The International handbook of self-study of teaching and teacher education practices,* especially the chapter by La Bosky, (2004), *The methodology of self-study and its theoretical underpinnings*.

The major features of qualitative research that may be characterized as arts-based, are outlined in Barone and Eisner's (1988) article, *Arts-Based Educational Research.* Here, these authors explain that although aesthetic elements and design features can be present in all research, the more pronounced they are, the more the research is characterized as arts-based. They explain that the most significant of these features are identified as:

- the creation of a virtual reality
- the presence of ambiguity
- the use of expressive language

- the use of contextualized and vernacular language
- the promotion of empathy
- the personal signature of the researcher/writer
- the presence of aesthetic form.

.... (Barone and Eisner, 1988, p. 75–78).

In my own work I have mapped out the processes of exploring experience as lived and told stories, and of writing educational narratives in the book, *The Art of Learning to Teach; Creating Professional Narratives,* (Beattie, 2007/2001). Here, I guide the writer through the processes of reflecting on his or her own stories, the stories of others, and of reflecting, responding, and doing the work of self-study research, and of writing an educational narrative. Throughout the chapters, writers are provided with narratives written from students' perspectives, and guided through the cycles of reflecting on these and on their own past and current experiences, writing about them, responding to feedback from others, and of doing the necessary writing and rewriting to engage in the cyclical processes of their own narrative inquiries. I have also used narrative and arts-based inquiry in a number of other research situations to explore teacher development and educational change (Beattie, 1995a), learning to teach and becoming a teacher (Beattie, 2007/2001), exemplary secondary schooling (Beattie, 2004) and the aesthetic and spiritual dimensions of educators' knowledge (Beattie, 2001/2007).

In a journal article entitled, *New Prospects for teacher education: narrative ways of knowing teaching and learning*, (Beattie, 1995c), I described the ways in which new knowledge about teaching and teacher education has been created in the field of narrative studies, outlined the parameters of the field itself, its connections to other related studies in education, and the possibilities it provides for programmes in teacher education. I also provided the historical context of narrative studies in the field of teacher development by outlining the research on teacher cognition which preceded it, and showed the connections between narrative inquiry and narratology, literature, and the many other disciplines where narrative studies have a long and well-established history.

In narrative, self-study research and in narrative inquiry with others, the writing of a narrative in which the interpretations and meanings are woven into a coherent and integrated whole, is an important and integral part of the inquiry process, for as Maxine Greene (1995) says:

> Learning to write is a matter of learning to shatter the silences, of making meaning, of learning to learn. (p. 108)

The process of writing and rewriting the narrative involves the writer in the uncharted, cyclical and continually shifting processes of the quest for meaning, as each new meaning made changes the past from which it has come and the imagined future to which it is moving. Tom Barone (1993) explains it eloquently when he says:

> ...each student, like the rest of us, is a person in the midst of writing and rewriting her own life story. Each is comparable to an artist in the middle of a creative process that moves through a resolution that is not pre-formulated,

> but gradually emergent. The end of the story of each living human being is yet to be encountered. The uncertainty that accompanies this process of self-creation is, therefore, as the literary critic, Frank Kermode (1967) noted, the source of much human anxiety. This is the anxiety of the artist, the poet, the storyteller and the schoolchild, who has dared to begin a work of art (here her life) without a clear sense of how to bring it to a meaningful closure.
>
> (Barone, 1993, p. 240)

Developing Students' Voices through Dialogue and Interaction.

> This above all: to thine own self be true,
> And it must follow, as the night the day,
> Thou canst not then be false to any man.
> Farewell, my blessing season this in thee!
>
> (Shakespeare, 1978, Hamlet, p. 205)

Students are encouraged to take advantage of the activities and interactions of this pedagogy which acknowledges the importance of the development of their authentic voices and self-awareness, of making their tacit knowledge explicit, and of developing their abilities to become increasingly more aware of others' perspectives and ways of knowing. These are all necessary to their growth and development as future narrative researchers, and this is reflected in the activities, assignments and three kinds of dialogues of the course, which are designed to help them to engage in the interaction of narratives, and in the exploration of the central concerns that give their lives unity and purpose. The reflective writing requirement of the course provides them with a framework for the establishment of a dialogue with themselves in which to explore the stories by which they live, and the influences, attractions, patterns and resistances they feel as they chart the landscape of their inner lives. It provides them with a context in which to be attentive to their emotions and feelings, and to develop the abilities to nurture and strengthen the qualities of self-awareness which are essential to the work of self-study research and of doing collaborative narrative inquiry with research participants. Daniel Goleman (1995) explains the importance of emotional awareness to all learners, and his words have special significance to those who engage in narrative, arts-based, research with others.

> Emotions that simmer beneath the threshold of awareness can have a powerful impact on how we perceive and react, even though we have no idea they are at work. (p. 55)

Through the solitary processes of their reflective writing, students can explore the details of their emotional lives by bringing their feelings and emotions to the surface, examining them, and developing the abilities to understand and manage them in the context of their whole lives. This private dialogue combined with the collaborative dialogues of the course, can also help students to be more attentive to the emotional lives of others, and to become more attentive to what is taking place in their interactions with others. The dialogues that students have with themselves in the reflective writing enable them to create a knowledge that is uniquely theirs by integrating their subjective knowledge with objective knowledge, and creating a personal practical knowledge that is embodied, embedded in a culture, and based in the narrative unities of their lives (Connelly and Clandinin, 2000). This inter-subjective knowledge is both theoretical and practical, and it is expressed by an individual in his or her particular situation and in the individual's personalized ways of knowing. It is a personal practical knowledge which Clandinin (1985) defines as:

> A special knowledge [that] is composed of both kinds of knowledge, [theoretical and practical] blended by the personal background and characteristics of the [individual] and expressed by her in particular situations. (p. 361)

The development of students' personal practical knowledge and of their authentic voices is also supported by the readings for the course which present the voices of others which will support these objectives, and which will inform, inspire challenge and stimulate their own ongoing inquiries. The readings are chosen to provide them with the concepts and ideas which will assist them with their ongoing inquiry and with their future research. They are also chosen to provide an overview of qualitative research methods, and specific examples of such methods as narrative inquiry, arts-based educational research, portraiture, self-study research, and various other qualitative research methods. Students are encouraged to enter into an active dialogue with all these texts, and to document the discussions, responses and arguments they have with the texts in their reflective writing journals. As they engage more deeply in these dialogues, many learn that this approach can be liberating and empowering, and can see how it helps them to develop their own unique voices. By responding to the readings of the course as they would to the voices of other more experienced researchers and writers and by entering into a dialogue with these authors as they read, students become less intimidated by them and more open to hearing what they say. Approached in this way, the voices of these experienced researchers and writers are less likely to overwhelm students' own developing and less experienced voices: they can be a source of inspiration and support for the ongoing quest for meaning and for imagining and designing their future research.

Having their authentic voices acknowledged in an academic setting can often be surprising for students. When the learning environment is openly accepting and welcoming of their voices, their diverse ways of knowing and their differences, students can learn to develop their abilities to communicate in a variety of ways, and to challenge existing hierarchies, theories and what is taken for granted in increasingly sophisticated ways. They also learn to value language and expression that is honest and authentic and to seek out new and unhackneyed ways of thinking, writing and speaking. Through the various processes of the three kinds of dialogue in the course, students practice the ways of developing their voices, learn to build bridges between their understandings and those of others, and learn to imagine ways in which to create future research that will enable them to make meaningful connections between their personal, professional and scholarly lives.

In the course readings, I draw on two published book chapters to provide students with examples of narratives where the authors acknowledge the connections between education and the arts, voice and identity, and between creative and scholarly activity in research and in professional practice. One of these chapters is Elliot Eisner's (1991b) *What the Arts Taught Me about Education*, and the other is my own chapter, *Beginning with Myself: My Own Story of Teaching and Learning* (Beattie, 1995a). In these two chapters, we describe the ways in which the arts have shaped and influenced our thinking and decision making, and have directed the course of our lives. They provide students with ways in which to begin to consider how the arts have influenced them, and in which many of their significant learning experiences have taken place in informal settings and in the context of interactions with others in relationships, family, work, culture and community settings. Reflecting on their experiences in the arts, many students are surprised to recognize the extent to which they have been influenced and shaped by these experiences. Similarly, they are surprised to recognize the ways in which their experiences with the arts have enabled them to develop their voices and distinctive ways of knowing. Some students also express their disappointment when they recognize that they have lost their connections with the arts and have lost their voices in the process. As they begin to re-establish these connections, they position themselves differently in relation to their graduate studies, to the processes of creating new knowledge, and to their identities as qualitative researchers. They also learn to relate to their own unique learning processes in new ways, and to consider the characteristics of the conditions and contexts for their future learning. As they make increasingly more significant connections between the development of their voices, the growth of their identities, and the creation of their narratives, their abilities to connect these to their professional practices and to their future research also become more solidly established. As they do so, they also begin to understand that the transformation of knowledge and the creation and re-creation of a self is an ongoing work of improvisation and of creativity.

The following excerpt from Laura Hegge's reflective writing, shows how her inquiry into the role of the arts in her life helped her to make new connections between her personal understandings and her professional practices. Laura was a high school English teacher who was in the Master's programme at the time she wrote this. She is now writing her doctoral thesis.

> The reflective practices introduced to me in my graduate studies have allowed me to better understand my struggles and successes in teaching by forcing me to make my tacit knowledge explicit. By exploring my personal connections to the arts, I have been able to see what it is I want to bring to my students as a teacher of the arts. By continuing to examine my own stories and meanings, I will be better able to provide the space for students to tell their own stories and to make connections with the stories of others.

> By navigating through the questions in the inquiry, I have found links between my own interactions with the arts as a participant and creator, as a teacher and as a human being. The arts are the means through which we express our individual humanity. They also provide meanings which allow us to float beyond our individuality and the cognitive realm of our right and left brains to connect with the deeper mind that runs like a current below the level of language and conscious thought at the very seabed of the universe. The arts cause us to question ourselves and to search deeper beyond the frame of our individual lives past the boundaries of time and culture into the depths of the ocean that is our common consciousness.

A. FOSTERING A DIALOGUE WITH THE SELF: CHARTING THE INNER LANDSCAPE

> Go into yourself and see how deep the place is from which your life flows—
> Rainer Maria Rilke

The unified framework of the written assignments, oral presentations and reflective writing of the course provides a context for students to engage in cycles of inquiry, to explore the meanings of their experiences, to receive feedback and responses from a variety of others, and to integrate their new understandings through the writing of a narrative. The processes of the three kinds of dialogues in the course—the dialogue with the self, dialogue with others, and dialogue between the dialogues—are designed to help them to do this individually and collaboratively. However, it is only when students create their narratives, by identifying the narrative themes and unities of their lives, and weaving their new understandings into a coherent, integrated, meaningful whole, that they make the connections between the different parts of their lives, transform their understandings, and transform themselves. The writing is an integral aspect of the inquiry process, for as Richardson (2000) says, 'writing is a method of inquiry in itself, a way of finding out about yourself and your "topic".' She says:

> Although we usually think about writing as a mode of 'telling' about the social world, writing is not just a mopping-up activity at the end of the research project. Writing is also a way of 'knowing'—a method of discovery and analysis. By writing in different ways, we discover new aspects of our topic and our relationship to it. Form and content are inseparable. (Richardson, 2000, p. 923)

Each student is required to document the details of the interdependent dialogues in their private reflective journals, to write the stories of the significant events in their lives, and to document their memories, arguments, questions and meaning-making. In doing so, they learn to explore the landscape of their inner lives, to connect to the sources of their creativity, and to learn, unlearn and re-learn. Through the processes of exploring their own lives and in reading about the lives of others, many students begin to acknowledge the complexity of their lives, the tensions and the competing demands which they seek to reconcile, and the ever-changing landscape in which they are living and learning. Many students also learn to adopt a more forgiving and compassionate attitude towards themselves and their imperfections, and to acknowledge that the quest for new meanings involves making mistakes, and having wrong ideas as a necessary part of their explorations, and of the process of having right ones.

For many graduate students, the expectation that they will write in forms other than standard academic prose can fill them with fear and dread. Many have never written in reflective or creative forms or in the first person, in an academic environment. Also, many are not accustomed to having the personal, emotional, moral, and aesthetic aspects of their lives acknowledged in graduate classrooms. As they become more confident and comfortable about engaging in a dialogue with their inner lives, students often find that this reflective journal writing allows them to hear their previously hidden inner language and music, to access long-forgotten memories and stories, and to come to greater understandings of how the realities of the worlds in which they are living are shaped by the stories they tell themselves about it. This writing allows them to generate the data for their self-study research, their interpretations and meaning-making, and the writing of their narratives.

Students need to know that their vulnerabilities will not be exploited in educational settings if they are to lower their defences and participate in ways where they can show themselves as they really are, with their weaknesses as well as their strengths. It is essential for them to have this fundamental reassurance and to know that their dull and gloomy sides are just as welcome as their bright and shiny sides. When they begin to write for themselves and to accept that the purpose of the written and oral dialogues is to help them to connect with what is important to them in life as a whole, because this also gives meaning to their academic studies, it allows them to participate more willingly and to benefit from the responses, perspectives and insights provided by their colleagues. It allows them to explore more deeply the ways in which their past experiences have shaped and conditioned their knowledge, their ways of interpreting and their ways of being, and to take responsibility for their interpretations, and when necessary, to re-create them in the light of their new insights and understandings.

Although some students are initially wary of the suggestion that they should keep a reflective journal as a requirement of the course, when they are encouraged to consider it as a private, unstructured, imperfect, series of explorations into what is meaningful to them in their lives, they are more willing to try it. Many feel less intimidated when they can learn to use the journal as a place to explore the darkness as well as the light, and to vent their frustrations, anger, and dissatisfactions with the world, as well as to celebrate its joys and successes. The reflective writing requirement also becomes less threatening when students find that they can explore and express their meanings through drawings, sketches, quotations, musical compositions and poems, and can use all these forms of expression to promote questioning and interpretation. Given that there are no rules for this writing other than putting a date on each journal entry, no expectations of perfection, or no involuntary sharing of the writing, many students learn that they have the right to make decisions regarding how they will document their meanings, and the authority to tell their stories the way they know them.

The distinctions between formal written assignments that are being assessed according to the criteria for quality work in an academic setting, and reflective writing which is done for the student's own purposes, is an important distinction for students to understand and embrace. In the reflective writing, it is important that they let go of their criteria for good writing, and adopt more playful, curious, and less judgemental attitudes towards their tentative thoughts, ideas, and expressions. When they can do this, it allows them to open up, and to use the writing to explore their meanings, to write about what they don't know as well as what they do know, to shed the familiar propositions, and to deepen their inquiries. This process of opening up to the dialogue in the writing also allows them to be more open to the dialogues with colleagues in classroom discussions and in the oral presentations. When students are willing to share their ideas and issues with others with honesty, they can receive valuable responses which can enable them to hear themselves in new ways, and to adapt, modify, and expand their understandings.

One of the most important ways I can help students to develop their voices and to overcome their fears of writing [and of making oral presentations], is by doing what I expect them to do, and teaching by example. When I can show some of the benefits of this kind of writing by doing it publicly, I have been able to alleviate some students' fears and to garner more willing participation for the reflective journal writing requirement of the course. By writing publicly on the blackboard as students write privately in their journals, I can show them how I use the writing to open up a dialogue with the ideas, questions, feelings, concerns and dilemmas I am dealing with in my life, and the ways in which I try to make sense of them through the writing. As I become more confident and comfortable with a group, I can bring some of what is alive and vital inside me out into the external world, and use the writing to access the images of my inner life. I can show students that one of the major benefits of this kind of writing is the circularity of the process, which allows me to revisit my own thinking, to re-think about what I have thought about, and to consider the many possibilities available to me.

This writing in public is not easy for me as any writing that I do spontaneously is always unfit for anyone's eyes but my own. Further, I explain to students that in my experience, good writing is all about rewriting. When I do it privately, reflective writing allows me to get the images, the metaphors and the language flowing by trying things out, generating lots of material, having lots of tentative ideas that go nowhere, and of searching for the gold among the dross. The process allows me to play with the ideas and the language, to make mistakes and connections between things, to rant, to argue, to remember, and to tell stories to myself. I explain that in my experience a writer can't sit around hoping to produce pages of insightful ideas the first time he or she sits down to compose, or expect brilliant thoughts to come out fully formed. For me, it is always important that I stay close to my personal purpose for the writing, and to remember that what I have to work hard at and what I am prepared to struggle and make sacrifices for, will often lead me to good writing eventually. The process is always one which

Yeats called 'a raid on the inarticulate', and of developing the ways in which to, in Yeats's phrase, "turn the bundle of accident and incoherence that sits down to breakfast" into "an idea, something intended, complete." When the raid goes deep into the issues that are at the core of my being and to what is non-negotiable there, the process can lead me to the articulation of new understandings and new intended and complete meanings.

I urge students to think of their reflective writing as a way of opening up the channels to their inner lives, and of working to find the lifeline that connects them to the source of inspiration and creativity in their lives. I explain that I have done this kind of reflective writing in public for my high school students, when I was teaching English, in order to demystify the writing process for them, and to show them that writing is done by human beings just like themselves. This practice held its own challenges at the time, but doing it for a group of graduate students, many of whom are excellent writers, holds even greater challenges. I provide an excerpt from my reflective journal here, where I describe one of those times when I did this public reflective writing for graduate students, and documented my reflections of continuing to do so as the course progressed.

Creating a Dialogue with the Self—in a Public Place

> As students wrote in their reflective journals, I wrote on the blackboard, and explored what I was thinking and feeling— in public. As I knew that I was going to do this, I had decided that it might be useful for the students to know how I had prepared for this particular class. I began to write my reflections on my experience of doing this, the choices I had made, and the decision-making processes I had used. I explored the processes of connecting my thoughts to the content of the course, to these individuals in this particular class, and of connecting the universal to the particular and back again as I prepared. As I wrote, I reminded myself that even though this experience was difficult for me, it was even more difficult for some of the students who had never done this kind of writing before. I hoped that by displaying the messy, non-linear, exploratory features of my own writing, seemingly without embarrassment or shame, the students would be encouraged to break free from the constraints imposed by their images of writing in the academic context, and from the necessity to produce perfectly formed thoughts in their reflective journals. As I wrote, I hoped that this spontaneous reflective writing would help them to break through the obstacles which were preventing them from accessing their own voices, knowledge and ways of knowing, and that it would encourage them to jump into the deep end and trust that they would not drown. How could they drown? They have nothing to lose in their private writing havens, I was thinking. I am the only one with something to lose!
>
> Reflecting back, I recall that I had used this blackboard writing technique for ten or fifteen minutes at the beginning of the class, and had tried to model the processes of exploring the inner landscape, as I was also expecting students to do in their journals. As I continued to do this, and listened to the

positive responses from students, I became more relaxed and confident in using the writing to think out loud, to explore my current thinking, to make connections between the theme of the particular class and the goals of the course, to reflect on the readings we had done for the particular class, and on the planning I had done for the class to connect the conceptual and methodological aspects of the research to the pedagogy. I could even write about my hopes that all this would be beneficial to students' learning. Then, I began to write about my ongoing connections with the arts...the books I was reading, the music I was listening to, the art I was looking at, the various concerts and operas I was going to...and their effects on me. The more I wrote in this way, the more honest and authentic my voice became. I began to hear myself using some good expressions, language that was contextualized and personal, and sometimes even pleasing to my own ear.

As the course progressed, I began to take increasing risks in the writing and to do what I encouraged students to do in their reflective journals, articulating my doubts and uncertainties, trying to clarify my puzzlements, and exploring ways to build bridges between my understandings and the dark places where things were murky. I wrote about the teaching practices that I believed had not worked very well, the gaps between my intentions and the outcomes, and my plans for what I would do next. I also wrote about my struggles to make better connections between the philosophical underpinnings of my espoused philosophy and theoretical framework, and my actual classroom practices: the gaps between the story I was telling myself and the one I was trying to enact.

Students in the class who had spoken of "hating reflective writing", began to relax and to talk openly about the arts (or lack of the arts) in their lives. I encouraged them to think of the arts with a small 'a', to think about play as the child's first attempt to be creative, and to recall times when they played, lived out lives other than their own, and created worlds in which to enact realities that were different to the ones they inhabited. Students began to tell me that they were writing stories of their childhood play and of creative and imaginative events in their young lives. They also started to wonder and write about why they had lost their connections to the arts because of their busy personal, professional and academic lives. Deeply shocked, and sometimes initially in denial, students talked and wrote about the circumstances under which they had lost their connections to things they had once valued so highly, and began to interpret the meaning of this in their lives. Many students wrote significant stories that acknowledged their deep connections to art-making at an earlier time in their lives, and acknowledged their feelings of loss and betrayal. Many students spoke of coming to recognize how the writing was helping them to reclaim their lost voices, their lost histories and their suppressed ways of knowing and being.

In the classroom dialogues and conversations which followed, students began to share excerpts from their private reflective journals, often telling stories of the ways in which their prior experiences in education had de-emphasized the

> expression of personal experience. Now, they learned that they could really acknowledge the significance of their personal experiences and could choose what to make public to their classmates, and what to keep private. This realization allowed them to open up to their inner lives in the writing, to engage in authentic dialogues which could always be private, and to reclaim their histories and stories of experience. They told stories of class, culture, gender, poverty, race, and an education system where they were expected to take in the knowledge of others but discouraged from thinking of themselves as makers of anything. Gradually, students began to understand that the reflective journals were a safe and private place where they could explore the stories they were living, and give voice to their interpretations and understandings. They began to trust their voices, and to develop them by using them to remember a time when they regarded themselves as makers and keepers of knowledge. The reflective writing provided them with a way to enter into the dialogue with their former selves, to be present to their earlier experiences, to probe and explore them, to make new connections, and to consider new ways of interpreting, and understanding them.
>
> As students became more confident in this dialogue with their inner lives, many spoke of how this was helping them to explore the ways that habit and convention had suppressed their voices and ways of knowing, and was helping them to look critically and creatively at their experiences and at the ideas they had accepted as 'real'. Some spoke of how the writing had helped them to recall other times in their lives when they thought of themselves as creative, as makers of things and ideas, described how it helped them to re-establish their connections to the sources of their inspiration and joy, and to rediscover the voices and the knowledge they thought they had lost. As they gained confidence in the distinctive ways of knowing they had learned through the arts, they also began to consider how they might use these in their professional practices and their future research. Increasingly, students opened up the dialogue between the various parts of themselves that had been socially and academically conditioned, which had presented difficulties for the development of their authentic voices, and had been felt as obstacles for the creation of a coherent, integrated, personal, professional and scholarly self. (M. B. Reflective Journal)

Writing with students in this public way allows me to show them that I am willing to be open and vulnerable before them, as I ask them to be before me. By demonstrating that I trust them enough to show them the rough and uncharted edges of my thinking, and the meandering, imperfect processes of my writing, I am encouraging the same attitude. I work to overcome my hesitation to do it because I want them to see how they can use the reflective writing to tell the stories of their experience as they know them, to have the experience of looking back at what they said, and of re-thinking what they thought. By sharing the tentative, rough and unfinished writing with them, my hope is that students will also become willing to share their unfinished thinking with me and their colleagues. Some students in these classes are far better writers than I will ever be, and it is often those students who are the most critical of themselves and who have the hardest time sharing anything that is not perfect. This sharing of what is imperfect and unfinished is important because it allows us to collaborate at the edges of each other's meaning-making, and in the making of shared meanings and understandings.

When students become less fearful of the writing process and more willing to use it to deepen their inquiries, they often find that it helps them to negotiate those places where old understandings meet new ideas, and in which new insights into stories, memories, and significant events of their lives, interact with older versions. As they tell more and more stories of their connections to the arts and to art-making, students become more perceptive about the role that engagement in arts experiences and art-making has played in linking the personal, private realm of experience to the public, conceptual realm in their lives. Then as they come to see that they are connected to many communities—(familial, professional, social, linguistic, cultural and academic)—many also learn to construct a research agenda that is grounded in the uniqueness of their personal and professional knowledge, and that can take advantage of their experiences and expertise in the arts to further their scholarly interests and future goals. Also, as they begin to respect and value their own voices, many students find that they are not so intimidated and overpowered by the stronger and more authoritative voices they encounter in the readings of the course and in the published texts of the academy: they gain increasing confidence in their own voices and in the music of their inner lives.

In an excerpt from the reflective writing she did in the context of the course, *Research and Inquiry in the Arts*, Nancy Dawe, a doctoral candidate in the Faculty of Music and an experienced music teacher, explains how the processes of her inquiry helped her to transform her understandings of her professional practice and her identity. She says:

> Until recently, I was not able to articulate my personal philosophy of music education. Admittedly, it was not something to which I gave much thought—neither during my teacher education programme nor during my time as a practising teacher. However, through my work in graduate studies, I have come to realize what it is that I value in terms of music education and how those values came to be. Through a narrative self-study process, I have begun to uncover the ways in which my life experiences, outside of my formal teacher education and professional practice, have informed the ways in which I create curriculum, develop relationships with students, and nurture spaces for emerging identities in my classroom.
>
> As a result of my inquiry, I feel grounded in the decisions I have made as a teacher, and I feel more comfortable with my identity as a teacher. I have not always felt that I have lived up to the expectations that were set before me during my teacher education. I have struggled to understand my true motivations as a teacher and to make sense of my approach to music teaching and learning—an approach that does not seem to be rooted in the knowledge and experiences I acquired during my formal teacher education. Discovering

> the concept of 'personal practical knowledge' has been one of the most powerful experiences of my graduate studies. It has enabled me to negotiate many of the tension points I had been experiencing surrounding my understanding of myself as a teacher. Further, it has only been through the discovery that knowing myself is critical to being able to know and teach others that I have come to terms with my own teaching practice and my teaching self. Through my narrative self-study, uncovering the life experiences that have informed my practice and that have shaped my identity as a teacher has been extremely liberating. It is my belief that my heightened self-knowledge will further enable me to create viable spaces for identity development in my classroom and to approach music education as transformative education.
>
> Through the process of writing a narrative self-study piece which explored the influences of the arts on my life, I discovered several significant lessons about teaching that I did not develop through my teacher education program—the importance of feeling empathy, of being an interested listener, and of making connections between music and the world. As a music education student, it always seemed to me that the relationships I would have with my students would be musical ones, that the stories I would share with them would be musical ones, and that the connections I would make would be rooted in our shared musical knowledge and experiences. Through my lived experience as a music teacher, I can now assert that there is so much more to being a music teacher than teaching music. I have always known that, but I never had the confidence in asserting that. My narrative self-study enabled me to make sense of who I am and to take ownership of what I value as a teacher.

B. THE DIALOGUE WITH OTHERS: ATTENTIVE LISTENING AND CONSTRUCTIVE RESPONSES

> Human beings tend to regard the conventions of their own societies as natural, often sacred. One of the great steps forward in history was learning to regard those who spoke odd-sounding languages and had different smells and habits as fully human, as similar to oneself. The next step from this realization, the step which we have still not fully made, is the willingness to question and purposefully alter one's own conditions and habits, to learn to observe others. (Bateson, 1989, p. 57)

The three oral presentations of the course are designed to help students to develop their voices, and to hear the voices and perspectives of others. They also provide a forum for interactive learning and for the stimulation of individual and collective reflection, interpretation, and meaning-making. They provide opportunities for the fluid interplay and interaction of diverse ways of knowing, and for developing an awareness and understanding of different ways of knowing and being. When students release their privately held ideas and perspectives from the cocoon of clarity of their own minds, they often learn that their ways of knowing and being are not universally shared. When they can learn to really hear ideas and perspectives that are different to their own, they can expand their understandings, re-cast their perspectives, and learn to tell new stories of themselves and of others that are more appropriate to their current and future realities, and to a world that has changed since they developed their constructs and understandings.

The oral presentations are designed to help students to re-connect to an earlier understanding of themselves as 'makers', to develop their abilities to voice their understandings, and to receive responses from multiple others. As they share ideas, theories and resources from their diverse backgrounds in the arts, humanities, sciences, and other academic disciplines, students learn to recognize the value each other's ways of knowing, and to become more responsive to each other. When students feel that the relationships and the community around them are genuinely respectful and trustworthy, they learn that they can be courageous enough to say what they really think, can open themselves up to expressing different perspectives and ideas, and also to accept that their colleagues can disagree with their ideas and understandings when this is done in respectful ways.

It is often a new experience for students to give and receive a wide range of oral and written responses to their work, to and from multiple others in the context of graduate education. It takes time for them to develop the levels of trust where they will put their prejudices and experiences into play, and feel comfortable enough to articulate unpopular, biased, or 'politically incorrect' ideas and perspectives. The oral presentations provide a context for them to receive and provide constructive and respectful responses to each other in the role of a soul friend/*anam cara,* and this can help them to consider things from a range of perspectives rather than from their own sole perspective. In this way, many students can let go of earlier ways of knowing in the light of their new insights, and can move from their understandings of known universes to the imagining and enactment of new ones. As the course progresses students also become increasingly more adept at providing feedback for each other's work orally and in writing, and to learn the processes of being collaborative narrative researchers in each others' inquiries. This culminates in the work they do for each other in the writing/research partnerships where they provide responses to the drafts of each other's final assignments for the course. This work also allows them to create a rich body of data —individually and collaboratively—, for the two formal assignments of the course: the writing of a narrative and the preparation of a qualitative research proposal.

Oral Presentation One: Something that Inspires me and Something I have made

In the first oral presentation *Something that Inspires me; Something I have Made*, students are invited to present an object or item that is a significant form of inspiration for them. This can be it a quotation, an excerpt from a novel, a painting, drawing, or photograph, or other similar motivator. They are asked to explain why it is a source of inspiration, and to explain its significance to them to the best of their ability. After this, students present an object or item that they have made, be it a poem, a painting, a piece of craft/art work, a website or other creation, followed by a description of what the process of creation meant to them at the time they made it, and what it means now when they think about it in the context of their roles as knowledge-makers and future researchers. Through attentive listening and respectful, constructive feedback in the form of written field notes, students provide support and feedback to each other.

Students are often nervous and fearful of the expectations of these presentations, and of exposing the details of their inner lives to colleagues and a teacher who are unknown entities in their lives. As teachers, we need to respect these feelings, and to model what we expect our students to do even though it requires that we show ourselves as whole human beings who have vulnerabilities and uncertainties as well as our academic status and credentials. In teaching by example, we openly acknowledge the challenges, emotional investment, fears, trepidations, and courage involved in an activity such as this one. By sharing our sources of inspiration, creative efforts and tentative meaning-making with students, we show that the process of making something concrete in the external world requires improvisation, creativity, intuition, and imagination as well as intellect. We also show that we value narrative and metaphoric thinking, expressive language, an authentic voice, and the use of arts-based ways of knowing to represent meaning in the academic context.

I have drawn here from the reflective journal I wrote after I made a presentation of "Something that inspires me and something I have made" to a class. I follow this with the writing I did a week later when I reflected on the presentations that students made.

Something that Inspires me: Something I have made

> For my inspirational piece, I chose the poem, *The Wishing Tree* by one of my favourite poets, Seamus Heaney. For the thing I had made, I had chosen a rough draft of a poem I had written very recently, entitled, *For Toni Morrison* At the beginning of my presentation, I handed out copies of the Heaney poem, and I read it aloud, lingering over the words and the rhythms. Then I read it again for the sheer joy of it, explaining how Heaney's words engage me at every level of my being, provide me with images of transcendence, and help me to imagine a better self. I told of my love for Heaney's language, ideas, images, and rhythmic patterns, and how they affect me as music does. I also explained that my love of poetry goes back a long way, my love of Heaney's poetry goes back to the first time I heard it, and this is a time that is long before he was awarded the Nobel Prize in Literature. I told of how I am always astonished at the image of the tree ascending at the end of the poem, as it connects earth and heaven and all those watching, trailing the comet's tail of wishes granted during its lifetime behind it. This image is one to which I return over and over again. It helps me to know who I am, and why I am here. It connects me to myself, to the earth and the sky, and to all that there is. When I read it or recite it silently to myself, I feel gratitude to the poet for making it present in my world.

In the second part of my presentation, I distributed and read aloud a draft of a poem I had written very recently in response to my intense inner feelings on hearing Toni Morrison speak at a convocation ceremony at the University of Toronto. I had called my poem, *For Toni Morrison* as I had written it to try to capture the meaning of my experience of being in her presence, and the emotions I had felt inside. The poem ended with these lines:

> Looking up I saw the Goddess,
> Slowly moving overhead.
> Smiling, gilded by the sun, she said
> The crown is bought and paid for,
> All you have to do
> Is wear it.

I found it difficult to read my own words and to talk about the frustrations I had felt in trying to find a language to describe the experience which I had felt so strongly, and for which I initially had no words. I spoke of my incoherence and incompetence, my struggle for language and my intense desire for clarity and coherence. I described the difficulties of finding any appropriate external expression for this intense inner feeling and truth. Giving myself time to breathe, I then invited students to bring their chosen items the following week, and told them to do their best to describe the sources of their inspiration and their creative processes as I had tried to do in this class. I reminded them that all their presentations would be listened to as attentively and respectfully as mine had been, thanked them for their attentiveness and interest, and for all the wordless feedback I had already received from them.

The following week, students brought their inspirational pieces and their art-making of many kinds to the class. There were paintings, drawings, hand-work, pottery, musical compositions, poetry, a web site, and writings. As they presented and spoke of their sources of inspiration and experiences in making, students showed the intensity of their connections to the objects and artefacts they had chosen. Increasingly, they became more comfortable in speaking about their connections to these, and of their significance in their lives. As the presentations progressed, students began to relax in noticeable ways, and to show both surprise and delight at the warmth and enthusiasm of their colleagues' responses. As they let go of their anxieties, they began to communicate with greater ease, and even though a few individuals prefaced their presentations with comments about their fear and discomfort, they seemed to lose the tension in their voices and bodies as they began to feel their own emotional connections to the objects and artefacts they were presenting. This increased as they began to pick up the wordless but welcoming responses and messages from their colleagues.

After the class, some students explained that the experience of choosing items for the presentation had caused them to realize the extent to which they were disconnected from the sources of their joy and inspiration, and of being determined to re-establish a connection. They spoke of my willingness to do the exercise first as a critical aspect of making it possible for them to do it before a group of their peers that they hardly knew, and of finding the courage to do it because I had done it first. Students also spoke of how the presentations which they had initially regarded with fear and intimidation had felt liberating and empowering once they got started, and were especially so when they were over and they had started to think of what the experience had 'brought out of them'. I encouraged them to document all these thoughts and feelings in writing so that they could be re-visited, and re-interpreted and re-created in the context of new insights and understandings.

Prior to the presentations, I had taught students how to make field-notes as qualitative, narrative researchers, so that they could provide feedback to each other's presentations. They had chosen partners ahead of time, and had agreed to record the details of each other's words and actions, paying attention to all that was expressed orally and visually, and also to that which was expressed through the body and the emotions. Students prepared their research notebooks by drawing a line down the page to remind them to differentiate between what they actually heard and saw, and the inevitable urge to interpret, judge, and bring their own meaning-making into the activity. I also wrote field notes for each student who made a presentation, and gave them my hand-written notes at the end of the class. Earlier, I had explained that this activity would provide them with valuable opportunities to develop the abilities to listen attentively and to notice nuances and details in another person's speech, and of the importance of this in preparing for their work with future research participants.

This process of making field notes provided students with hands-on practice in learning qualitative research skills and also provided each of them with a range of valuable responses and different perspectives on how their words had been heard and their actions perceived. For many students, this stimulated new levels of reflection, exploration, interpretation, and meaning-making. Several students responded to their colleagues with gratitude, and spoke of valuing the hard work, commitment, and generosity of spirit which they felt. The intensity of these processes of presenting, of providing meaningful feedback to each other, and of collaborating in the intimate relations of this activity, had the effect of creating threads of connectedness between us all, and a web of connectedness where we were connected to each other in new ways, and also connected in new ways to ourselves.

As I continue to reflect on this activity and the follow-up discussion with students, I see that it provided a context for students to continue to build trusting and respectful relationships with themselves, with each other and with me. It allowed us to acknowledge and value the emotional, aesthetic, moral and spiritual aspects of each other's lives as well as the intellectual, and to create a new vision of what relationships could be in an academic environment. The activity had also provided me with a context for modelling narrative questioning...for asking questions that ask for more of the story, acknowledging that it has past, present and future dimensions, that show genuine interest, respect, desire for the expansion of meaning, and which also acknowledge that each individual knows his/her own experience like no one else does. I also noticed that students were picking up the qualities and tone of my questions and asking their own questions of colleagues that looked for more meaning and a fuller version of the story being told. Increasingly, the questions which had an implied criticism or judgement embedded in them, or were imbued with a kind of interrogation, became more rare.

I am starting to appreciate the ways in which these oral presentations enable us to create the kinds of relationships and learning community where students can learn with all aspects of themselves as human beings. Students learn to articulate their understandings, hear how their voices are being heard by others, and are encouraged to deepen their inquiries into their relationships with their creativity, connectedness to the arts, and understandings of themselves as makers. By doing my presentation first, I am required to 'take a leap into the dark', and to try to look fearless as I share my sources of inspiration and my creative products, in all their imperfection. In preparation, I have to continually remind myself that I am only doing what I expect my students to do, and that I should trust the process and take the risks because it is what I tell students to do, and expect that they will do.

Each time we do this oral presentation in the class, I am reminded of how powerful the experience can be for each individual in the room, and this includes me. I am also reminded of how valuable it is when I show (rather than tell) students how much I treasure my connection to the arts, my lifeline to the sources of my creativity, and my experience of the quality of a life that accompanies the process of creating something. I am also aware that these presentations allow me to show the importance of a life where the personal, professional and scholarly are intertwined, where a strong connection to creativity and making is fully present, and enjoyed as an ongoing source of inspiration, and a process of making and re-making new knowledge and understandings, and of remaking the self. (M. B. Reflective Journal)

Oral Presentation Two: Creating a Museum Exhibit of My Life

In the second oral presentation, *Creating a Museum Exhibit of My Life*, students are invited to present a collection of objects that will serve to illustrate their connection to the arts, their learning through the arts, and the role of the arts in their lives as persons, professionals and new educational researchers. Each student sets up the exhibit in the classroom ahead of time, and in turn narrates the journey through the small exhibit, holding each piece and explaining its significance to the group. Students make tape-recordings of their presentations, and research/writing partners provide written feedback to the presentations in the form of field notes. In the context of the whole course, the timing of this presentation is critical as it requires well-established collaborative relationships among students, and a well developed community where collaboration and shared meaning-making, [without aggressive questions or selfish behaviour] can almost be taken for granted.

As students learn to articulate their knowledge in authentic, personal ways, and to hear responses from others, they learn how to learn from and with each other. They also learn that through this collaborative interpretation and shared meaning-making, they can do together what no one individual could do alone. Students begin to see that through the telling of their stories, listening to the stories of others, and receiving feedback, they are engaging in the processes of self-narration and of uncovering their self-knowledge; in the circular process which Gadamer (1975) refers to as a 'fusion' of old understandings with new ideas (p. 30). They gain increasing understandings of how this process involves the continuous re-construction and transformation of experience and the construction of new levels of understanding. As they allow themselves to delve deeper into their inquiries they come to recognize that they are involved in the continuous construction and re-construction of their identities and of a narrative that requires the re-ordering of the past, present and future.

I provide an excerpt from my reflective journal here to provide a description of the oral presentation entitled, *Creating a Museum Exhibit of My Life*, and my reflections on this.

Creating a Museum Exhibit of my Life

In the presentation, *Creating a Museum Exhibit of my Life,* students presented collections of artefacts which are significant to them in the context of their developing inquiries and which show the relationships between the personal, professional and scholarly aspects of their lives. The activity allowed them to access their ways of knowing through the aesthetic, emotional, social, moral and spiritual dimensions as well as through the intellectual. This is in contrast to the ways we usually work in graduate studies where we generally begin with the intellect and often stay with the intellect.

Students have several weeks to create this collection which often includes visual materials, music, personal and professional mementos, books, toys, documents, crafts, art-work, writings, and other items. They display their artefacts as if they were a museum exhibit of their lives, and as individuals present each artefact, they explain its meaning and significance from their personal perspective and reflect on its meaning in the context of the ongoing inquiry. Because they are more accustomed to beginning in the world of the intellect in graduate education and of disregarding the world of feelings and the aesthetic, some students begin with academic theory and language, and by connecting their explanations to the cognitive objectives of the course. When they accept the invitation to go beyond this, to begin with the personal, they begin to tell the stories around the object, to make increasingly significant links between the object, the people in their lives, and various aspects of their lives. They are often very surprised at the depth of their own thinking, their emotional responses, and the interpretations they do in front of a room full of people who are only a few steps removed from being strangers in their lives, but with whom they have been developing increasingly more trusting and collegial relationships.

Students audio tape their presentations, their research/writing partners take field-notes, and they write their own reflections on the experience immediately after the exercise. In their reflections, I encourage them to focus on their immediate reactions to the experience itself, to consider the effect of the reactions of their colleagues, and to write about how they heard their own voices in this arena. When I ask them about the experience, students invariably tell me that the first thing they write about are the fears they had prior to the presentation. Then they tell of the surprising features of the experience itself and of being amazed at what the immediacy of what the experience 'brought out of them'. They tell of situations where they could hardly believe the things that they heard themselves talking about in public and in an academic environment. Many also tell of being very surprised at the ways in which they had responded so viscerally and emotionally to their chosen artefacts, and were left considering the power of these objects to evoke memories, and to activate their imaginations as well as their intellects. Students also speak of the value of hearing the presentations made by their colleagues, and of the opportunity to provide responses to others where they felt that they contributed to their colleagues meaning-making. They also talk about all the new questions that opened up, and of the frustrations as well as the joys of an inquiry that gets deeper and which seems to be never ending.

I am aware that this activity is highly dependent upon the quality of the relationships and sense of community in the classroom. Each time we do it, I remind myself that the scheduling of this activity has to be absolutely right, and with each group I teach, this 'right time' is a different time in the course schedule. Everything depends on the quality of the relationships that have been created, the conditions of collaboration and of community which have been built, and the levels of trust, respect and safety that students feel. This affects the levels of exploration, interpretation and meaning-making to which students are prepared to go in public. It is important that they have already experienced a range of classroom activities where they have voiced their ideas and meanings, taken risks, and received constructive and insightful feedback from others.

I observe the extent to which students' learning is enhanced by the quality of the responses—spoken and unspoken—that they receive from their colleagues and from me. Using a narrative approach to questioning and responding, I have tried to teach by example, and to encourage students to ask the kinds of questions that will encourage their colleagues to tell more of the story, to go deeper into the meaning of the experience as they know it, and to explore the many possible interpretations available to them. Increasingly, students learn that in the role of co-researcher and soul friend to each other, they are of value to their partners when they can show that they are attentive to the details and nuances of what is said and not said, to what is written on the lines and between the lines, and responsive to the patterns and themes, and to the silences and the spaces. Students learn the difference between the kinds of questions and feedback which invite the telling of fuller versions of the story and those which have the effect of shutting things down, and learn to develop the abilities to engage in the former, and to disengage from the latter. (M.B. Reflective Journal)

Oral Presentation Three: What is a Thesis?

In the third oral presentation, *What is a Thesis*, which is scheduled to run throughout the course, each student presents an example of a high quality, narrative, arts-based, holistic thesis. This course requirement is designed so that students will read and examine a recently completed thesis that is of high quality, is meaningful to them, relevant to their own research interests, and which will also be useful and valuable to their colleagues. This calls for a close reading of the thesis, and for outlining the nature of the research, the conceptual framework on which it is based, the contribution to the literature and to professional practice, and the significance of this work to the presenter. Students provide oral feedback to each other's work at the end of the presentation, as they do to the other presentations, asking thoughtful questions, and working to promote each others' understanding. Students also provide written feedback to each other through the internet between classes.

The discussions following the presentations allow for the kinds of dialogues where students learn to distinguish between the different kinds of research, and also develop their understandings of work that is of high quality and that which is of lesser quality. They also learn of the wealth of existing qualitative research that is narrative, arts-based and holistic, see how the various parts of a thesis are connected to each other, and the ways in which they fulfil the criteria for high quality research. Many students explain that this course requirement has the effect of de-mystifying the research and thesis writing process, admit that they had never read a thesis before, and express surprise at finding that reading a thesis can be pleasurable and highly informative. They explain that the processes of presenting a thesis to their colleagues in the class and of hearing the details of the wide variety of qualitative research presented by others, had helped them to make the image of their own future research and a completed thesis into a real possibility for them. Many speak of how it had also helped them to plan their future research.

Fostering the Dialogue with Others

By beginning with an inquiry into the ways in which the arts have influenced their lives, students who have been disconnected from the arts, gain new understandings of the distinctive ways of knowing they have created through the arts, and transform their understandings of the ways in which they can bring their distinctive ways of knowing and being into their work as educational researchers. Collectively, the three oral presentations provide them with a wide range of opportunities to engage in the dialogues with others which enable them to deepen their quests for meaning, and to receive a wide range of responses from multiple others. As they learn that their creativity, intuition, and imagination are just as welcome as their intellects, students are more inclined to introduce playfulness, fun, humour, and laughter into what they do. Increasingly, they accept that they can be spontaneous, can take risks and have things go wrong, and that mistakes, unexpected hitches, and failed efforts can be understood as steps on the road to eventual success. Some students make great strides in what they can accomplish in a short time when they avail of the opportunities to experiment and explore and to respond to the wide range of valuable feedback they get from their colleagues in the class.

Seeing other peoples' work can be very valuable in helping students to see and understand at a more conscious level what they have done themselves. Also, when they see how their work has the power to affect and inspire their colleagues, and to engage them at all levels of their being, they begin to assess the merits of different kinds of research, and to consider the ways that certain kinds of qualitative research can engage their research participants and future readers with the whole of their humanity. The discussions of the class and the interactions within the dialogues provide valuable contexts in which students learn to distinguish between the kind of research that engages only the intellect, and that which also engages the emotions, the spirit, and the moral, aesthetic, and spiritual dimensions of the reader. As they become increasingly more knowledgeable about the various kinds of qualitative research, and the variety of forms of representation available to them as qualitative educational researchers, they begin to seek out those ways of doing research which can promote the empathic participation of the reader in the lives of the persons they are writing about, as well as their intellects.

C. CREATING A DIALOGUE BETWEEN THE DIALOGUES: INTERACTION AND INTEGRATION

> The vision of human wholeness is an ancient one. It can be found in the worldview of indigenous peoples, in Greek culture, in Buddhism, Hinduism, and Taoism, and in the American transcendentalists. Each element in our body is interconnected and our bodies are connected to all that surrounds us. These interconnections form the whole. Marcus Aurelius (1997) saw this: "This you must always bear in mind, what is the nature of the whole, what is my nature, and how this is to that, and what kind of part is it of what kind of a whole: and that there is no one who hinders you from always doing and saying the things that conform to the nature of which you are a part." (p. 9) (Miller, J. 2006, pp. 156/157)

The writing of the narrative involves the student writer in a new dialogue between those dialogues that took place with the self, and those external dialogues with texts, with colleagues and with others. It is only when they write their narratives that they draw the disparate parts of their lives together, confer order on their experiences and interpretations, come to new understandings of how the parts are related to the whole, and create a new, coherent, integrated whole. As they write and rewrite their narratives, students become increasingly aware of the power of the process to help them to bring form, coherence and harmony to what may seem to be disparate aspects of their lives, to work to reconcile opposites, and to integrate the knower and the known. As they create these temporal portraits in time, they synthesize the meaning of their experiences, bring a stronger sense of focus, integration, authenticity and wholeness to their lives, and gain an appreciation of how these narratives they are creating will always be works-in-progress, for the end of the story can only ever be imagined. As the horizon towards which it moves continually shifts and changes, the end of the individual's life has to be re-imagined continually, and the parts have to be reconstructed over and over again into a new whole.

The creation of their narratives involves students in the dynamic interplay of the dialogue between the dialogues, in finding the right voice with which to articulate the forming and reforming of their understandings, and in the making of new connections and new meanings. This process is one where the writer makes connections between 'their roots and their reading', their reflections and their writing. As Seamus Heaney (1980) says about his own growth as a poet:

> Finding a voice means that you can get your own feeling into your own words and that your words have the feel of you about them; and I believe that it may not even be a metaphor, for a poetic voice is probably very intimately connected with the poet's natural voice, the voice that he hears as the ideal speaker of the lines he is making up. (p. 43)

Creating a narrative is a process of making sense of a life in the midst of that life and within the wholeness of the life as it is currently understood. It is a process of synthesizing and integrating what is known, of merging the knower and the known, and of making something new. As students construct and re-construct what they know, they also construct and re-construct themselves, as each completed cycle of inquiry leads into the next cycle of imagining, contemplating, interpreting, articulating, and enacting the persons that these individuals now see that they can become. Drawing on all the materials they have created through the dialogues of the course, individuals work to identify the themes and tensions in their lives, seek to reconcile opposites and discordant qualities, to integrate them, and to form them into a coherent, meaningful whole. The process can be filled with the mixed feelings of hope and tension, given the uncertainties of the journey and the undisclosed destination which is always changing. The writer must continually make connections between what has been created and what is imagined, must live in the tension between them, and must struggle to give shape and form to the emergent meanings. When writers stay close to the source of creativity and inspiration and engage wholeheartedly in the work of bringing the emerging insights and interpretations into new forms and understandings, the process of writing and rewriting the narrative can be both engaging and empowering, and can help them to make their way home to themselves.

I have written about the writing of a narrative elsewhere (Beattie, 2007/2001), and have explained how the cycles of writing and rewriting provide a framework for making connections between the themes and threads of individuals' lives, for recognizing their specialized knowledge, skills, and sensibilities, and for creating meaningful connections between the various aspects of their lives. These cycles of writing and rewriting can inspire deeper levels of inquiry, and can help students to consider the connections between the purposes of their inner lives and their actions in the external world. When their narratives have aesthetic and artistic qualities, they can help readers to hear their unique perspectives and voices, to vicariously experience their explorations, and to gain insights into their own unique quests for meaning. Like literary works, these narratives can engage readers intellectually, emotionally, morally, aesthetically and spiritually, can show them who they are, help them to imagine who they might become, and suggest how the stories they live out in their lives might be otherwise. They can sometimes help readers to change the stories they are living, and to change their lives.

Through these formal assignments, and the activities and oral presentations of the course, students learn the ways of doing narrative self-study research, and of collaborating with each other to learn how to do narrative, arts-based research with others. Within the research and writing partnerships they create with colleagues, they learn how narrative researchers work to explore stories, and to identify significant patterns and themes, continuities and contradictions in those stories. They learn to use mind-mapping techniques and visual thought-webs: they read and respond to each other's writing drafts, and collaborate in each other's meaning-making. Students learn that the processes of doing this kind of narrative, arts-based research and writing, can be creative and artistic processes when the researcher wishes it to be so, and has the abilities to make it so.

D. COLLABORATING IN STUDENTS' INQUIRIES IN THE ROLE OF CO-RESEARCHER AND SOUL FRIEND

> "Hope" is the thing with feathers-
> That perches in the soul-
> And sings the tune without the words-
> And never stops-at all-
>
> Emily Dickinson.

In the role of co-researcher and soul friend, the teacher can enter this dialogue between the dialogues by providing one-on-one written feedback to the penultimate draft of each student's narrative, prior to assessment. In this role the teacher can provide the kind of responses that will stimulate new thinking and connections and will help students to take their inquiries to deeper and more significant levels of meaning. This involves listening actively and attentively to what is said and not said in the text, honouring the complexity and uniqueness of the life stories, and of continually checking for understanding throughout. In this role, the teacher can help students to identify new connections, provide responses to their pattern-seeking and the exploration of themes, and suggest contacts and new resources. In this collaborative, non-judgemental role, the teacher can also help by highlighting the parts of the writing where the author's voice is clear and the insights are authentic, and indicate also those parts that have an inauthentic ring, or where the reader feels the presence of untold or silent stories in the text. In this role of co-researcher and soul friend, the teacher can also provide the encouragement, and inspiration which most writers need in the final stages of their writing, and which can give them the confidence and enthusiasm to look for those deeper levels of integration and meaning-making.

Over the years, I have worked to develop my abilities to provide feedback to students' oral and written work in this role, and to teach by example the differences between narrative and paradigmatic ways of knowing, and of responding. Supported by Connelly and Clandinin's (2000) work in narrative inquiry, I have developed ways to do this in the written feedback which I provide to the penultimate drafts of their narratives. I have written elsewhere about ways in which students can provide these kinds of responses to each other's written work in the context of the writers' workshops where they can collaborate in each other's meaning-making (Beattie, 2007/2001).

A narrative way of responding to students' writing is one which focuses on the meaning that is embedded in the narrative history of stories and events. In responding to their writing in the role of a narrative co-researcher and soul friend, the teacher is present in a way which shows that he/she has the student's interests at heart, is working on the student's behalf, and is using a language and a voice that is respectful, supportive and encouraging. This role requires the continual development of presence and attentiveness, of the ability to hear the resonances, resistances and silences between the lines, and to see glimpses of things that hint at how subtle details might be parts of a larger, unexamined whole. In this approach, the questions and responses invite the expansion of meaning and the telling of new (sometimes partly hidden) stories. It also includes paying attention to emotional resonances in the stories told, of hearing the untold or incomplete stories, and of trying to help students to go deeper in their meaning-making, by inviting them to 'say more'. In these written responses to students' work, I have worked to develop ways to invite them to acknowledge that narrative ways of knowing always have a sense of tentativeness, and that there are multiple possible interpretations of any event from many different perspectives. I have looked for gentle but probing ways to ask students to consider other possible meanings, to look at issues from a variety of perspectives, and to explore other possible interpretations.

Here, I provide an excerpt from the narrative of a former student to show how the teacher in this role can collaborate in the final stages of the dialogue between the dialogues in a way that encourages new levels of connections and which can deepen the student's inquiry. The excerpt is from the narrative written by Robert Lompart, a visual artist, secondary school art teacher, and Master of Education student who was enrolled in the *Research and Inquiry in the Arts* course. Rob was a reluctant writer at the beginning of the course, and he explained that his ways of knowing and understanding were visual. His lifelong enjoyment of visual art and of his own art making had always provided him with a rich quality of life, yet his professional life as an art teacher, his graduate studies, and new role as a father of a baby girl were creating a severe lack of time for these, and this was causing him some frustrations. Additional writing was the last thing he needed.

In the penultimate draft of the narrative to which I responded, Rob had written three sentences about the first time he had seen the painting, *Passenger Pigeon Hunt*, by Antoine Plamondon. He wrote:

> An historical painting that I find conceptually interesting is a painting by Antoine Plamondon. *Passenger Pigeon Hunt*, painted in 1853, and now part of the permanent collection at the Art Gallery of Ontario, casually portrays three boys enjoying an afternoon of passenger pigeon hunting along the St. Lawrence River. I assume that the artist intended this to be a relatively pastoral painting, but almost 150 years later the discourse presented by this painting is immense.

As I read Rob's words, I could hear him explaining how the painting had affected him visually and intellectually. Beneath the lines, I could also hear an emotional resonance, could feel his passionate response to the aesthetic qualities of the painting, and the sense of loss that he was intimating, but not articulating. In my written responses to his writing, I told him of these resonances I was picking up beneath the surface of his words. I asked him to say much more about his actual experience of seeing the painting for the first time, to describe what he saw and felt in greater detail, and to draw on all his senses in doing so. I urged him to probe more deeply into the meaning of the feelings and thoughts that were evoked by the painting at the time he saw it, and again as he was remembering it in this new context of his current inquiry. I also urged him to explore the emotional and other connections he might have felt then and now, as well as his visual and intellectual responses. Then, I asked him to consider why this particular painting held such a significant place in his life, and how it might be connected to some of the central issues and purposes of his life, given that he had seen a lot of significant artworks first hand in Canada and elsewhere.

Rob responded to my suggestions and invitations by writing an expanded version of the piece where he gives a much fuller account of his response to the painting, and his subsequent reflections on its significance to him. This excerpt from his final narrative shows how he responded to my comments, questions and suggestions, and used them to make significant new connections and understandings.

> One artwork that is significantly meaningful to me is a painting by Antoine Plamondon, entitled *Passenger Pigeon Hunt.* This painting casually portrays three boys enjoying a day of pigeon hunting along the St. Lawrence River. I remember the first time I saw this painting hiding on display near the back of the historical Canadian collection at the Art Gallery of Ontario. I remember being drawn towards its large size and its smooth and shiny varnished surface—the picture has an immaculate quality—and examining its carefully rendered details: the gentleness of the boys, the fineness of their clothing, the workmanship on their gunstock and powder horn, but most of all the beautiful details and vivid colours of the birds, taken and presented before me.

> What continues to resonate most for me, today, is that when this painting was created in 1853, it was likely intended to be a pleasing pastoral account of life in Lower Canada. Today though, I am haunted by the thought that the trophy birds are Passenger Pigeons—now extinct—and by the gesture of the boys towards the valley—the energy of their youthful anticipation penetrating through the stylistic refinement and restraint of the day—towards a flock of living Passenger Pigeons that I have never had the opportunity to see. The painting is more powerful than the presentation of the details it portrays.
>
> Plamondon's painting catalyzes for me, all the scientific censuses and literary passages of millions of Passenger Pigeons that once darkened the midday sky over Canada and the passing of the last Passenger Pigeon in 1914. Everything that I know and feel about Passenger Pigeons is harnessed and released by this one painting, in an instant.
>
> Almost every artwork that has had an aesthetic impact on me has been as a result of a direct experience with the artwork. Each artwork allows me to make connections about my understandings of the world, and to construct new meanings through my own interpretation and translation. The learning is multifaceted: it creates and recalls facts and details, connects to memories and evokes opinion and emotion.
>
> Experiences with art have provided me with a significant means through which I have constructed rich meaning and understanding about myself and the world…
>
> In my teaching, this understanding enables me to help students to develop awareness of their own aesthetic understanding, and to understand the role of the aesthetics in art. Many students have limited exposure to art and it is important to me to have students experience as much artwork as possible so that they can experience their own connections. Often I will provide opportunities for students that allow them to work with an artwork of their choice, as opposed to touring the whole class through one artwork. This allows students to begin to find understanding that makes sense to them.
>
> What began as a personal inquiry into understanding the significance of my experience with the arts, allowed me to understand what I value from the arts, and to expand my understanding of using the arts. This has expanded to my understanding of using the arts in the process of doing research with others and creating meaningful formats for representing the research. As a result I have a greater appreciation for the role of the arts in my life, and the value the arts bring to educational research.

Rob's expanded version of the three sentences he initially wrote shows how he used the responses I made to his writing to deepen his inquiry into the role of the arts in his life, and to make deeper connections between his responses to the painting, and to his life as an artistic, morally-based art educator and beginning educational researcher. My responses to his initial three lines had included all the ways of listening to stories and listening for stories that I have worked to develop over the years; the stories told and untold, and the stories that are partially hidden beneath the surface. In this role of co-researcher and soul friend, my responses were focussed on collaborating in his quest for meaning, and in the creation of a new dialogue where through our interacting narratives:

> Lives meet lives..... and interact and inform one another, influencing and changing one another in the process as the energies of each are harnessed in the service of the other, and [in which] new possibilities, relations and forms are created. (Beattie, 1995a, p. 143)

The process of engaging in this interaction enabled Rob to come to new understandings of the importance of the direct experience of the painting to engage him at levels that are beyond the intellectual and visual, and which also include his ecological, moral, and spiritual sensibilities. It helped him to make connections between his new understandings and his professional life as an art teacher, and also to connect this to the recognition of the primacy of direct experience with the aesthetic in students' lives in order to help them to make their own connections and new meanings. The process also helped him to make valuable new connections to his future research and to the fine Masters' thesis he subsequently wrote.

In the expanded version of the writing, Rob eloquently describes the power of art to help him understand himself and the world around him, and also to stake out the source of his creativity and uniqueness as a human being. It helped him to recognize that his experience of seeing the visual representation of the now extinct Passenger Pigeons had transcended time and place. The realization that neither he nor his baby daughter would ever see one of those birds, once so numerous, they would darken the sky when passing, has great poignancy and a sadness in the telling. His new writing shows how the responses to his work allowed him to go to deeper places in his inquiry, and to use his own distinctive voice to express the meaning of the transformation of his understandings. It shows how he integrated his new meanings into his existing knowledge and understandings, created ways of knowing, and a new self.

Providing responses to students' writing in its final stages, in this role of co-researcher and soul friend, allows the teacher to participate in intimate ways in the dialogue between the dialogues at a significant time in the process for student writers. This work can be mutually beneficial as it also provides the teacher with a framework in which to enact a unified philosophy of research and teaching which acknowledges the emotional, aesthetic, moral, personal, and intellectual dimensions of students' lives. Through interacting narratives, this process can be a context which stimulates curiosity, imagination and the joy of learning for both the teacher and student, and it can be deeply satisfying, inspirational and renewing for a teacher, as it requires the continual adaptation, improvisation and creative processes which result in new learning. As Dewey, (1916) said:

> The alternative to furnishing ready-made subject-matter and listening to the accuracy with which it is reproduced is not quiescence, but participation, sharing in an activity. In such shared activity, the teacher is a learner and

> the learner is, without knowing, a teacher—and upon the whole the less consciousness there is, on either side, of either giving or receiving instruction, the better. (p. 188)

Interacting Narratives: Collaborating to Learn.

The teacher in the role of co-researcher and soul friend can be present in all the dialogues of the course, and in her own distinctive voice and from her unique perspective as a learner, Winifred Hunsburger tells of how the various kinds of dialogue of the course enabled her to make important connections between the personal, professional and scholarly aspects of her life. In this excerpt from the narrative she wrote in August, 2004 in the context of the course, *Research and Inquiry in the Arts,* she presents insights into the ways in which the writing of the narrative enabled her to 'claim herself', and provided the foundation from which she wrote a research proposal which was grounded in who she is as a human being, and where she was at home to herself as a person, professional and scholar. At this time, Winifred was a doctoral candidate and elementary school teacher. Four years later, in April, 2008, she completed her doctoral thesis, *Inquiry Learning: A narrative inquiry into the experiences of three teachers*. Winifred shares the journey of that inquiry in the chapter entitled, *Learning through Inquiry: A Recursive Path,* in this book. In August, 2004, she wrote:

> The first oral presentation of the course, and the readings, were really only laying the groundwork for the two major assignments—the narrative of how the arts had helped shape the educator I have become, and the research proposal. The two were intimately linked, and I certainly couldn't have accomplished the research proposal without having written the narrative first...
>
> Writing the narrative was an extraordinary experience. Having the direction to look at how the arts had influenced or shaped me was really what made it work for me. It made me look at my life through a particular lens. This narrative was an inquiry, an investigation. The interview with the other student worked for me in a rather odd way. I was frustrated she didn't ask me good questions about my arts experiences or how the arts had influenced me. This bothered me immensely. However, when I came to write the narrative, I realized that this frustration was pointing me towards what I needed to write about and so it became a very personal inquiry.
>
> Following the threads of my music and theatre experiences through to my professional life in the classroom was a terrific adventure. I decided to begin it with a really wonderful experience I had had in the past year where I really felt like I was at my best in the classroom and see where it took me. It also happened to be one in which I had integrated visual art and mathematics—so it seemed ripe for an investigation of art and education. I knew from my experience with presenting the website I had created in the oral presentation, 'Something that inspires you and something you have made', that if I worked

with something that I felt excited about I would be able to get at the heart of things. And I think that is really what happened. Once I looked at that experience and saw how I was something of the behind-the-scenes stage manager—how I was the patron of these students—the rest seemed to rush out of me.

The narrative allowed me to 'claim' myself, to recognize myself, and I think in that, I was then able to recognize and experience what it was that arts-based research could do. I began to understand how this kind of research could help me to get at things from the inside, to explore how people bring meaning to experience, how tacit knowledge becomes explicit, and how they build their knowledge.

Writing the final product for the course, the research proposal was the most profound experience. The feedback I got from Mary continually urged me to: 'Think about what you love', and I knew that I had to be authentic if it was ever going to work. Then I got away from writing for someone else and began writing it for me. That has to be the most important thing any teacher can do for her students. I wrote myself into that proposal. It gave me the room I needed and the inspiration and determination to include all the disparate bits of myself in there. In thinking through the proposal I knew that it had to include a narrative creation; an exploration of the kind of teaching that makes me sing—inquiry learning which is also related to my role at school as an inquiry leader; it also had to somehow relate to democracy and education.

Because I was able to be myself in this proposal rather than trying to fit a mould, I was able to put those things together in a way that seems natural and that they would flow in and out of each other in a completely sensible way. That was what was transformative, as it let me work with myself, what I know and who I am. Not only was I was able to get it on to paper in a narrative, but to move beyond that into a research project that will delve further into my own understandings and observations and allow others to do the same as I work on it. It is one thing to look into the narrative mirror and see yourself for the first time, but then what are you going to do with this knowledge you have about yourself? If the process it is to be truly transformative, there needs to be a next step that responds to my question of: 'Where do I go from here?' That is why I am so very keen to go to that next step by doing the research and writing the thesis.

AFTERWORD: PREOCCUPATIONS AND PURPOSES

If we understand our own minds, and the things that are striving to utter themselves through our minds, we move others, not because we have understood or thought about those others, but because all life has the same root. Coventry Patmore has said, 'The end of art is peace', and the following of art is little

> different from the following of religion in the intense preoccupation it demands.
>
> (Heaney, 1980, quoting W. B. Yeats, Samhain; 1905, in Explorations)

The development of a narrative, arts-based pedagogy is an ongoing journey that will always be a work-in-progress. It has its origins in what I learned in a kindergarten class, was nurtured by the other inspirational teachers I have known throughout my life, and is continually developed in my practice, my preoccupations and my purposes. This approach to pedagogy is continually being re-imagined and re-enacted in the work of creating learning communities for each new group of students I teach, in creating relationships and a community where individuals can be awakened to the fire within themselves, and can feel the warmth of the fire at their back and the presence of their soul friends by their sides. I believe that it is only when students feel the care and connectedness of relationships and community, that they can truly learn to claim themselves, and to create the new stories that will enable them to live more connected, fully integrated and meaningful lives. These conditions are especially necessary for graduate students to learn the complex, interpersonal processes of doing narrative, arts-based research, where they collaborate with research participants to explore their stories, and to interpret and represent them in meaningful and resonant ways. They are also necessary for both graduate and undergraduate students as they conduct self-study research into their own lives, gain increased self-knowledge, make connections between their personal values and purposes, and create new understandings of the possibilities available to them in their professional and scholarly lives. In the telling and re-telling of stories of the past, and in the co-creation of new stories for these lives, students can give up the stories they hold when they can replace them with richer and more significant versions that are more suited to their current environments and the futures they envision. As they do so, they learn how to create the kinds of learning communities and research projects in their own lives where others will be inspired to tell and retell the stories through which they transform what they know and transform themselves.

I have been blessed to have had many teachers who were soul friends to me, who stimulated my imagination and intellect, and inspired my love of learning, of teaching, and of the ongoing quest for meaning. Their legacy and their voices live on at a vital level in my personal life and in my professional and scholarly work. My hope is that I can inspire my students and readers as they have inspired me.

PART TWO: THE DIALOGUE WITH THE SELF: CONNECTING INSIGHT AND IMAGINATION

In the dialogues that we have with ourselves, we identify our own authentic voices, explore the stories by which we live, the central concerns that give our lives unity and purpose, and create and re-create not only our knowledge and understandings, but we also create and re-create ourselves.

- Chapter 3: Beginning with Myself: The Power of Music: A Reflection, Renewal and Transformation by Michelle Pereira: *Michelle Pereira*
- Chapter 4: Dancing Through Life, One Story at a Time: *Melanie Markin*
- Chapter 5: The Power of Stories: Tracing the Creative Thread and Healing the Self Whole: *Carly Stasko*
- Chapter 6: Being Seen: *Bob Phillips*

MICHELLE PEREIRA

3. BEGINNING WITH MYSELF

The Power of Music: A Reflection, Renewal and Transformation by Michelle Pereira

The personality that is engaged in the work of the soul is buoyant. It is not burdened with negativity. It does not fear. It experiences purposefulness and meaning. It delights in its work and in others. It is fulfilled and fulfilling.
(Zukav, 1990, p. 236)

INTRODUCTION: AM I STILL ME?

I've finally received the phone call I have been waiting for. Surrey Opera Company has chosen me to understudy the role of Musetta in Pucinni's La Boheme and I couldn't be more thrilled! I've always been told that I should audition for the role of Musetta as my voice and appearance match her "look", so, I have always included her aria, "Quando m'en vo" (Trans: When I go), as a standard audition piece. I can't wait to play her; I have already practiced how I will flip and twirl my long dark brown hair and give coquettish looks to the audience with my brown eyes. My Italian mother and British father have given me the voice and the look that enable me to play roles where I not only sing the part, but can also look the part of the female romantic interest or coquette. I've worked up the courage to ask my boss for flexible hours and she's agreed! I will have to ask Barrett to help me learn the role-I am stressed, excited, worried and happy. Could it finally be happening? What an amazing opportunity. If I impress them enough-who knows-my potential knows no bounds! The better I feel-the more I take on-and the more stressed I feel. Will I always be stuck in this torturous cycle? I want this to be the opportunity I need. I promise that I will work myself to the bone for this project and be totally dedicated. This is why I am here. This is why I moved to England. This is a great feeling, but I am scared it will all unravel.

Today at the gym, Jorge has told me he wants to move back to Canada. He has told me he is unhappy and has presented me with an ultimatum. He is forcing me to choose between our marriage and my potential career as an opera singer. He doesn't like living this way, he wants stability; he wants to stop having to pay for groceries on our maxed out credit cards. He doesn't like what my pursuit of a career in opera is doing to me, physically and emotionally. He loves me but he is scared for me. My passion and desire to

M. Beattie (Author/Ed.), The Quest for Meaning: Narratives of Teaching, Learning and the Arts, 75–91.

> sing opera professionally has served to alienate the one person who has believed in me and supported me unconditionally, until now. I am heartbroken. I don't know what I will do. I want to stay. I've just sent off my resume and photos to all of the professional opera companies in England..if I leave now, and go back home, I will be a failure. My greatest fear will be realized, and I will be nothing. What will I do? What will I become? I don't know what to do, but I don't think I am ready to give up yet.
>
> (Pereira, M. Unpublished Professional Journal, January 2008)

I've decided to introduce myself through the above excerpt to provide a glimpse into my life and a sense of who I was when I was pursuing opera professionally and living in London, England. Reading the words now, I am aware of the desperation woven throughout. Within the joy of music making, I am pleading with the universe for success within the profession of music. It has now been six years since I left London, where I had lived for two years, and moved back to Canada, a few months after I turned thirty. Coincidently, thirty is believed to be, by some people in the opera profession, the age in which a singer must decide if she will continue her pursuit of becoming an opera singer. I've often heard opera singers (the successful ones - the ones who are able to earn a living from singing) comment about this. I've heard that if a singer hasn't found success by thirty, she needs to seriously reconsider her career path. Revisiting this excerpt, I finally feel a sense of...something other than pain. I believe it is acceptance. Acceptance allows me to reflect upon my experiences in London from a different perspective. I have also included the excerpt to illustrate the realities and struggles I faced while pursuing this career; the financial sacrifices, the familial negotiations and the conflicting internal dialogue inherent within my pursuit. They are all integral to who I am.

Until this year, I had always carried the weight of my musical identity with a sense of shame. I could only see myself as a failed musician and it hurt deeply. In fact, it hurt so much that I couldn't listen to classical music or even attend classical concerts. I closed myself off to the part of life to which I had always been devoted. Closing the door on my passion and, in effect, my spirit, was very painful. I experienced a grieving period..grief over the loss of my dreams, the loss of my identity and the loss of part of myself. Being a musician, being an opera singer, was woven into my very being. Music was as much a part of me as my lungs, my mind, or my hands. For quite some time, I existed in a foggy daze, not understanding what had happened or how I ended up *here*. I carried my shameful secret around with such sadness in my heart; afraid to enter worlds I had previously known. Thankfully, the fog has finally lifted. The experiences I gained from my time as a performer are very much part of who I am, but I no longer feel shame about these parts of myself. I feel compassion towards myself, and a sense of having healed.

The process of completing my Masters' degree in music education, has confirmed what I have always known: that I am a teacher. This is a label and an identity I state with pride and which I am anxious to bring into practice. In my teaching, I am interested in fostering relationships built around care with students and I look forward to inspiring a new generation.

I don't think I could have reached this point in my understanding without having engaged in self-study research. I have been able to reach these understandings and to embrace my new identity within the music community through the inquiry. My self-study research has allowed me to reflect, reframe and re-imagine (Richardson, 2006) my experiences as a musician, as a teacher, and as a perfectly imperfect human being. My identity has been renewed and I have been able to reclaim the part of my spirit that was shut out. In fact, as a result of my self-study, I no longer view myself as a failed musician; rather, I look at this necessary re-telling of my story as a gift. Self-study has allowed me to channel my sensitivity and compassion towards myself and has allowed me to reconcile my past, present and future into a new narrative.

The Research Class at OISE: Which Persona Will I Choose?

When I entered the classroom at OISE I didn't know what to expect; I was both nervous and excited. I viewed the Collaborative Narrative Inquiry into the Arts class as a good test. I suspected that in the first class we would have to go around the table and introduce ourselves and wasn't sure I wanted to mention my connection to music, or to my past. I could identify as a Masters of Music Education student, allowing the class members to make their own assumptions about me. I struggled with my identity but ultimately, I chose to be honest and declared that I was in the midst of a transition within the music community.

The processes of inquiry, and of engaging in self-study research methods forced me to look at myself in a non-judgmental manner. Illumination over the duration of the course occurred in a symbolic and metaphoric way. The class seemed to have awakened me to a way of thinking and of knowing, of which I hadn't previously been conscious. Through my writing and research, I realized that I was holding onto my pain with a tight grip. Through discussions in class, I also realized that my journey could actually be perceived as a positive one. My final paper consisted of a research proposal and in it I chose to locate my study in the positive rather than the negative. I know there was something incredibly freeing about that decision.

The pivotal moment of the semester came near the end (the timing is important to note as this moment occurred upon completion of my narrative, self-study research paper). For the Thesis Presentation assignment, I presented Carole Richardson's (2006) dissertation and at the close of my presentation, I sang an aria. I felt something more than joy in that moment; I felt a strong connection to every person in the classroom. As I sang, I was able to go back in time to the joy I used to feel when singing. This moment wasn't about being perfect or winning a role in an opera. It wasn't even about performing. I wanted to connect with the people I had come to know during class and wanted to share my voice with them. In fact, I *needed* to share my singing voice with them, especially as I had already shared aspects of the painfulness of my journey. I hadn't realized, until then, how disconnected from the actual art of singing I had become. In that moment, I reconnected with the art and joy of singing.

I present an excerpt from my narrative self-study research paper, written as part of the coursework for the class. It provides insights into my journey of discovery and connection to the arts, and to making connections between the personal, professional and scholarly aspects of myself.

The Power of Music: A Portrait

When I listen to Beethoven's Emperor Concerto, I am transported to an open field on a cold winter day. The day is so cold that even the snow longs for warmth. The rooftops have a fresh dusting of snow on them and icicles dangle gracefully as they glisten and reflect the sunlight. Smoke lazily exits chimneys to the rhythm of the gentle and quiet piano part that appears so perfectly in the middle of this musical masterpiece; immediately following the explosion of the orchestra with the militant strings aggressively repeating their theme. I can hear the crunch of the top layer of snow as I step respectfully on the downbeat (thus creating an instrument of my own in the midst of this tranquil sound that the piano is producing.) The theme that is playing in variations hypnotizes me and I am at the mercy of magical sound. There is purity in these forceful rhythms and mesmerizing harmonies that make my heart flutter with love. The piano's grace is my pendulum. I cannot resist this. I smell wood burning in a fireplace and envision people skiing, walking or skating in solitude, meditating. This listening journey is one that must be taken alone. The music speaks to me-it is as if Beethoven himself is whispering intoxicating secrets in my ears. These secrets calm me and deliver a peace I have rarely known. No matter what is happening around me, outside of my experience, I have reconnected with myself. I have survived this experience and emerge humbled, energized and wistful…renewed.

I believe this is the closest I can ever come to describing (with words) the feeling of music. When I sing, the act transcends everything. Time and space are no longer in effect and the power of the sound derived from the ritual of singing transports me to a higher spiritual level. It is as if there is a tornado constantly swirling within me but when I sing I am in the eye of the tornado; in the calm and peaceful safe spot, which is centred and balanced.

REFLECTION

I want to belong. Desperately. I am the girl in the chorus watching the soloist soar. I am the girl in class not quite understanding the cruelty of the Hungarian trained music technician. I am the girl in the red dress, hair piled on her head with a rhinestone clip baring her soul to the world while her heart pounds so hard she is sure the audience can see it beating. I am the girl who has learned the repertoire and rehearsed everything to perfection who cannot breathe as she begins Bach's Bist du bei mir (Thou Art my Joy). I am the girl who receives praise and tears of emotion from new fans after the Schubert lieder (song) who goes home alone with a headache and heartache. I am the girl

> who guiltily receives praise and who readily accepts the criticism that inevitably comes from those who know. I am the girl who is painfully aware that you cannot rest on your laurels. I am the girl who just wants to sing. I am the girl who is tired. I am the girl who wants to belong.
>
> (Pereira, M. Unpublished Professional Journal, 2007)

CONUNDRUM

> The arts are not for a privileged few but for the many... that their place is not on the periphery of society but at its centre, that they are not just a form of recreation but are of central importance to our well-being and happiness. In the panel's view, this status will not be widely achieved unless artistic excellence is the constant goal of every artist and every arts organization, and mediocrity is recognized as the ever-present enemy of true progress.
>
> (The Rockefeller Brothers Fund, in Tindall, 2005, p. 52).

I am a classically trained opera singer. My undergraduate degree states that I have a Bachelor of Music with a major in Voice Performance. Even now, eleven years later, I am proud to state this. During my undergraduate program I was introduced to various forms of discipline, abuse, joy, love and heartbreak. I always joke, to whoever will listen, that my degree was earned through hard work, blood, sweat and tears. I mean that literally.

There is a lot of pressure when I am identified as a singer. When people find out that I sing classical music, especially opera, there is a joy in the other person's face. This moment is wonderful, because I am able to make a connection through a love of music with another person. However, there is another side to this moment. When I label myself as a *singer*, there are expectations attached to that identity, of which non-singers are unaware. For example, I am always asked to sing at events on a spur of the moment basis. I am so well trained that I cannot possibly entertain the idea of singing on the spur of the moment! There are many factors to consider: is the voice properly warmed up? What time of day is it? What are the acoustics in the venue? Are my vocal chords lubricated? What if I don't live up to their expectations? Of course I realize how ridiculous this sounds to non-singers but this is the truth.

Musicians, music educators, and society have done a fine job advocating that music is special. In doing so, society has placed classical music and musicians on a pedestal. On this pedestal, only good exists. There is a collective denial of the bad things that do exist in the training of professional musicians. There is a denial that the art that once brought us joy can sometimes deliver heartache when we try to perfect it. The hierarchy and traditions (which include issues of power and a culture of isolation and perfection) of classical music are intrinsic in our training of musicians. The allure of becoming a professional musician dictates that we must sacrifice and endure hardships in order to reap the benefits. Sometimes this means enduring a *pedagogy* that includes abuse (physical, sexual and/or emotional).

In order to achieve great things why must I sacrifice, and why am I scared into silence? Why am I forced to choose my art (my potential livelihood, my identity/

label as special and talented, and all of the years invested) at the expense of my spirit? I don't believe that this should exist and through my story I hope that others will find the courage to sing their stories and also find the strength to rebel against the violations that are common in the training of professional classical musicians. I know that I am not the only one who has faced these difficult issues.

REFLECTION

> In Rome, the conductor yells at me repeatedly, throws his baton at me, and tells me he thought he hired a singer not a squealing pig (or some similar derogatory term-I can't quite make it out-his Italian accent is thick); he has decided that he doesn't like me. He also throws chairs at certain members of the orchestra. I am not special; he is equitable and generous with his hatred. Each rehearsal is a power struggle between us and I force myself to attend each rehearsal because if I can manage to endure this, it will be an amazing reference. I embrace my identity of singer and cling to it desperately. Tears threaten to make an appearance but I swallow them painfully. Right now I need to focus on producing quality sound, not tears. During breaks I talk to one of the string players, he is visibly shaken by the conductor's behaviour. We sneak off to explore the city during our free time and we find peace. The peace comes from knowing that we are not alone in our suffering! He lets me know that the orchestra thinks I am amazing-I have become a sort of hero to them. No matter what the conductor throws at me (literally and figuratively) he cannot break me. They find strength in this. This makes me feel embarrassed. I want to be known as the girl who can sing, the girl who has talent, not the girl who survives. He assures me that if I wasn't such a talented singer, the orchestra would not think twice about me. This helps my fragile ego and propels me to continue.
>
> At the performance, the conductor is frowning at me and waving his weapon (the baton) wildly at me. But, I have a secret; I am empowered by the orchestra (my secret supporters!) I am also energized by the audience-they are sending me positive energy.
>
> After I finish my aria, the orchestra rises to give me a standing ovation. The servants have triumphed.
>
> (Pereira, M. Unpublished Professional Journal, 2007)

Unusual Connection-Crisis as Opportunity

The doctor in the emergency room at the hospital, as gently as he could, told me that I had just suffered a panic attack. Simultaneously, I felt anger, shame and humiliation. How could I have something mentally wrong with me? How could I be doing this to myself? Didn't the doctor realize who I was? Didn't he know that I was an opera singer? Didn't he know that I had sung in front of hundreds of people in Rome and Canada? Didn't he know that I had recorded for the Canadian Broadcasting Company's Young Artists in Profile concert series? I wish I could tell this story differently. I wish I could describe a scene in which I handled the diagnosis with grace and dignity. However that is not what happened. I begged for a brain scan and I prayed that they would find something other than this mental health diagnosis. Alas, the reality was that I had suffered a panic attack and agoraphobia followed.

Agoraphobia is a strange condition to experience. A good definition I have found to describe it is "the term 'agoraphobia' means "fear of open spaces", but is more appropriately described as a fear of being any place where one might feel alone and vulnerable to fear and panic" (Capps & Ochs, 1995, p. 3; quotes in original). During the period in which I suffered with it, everything I knew or at least thought I knew was turned upside down. I felt I was no longer the person I knew myself to be and as a result, I had to renegotiate my identity. I suffered from agoraphobia for three months, a time during which I could not leave the house due to fear. As horrible as agoraphobia is, I often describe my experiences with a sense of humour. I believe this is my way of coping with the fact that I have, indeed, suffered from this mentally debilitating condition. I also feel the utmost respect and compassion for anyone who is suffering with or has suffered with this condition.

The fear I experienced during those three months can best be described as sheer terror. As soon as I attempted to leave the sanctuary of my home, I was gripped with an overwhelming sense that I was going to faint or worse...die! At the same time, however, I was still struggling with negotiating the identity of who I knew myself to be. Therefore, as real as the feelings of terror were to me, there was always an inner voice grounding me. So, the part of me that problem solves and strives to be perfect sought to find group therapy for agoraphobia. It is an isolating condition, so my thinking was that if I could find a group, perhaps an 'agoraphobia anonymous', I could be well on my way to healing. At the time, it made perfect sense to me, however, obviously this idea is flawed. For example, if the support group consists of people suffering from agoraphobia, people who have a fear of open spaces...a fear of leaving safe havens, then how in the world will they meet for group therapy? When that reality dawned on me I laughed so hard. I realized that I had a choice: get better and participate in life, or continue existing in my new reality.

Part of the pain of suffering from panic attacks and agoraphobia, for me, at the time, was the knowledge that somehow I was creating this reality. I decided that I needed to see a therapist and with the help of my mother sought counselling. I needed someone to drive me and accompany me to the appointments. This was my way of coping. My thinking was that as long as I wasn't alone in the open spaces of the outside world, I would be okay and wouldn't faint or die. Driving to my counselling appointments is not a time I like to remember. I was gripped with panic the entire time. I also sobbed the entire time and used coping mechanisms such as deep breathing, closing my eyes to shut out the world, and repeating my mantra, "everything is going to be okay". This part is difficult to describe because unless you have experienced this condition, it seems bizarre. My mother was the one who ensured I attended all of my appointments, and I know that although she didn't understand what I was going through, she could see and sense the anguish I was in.

Crisis as Opportunity-Origins

It began as I drove down the country roads singing along with the wonderful soprano, Tracy Dahl, who was singing Mozart's *Vorrei spiegarvi, oh Dio* (*If I, O Heaven, Could Tell You)*, K. 418, which is one of his concert arias for coloratura soprano. This is a difficult aria, it is Mozart's trademark, and it is deceptively complex. The difficulty of this piece is that it is mostly written in the coloratura's passagio, the place where the voice breaks between registers. Once you can figure out how to sing *up there,* how to navigate through the passagio, can support your breath as you climb up to the high C note from the passagio, then you can float, spellbound by the sound that you are creating. Vibrations of perfectly balanced sound escape from your mouth, but this only happens when you have attained a certain level of proficiency. I had been studying voice for twelve years before attempting to sing this piece, and knew that it requires a high degree of vocal prowess. On that day, one moment, I was in my singing zone. In the next moment, I passed out. When I recovered, I drove myself to the closest gas station and unintentionally frightened the cashier who could see my heart beating speedily through my shirt, and my sweat dripping onto the dirty grey tiles. The ambulance and firemen came and I began my transformation.

Reflecting upon this experience, I realize that one-year prior to the above incident, I had been singing the same aria by Mozart, on the same country road and on that day we experienced a minor, uncharacteristic earthquake. As a result, deer came running wildly out of the safe refuge of the ravines. I was driving along happily singing when a doe landed on the hood of my car. After locking fearful eyes with me, she galloped off. In performer mode, where I have been trained well to suppress emotions, I started up the stalled car again, and drove to my husband's workplace, which was very close to where the doe and I had collided. I calmly told him what had happened. When he came outside to look at the car, neither one of us could believe the amount of damage that had been done.

When the doctor labelled me as someone suffering from anxiety, I was given a prescription of Valium and became agoraphobic for three months. It could only be for three months, because in three months I was moving to London, England to pursue opera professionally.

I approached therapy the same way I approached my professional training. I wanted to be the perfect patient and I wanted to be the best. I also wanted to experience a recovery that was faster than any other client. I wanted to overcome agoraphobia so that I could get on a plane and fly to London, England and start my life as a performer. I achieved all of that. However, thankfully, my body and nature conspired to continue to send me messages and eventually I listened. The message is simple: I am a teacher in my heart and spirit; I do not have a tough skin; my empathy, compassion and intuition enable me to teach...**listen to your spirit**.

REFLECTION

> In grade one we had music class. The music teacher would let us sing our hearts out to the music she chose for us. One day, as we were singing through the repertoire, she stopped the choir because she heard a beautiful voice. She went from child to child and asked each of us to sing part of the melody that we had been singing. When it was my turn, I gleefully sang the melody and my voice was met with smiles and praise. She stated that I had the voice of an angel, and that I sang like bird. She said that she could listen to me sing all day. All I knew was that I loved to sing, to make music, and I looked forward to music class each time we went.
>
> (Pereira, M. Unpublished Professional Journal, 2007)

How Music Seduced Me

Music seduced me at a young age. Ever since I can remember I have wanted to sing. I never wanted to sing anything but classical music and I have no idea why. My parents are not musicians but they did expose me to the most beautiful music through live performances, television and records. I do have a vague memory of watching Bizet's Carmen with my Dad, and I remember watching Carmen sing her famous Habanera and wanting to be her at that moment. She was beautiful, mysterious and powerful. My parents enrolled me in the local Children's Choir and I was able to sing the music I yearned for.

When I was sixteen years old, I found that singing in a choir no longer satisfied me. I wanted more of a personal connection to music, and I wanted to nurture my voice. I became aware of "the voice" (all singers refer to their instrument in third person.) A singer never refers to "my voice", because at a certain level of development it becomes "the voice"! Perhaps this is what protects our souls from the criticism that is embedded in our tradition. When we remove our voice and disconnect it from "my voice", somehow the critique becomes less personal. The *(my)* voice was pretty and powerful and craved more than to blend in with others. The voice was ready to be nurtured and pandered to. I wanted private lessons. I needed to sing as a soloist. I saved money from a part-time job and I found a voice teacher. She was wonderful. Her name was Margaret. She was tough and gruff and smoked cigarettes and she looked worn out and tired. But, when she opened her mouth to sing, my goose bumps always accompanied her. Her tone was warm liquid and it enveloped me with a sense of calm. The first thing Margaret said to me, as I stood in front of her with all of my hopes, was "Why do you want to sing?" Without thinking or pausing, I told her that I didn't want to sing, I ***had*** to sing, and it was because I couldn't imagine doing anything else, I couldn't imagine my life without singing. I told her that when I closed my eyes I could see myself on stage making people feel alive. She seemed to like that answer and we developed a great relationship.

Although I am sure I frustrated her, I know that she believed in me. She was the first (*magical*) musical person to believe in me and I have never forgotten that. She made me feel hope that one day I too would belong to music.

Margaret looked like the stereotypical Wagnerian soprano. She had dark and curly shoulder length hair and her body was robust and stout. She wore a mask that told you she was tough and strong. She stood with her shoulders back and her spine rigid; she moved with grace, regardless of the weight she carried. Her body was alert, ready to produce sound under any circumstance. She had one of the most beautiful mezzo-soprano voices I have ever heard. It was infused with deep and rich tones that soothed my ears. Youthful ignorance and naiveté led me to pose the bold question "Why didn't you pursue a professional singing career?" Her answer, as she stared at me intently, was that nerves and anxiety prevented her from it. She would become sick to her stomach before every performance and realized she didn't want to live that way. I felt sick when she told me that. You can conquer it, I thought. I had nerves, and I wasn't even close to being as good as she was at my age. Somehow I managed to stand on stage at the infamous Kiwanis Music Festivals and sing my soul out, while my knees and hands shook, and sweat poured from every pore in my body.

As we all know, with age comes wisdom and I now know that for Margaret the decision not to pursue a career in opera, took more courage than it did to continue with it. She put her health (mental and physical) before a job and she found a great career as a singing teacher, inspiring young singers to follow their dreams.

Becoming a Singer

When I graduated from high school and entered the next phase of life, University, I enrolled in general studies. This entailed attending a variety of courses in many fields and I didn't find my niche. One day, as I was walking around campus and doing some soul searching, I came to the conclusion that I wanted to study music. I realized that I was envious of the people I had met who were studying music. For me, it seemed as if a new world was opening up; a brilliant world where one could actually obtain a degree in MUSIC. A degree in music would surely prove that I belonged to that world.

At my next lesson, I informed Margaret that I was going to get my Bachelor of Music. She encouraged me and I gleaned pertinent information from her. She found an accompanist for me and helped me to prepare for my Faculty of Music audition. Soon, the big audition day came and I was nervous: very nervous.

I proceeded with the audition and I was horrible. The head of the music department asked me why I was auditioning, as it was evident that I had no formal music training. I looked at him directly in the eyes and told him that if I was admitted to the program I would give 150% at all times. I told him that this was a challenge that I needed to undertake and that even though I had never been formally introduced to music, music had seduced me and I was desperate to obtain a Bachelor of Music no matter how hard I had to work to earn it. As I left the audition, people had gathered outside the door and on my way out, I heard people exclaiming that I had a beautiful voice. I noticed as well that they were stealing glances in my direction. Weeks later I received a letter of acceptance. When I read the acceptance letter I cried out of sheer joy.

All of my professors were professional musicians and none of them had teaching degrees. I always found that ironic, that at this higher level of education, my professors were not required to have teaching certificates. My voice teacher had a career in lieu of education, and the cycles that music performers are taught were repeated with each generation. My lack of formal music education caused me to be at a disadvantage in the music program. I did not fit in with the professors and I did not fit in with the students. I felt that I did not belong. I soon discovered that I needed to hide the fact that I did not have the music theory and music history knowledge prior to University. This was a new experience for me. How could the mechanics of music make me feel so badly about myself, and yet, singing was pure joy? How could these two things be related?

Musicianship Class: Practical Music Making

> No matter what the style or complexity, music can be most simply described as organized sound; and the purpose of studying harmony and theory is to learn the methods by which sounds are organized in both large and small ways
>
> (Wyatt & Schroeder, 1998, p. 6)

> I remember being locked out of a classroom for being one minute late for musicianship class, and receiving an F grade for that day. I remember running to class every day after that. One day, in particular, I remember falling on the hard concrete on the steps of the subway platform, dirt caked on my face and tears spilling from my eyes in a desperate attempt to make it to that morning class with the Hungarian music specialist (a renowned musician in Hungary, not a renowned educator). I remember sitting at the piano to play one rhythm line, tap the second rhythm line, and sing the third rhythm line. I remember making a mistake and feeling as if I was going to faint. I didn't know my heart could beat so fast. I remember the professor making an example of me by telling the other students that he hoped no one was as bad as I was, and then asking me to repeat the exercise, this time with him yelling at me for inspiration.
>
> (Pereira, M. Unpublished Professional Journal, 2007)

This experience made me feel humiliated; it made me feel as if I didn't deserve my talent. I experienced feelings of anxiety and sadness during this time and I felt there must be something seriously wrong with me. For a while, every time I opened my mouth to sing, my voice sounded shaky. Musicianship is the process of building a foundation of aural skills and music theory; of developing basic music skills. The students in the class would cringe every time I had to perform my musicianship exercises. I experienced such intense despair; I remember I almost withdrew from University on at least three occasions. My confidence had slowly and meticulously been chipped away.

Solace was found in the comfort of my voice teacher's studio. He was an ally to me, he believed in my voice, my drive and my talent; he didn't know my horrible secret-how terrible I was in musicianship class. His mission at this phase of his teaching career was to create intelligent singers. In his studio, I was introduced to phonetics, physiology and vocal pedagogy. When the other voice studio was rehearsing, his students were at the hospital engaging in laryngoscope investigations. We recorded our vocal chords in action and became well versed in maintaining our healthy instruments. While the other studio's students were vocalizing, we were measuring our vibrato on his state of the art Apple computer program. There was pressure in every lesson to make perfect sounds. I became afraid of making a mistake, even when practicing.

Although I was accepted with open arms at my voice teacher's studio, others were not so lucky. During master classes, those who didn't possess talent, those who didn't embrace his style of vocal pedagogy, those who dared to speak against his technique, were punished. Each month my voice professor's studio size diminished, as he would expel the students who disagreed with him about his methodologies. As is often the case in the unique teacher-student private studio relationship, the relationship was more akin to master-servant.

I learned that singing is a sport and a science. I learned that singing encompasses the use of the entire body, not just the throat and the upper torso. I learned music theory, music history, how to play the piano poorly, and how to read music! I learned that my voice teacher wasn't liked very much in the department. I learned that politics ran rampant throughout the music world and especially in the music department. I learned that each teacher believes that she or he is correct and everyone else is wrong. I learned that students would defend their teachers fiercely. I learned that some singers could be desperately cruel. I learned not to trust people. I learned that I still didn't belong to this musical world. I learned that if you were "not good enough" you would be recommended to music education. I learned that I was a good listener and I became a sort of mentor to some of my peers. We even held master-classes for each other and respect was at the heart of these collaborative sessions. We knew the sacrifices we had made, including the repudiation of unwanted sexual advances from our various professors and conductors, and we helped each other through the tears. By acknowledging and allowing our pain, the musical experience became authentic.

BATTI, BATTI, O BEL MASETTO (BEAT ME, BEAT ME, MY BEAUTIFUL MASETTO)

> My teacher has asked me to visualize as I sing my recital repertoire. He has asked me to go back to a time when I felt free, when I felt peaceful and happy. I always turn to nature. One of my favourite memories of feeling free, at peace and happy is when I used to ride my bike around the Reservoir; the feeling of the wind in my hair, the sound of the wind in my ears, the feeling of power and freedom. As I sing Mozart's Batti, Batti o bel Masetto, the beautiful aria from the opera Don Giovanni, I remember that feeling. Except. Except that my teacher keeps on interrupting me:

"You're flat on the F#, you're not breathing properly, the vibrato in the beginning of your notes is uneven, I must hear the full spectrum of sound with every note you sing, lie down on the floor and try it, stop jutting out your chin, your tongue looks too tight, sing into this microphone and I'll show you how your vowel isn't pure...You aren't emoting....... EMOTE ....."

Sometimes the sixty-minute lessons felt like torture and sometimes they felt like pure bliss. How can a joyful experience be so painful at the same time? This is the paradox I search to untangle.

Longing for Connections

By the time I graduated from University and began to perform semi-professionally, I enjoyed the audition process. Instead of dreading the panel of disinterested judges who madly scribbled things on their notepads, I began to look at auditions as a way to connect with other musicians, and as an opportunity to sing in front of others. The intensity of competition at this level is remarkable. However, I always managed to connect with some of the other singers and would always offer them genuine advice and compliment them afterwards. I longed for a connection with other people who were experiencing what I was experiencing; people who were seeking what I was seeking. I spent most of my time in a studio by myself where I would review phonetics, languages, libretti and notes; in a chamber of self-imposed isolation. When I wasn't by myself, I was either with my vocal coach, who also did not possess a teaching certificate, or my voice teacher who was a recording artist, and also without a teaching certificate. I was being told that I was imperfect, and that I wasn't good enough.

REFLECTION

I am supposed to meet my new vocal coach backstage at the Royal Opera House, Covent Garden in London. I am so excited that I want to scream. I think of the myriad of singers that have walked through these doors. I will have to audition for him, of course, but I have solid references, solid technique, a warm sound, and a tough skin. After passing security, I see him waiting for me. As we walk to the practice studio, he opens the door to the stage and I see the hall from the perspective of a performer. He tells me, as he lets me bask in this moment, that this is where I might be singing one day. Back in the studio, we begin with the Bellini and he remarks that although my voice is small, he can work with me, and he comments that I have potential. Not satisfied, he comments again on my small voice and alludes to the fact that it doesn't match my bigger body. I take it in stride, as I am a well-trained coloratura soprano. If I dwell too long on the "small voice" comment, I am afraid I will cry or yell, so, I bury my reaction in a place which I am sure is overflowing. Over the months I end up dreading my walks up to the backstage of Covent Garden, Royal Opera House. I never know what will happen in each lesson.

(Pereira, M. Unpublished Professional Journal, 2002)

Teaching

When I lived in London, England, possibly one of the most expensive cities in the world, I found work as a teacher at a Day Centre for developmentally disabled adults. Ironically, I secured that position without a degree in education and with no references. I needed a day job because even though I had been singing for fifteen years, with a list of impressive references, I couldn't yet make enough money solely from singing. My intuition and common sense guided me into teaching. All my life, family and friends have been telling me that I am a teacher. That hasn't been what I've always wanted to hear. I wanted to hear that I was a natural performer, that I belonged on stage, connected to music. When I graduated from University, I needed money and I found a job at a local college as a Disability Services Officer. In this role, I helped students in various capacities. For example, my office was a testing centre for students who needed extra time to write; I scribed and clarified for students; I provided an informal counselling/tutoring role. This job didn't seem like work to me, it felt like connecting with people and helping people, and I felt good at the end of each day. In the beginning I denied how good it felt, because I (ignorantly) thought that if I liked helping people in this way I wasn't a true performer!

In London, I looked forward to the days that I taught. Together, the students and I made music by clapping and singing, we made pottery, we planted seeds and trimmed gardens, and we managed a shop where we sold our plants and pottery. The feelings I had when I was with my students were akin to the feelings I experienced when I was allowed to perform; when I was deemed good enough by the experts. This was difficult to admit because of the shame associated with shifting within the musical community. The current view is that if you are a performer, then you are a performer. If you cannot make it as a performer, if you've failed, then you fall back on teaching because there is something wrong with you. These assumptions make me angry. I now realize that I can be good at more than one thing! When I pursued a career as a professional musician, my life was filled with angst, and I was filled with desperation, anxiety and sadness. When I decided to pursue a different path, I sought counselling as I recognized that I was experiencing the stages of grief. The decision to leave my dreams behind was one of the most difficult decisions I've ever had to make. Through volunteering at public school, and through teaching disabled adults in London, I found comfort and a natural fit. When I teach, I don't feel like I am fighting against something, I don't feel as if I have to prove something. Unexpected moments in teaching provide joy and learning whereas unexpected moments in performance provide neuroses and criticism. When I teach I feel connected to other human beings. I feel relief.

REFLECTION

During my transformation this year, I have had a moment of insight. Some of the teachers that I have been experiencing while attempting to achieve my dreams are not true teachers. Their identity is failed performer or successful performer or simply performer. This identity is always at the forefront. The

> teaching is secondary. Each student is a vehicle for his or her ego. The student that displays talent, determination, and drive could be the one that catapults them into the spotlight again. I am appalled to discover that there is no governing body that monitors the teaching of music.
>
> (Pereira, M. Unpublished Professional Journal, 2007)

Conclusion

Music and I have separated and reconciled over the past few years. Our relationship has been filled with passion, glee, and pleasure; it has been tinged with regret, sorrow, and anger. We have a tumultuous relationship. For the few brief moments that my heart melts and I let down my guard, music is my saviour and always welcomes me with open arms. My desire to sing opera professionally spread into every aspect of my life. I made many sacrifices and always felt alone in my pursuit. I was trying to belong to something.

Through my narrative self-study research I have finally realized that it is not music that makes me angry. I am angry at the accepted traditional mode of teaching and the culture we have fostered and the tradition that values product over process, that values perfection over human spirit, that I am angry with. This is a strange feeling because I have spent a long time being angry at music. I am relieved to discover that I am not, in fact, angry at music. I can renegotiate my relationship to and with music! I feel hopeful and I feel liberated as a result. I am awakening a desire within myself to continue my studies; I would love to pursue this. At the same time my confidence has been restored. My shameful badge of failure has been replaced with a badge of courage. My inquiry and self-study have served to illuminate my strength.

Beginning the self-study was difficult because I was forced to look within-to remember painful things. As I started writing and looking back at journals kept along the way, knowledge began to blossom metaphorically and intuitively for me. As the painful events screamed at me, joyful moments slowly dug their way out of dark corners and depths of my memory. Reconnecting to the joy of music through self-study research has been pivotal for me as well in terms of my art. In fact, the other day I caught myself doing it again: singing. I was singing! I started singing the opening measures of Verdi's "Caro nome che il mio cor" (Treasured memory of his name) from the opera Rigoletto; I have to admit, it felt great. It didn't sound too bad either! I was singing for the sake of singing!

Beginning with the investigation of these issues and through the process of generating personal accounts of these experiences, I am hopeful that my own healing will continue. By redefining and questioning our current methods and beliefs we can begin to question the accepted definition of the music teacher. Slowly the musicians' pedestal is lowered.

REFLECTION

> To educate as the practice of freedom is a way of teaching that anyone can learn bell hooks (1994, p. 13).

> I am holding my breath and now I feel dizzy; I am afraid of rejection but... I can breathe. The news is good! I have just been accepted into the teacher education programme at The Ontario Institute for Studies in Education at the University of Toronto, and I am ecstatic. This feels different than other acceptances I have received in the past... when I was a singer. This feels exactly like where I need to be. I feel secure and confident...there is no anxiety. I keep on picturing myself as a teacher in my classroom! And I can't stop smiling every time I envision it. My classroom is going to be a place of joy, comfort, community and respect. Everyone, regardless of age and abilities wants to feel cared for, listened to and respected and every human being deserves that. The children are going to enter the colourful classroom and be surrounded by lots of colour, and pictures of nature. Maybe I'll bring some nature into the classroom too, plants, rocks, and sand. The children's work will adorn the walls. An abundance of books will greet the children and every day they will have time to read. Elementary school is going to be a wonderful place to foster a love for learning.

> Even though I am not going to be a 'music teacher', I am going to find a way to incorporate music into my classroom. Perhaps I will start the day with songs, have lots of books with music, have songs to end the day. I could play music for the children too...the possibilities seem endless. I want to remain flexible on this new journey, and remaining open and flexible in the moment is going to be a key component in my teaching. My classroom is going to be a safe, warm and inviting space where ideas will flow. My job will be to guide student learning; I need to provide leadership and guidance as students develop and explore. I know that maintaining a culture of empathy and respect in my classroom will be essential, and I am going to embrace diverse learning styles with an emphasis on creativity and tolerance. Okay, I just have one more year and then I am going to have a real career! I am going to be a teacher and I can't wait!
>
> (Pereira, M. Unpublished Professional Journal, 2008)

AFTERWORD

It is April 2009, and I am completing my internship in the teacher education programme. This is the final requirement of the programme, I am close to becoming a certified teacher and I feel like I have come home. I cannot remember a time I have felt this consistently at peace. I have successfully completed two practice teaching placements over the past year and I have had the most amazing experiences. I love teaching and I adore the children. Every day I am in the classroom I learn...I am proud to say that I both teach and learn. The most amazing things have happened to me over this past year. Perhaps the most surprising thing for me is that my music identity has merged with my teacher identity. Music has swirled around me and dangled its tantalizing allure, and once again I found I could not resist its call. I have used music in all of my teaching experiences; however, I have included music in my own style and in my own way. I have integrated music with literacy and I am already thinking of new ways in which I can integrate music into more lessons...I have even started to visualize myself as a music teacher!

I realize now, that while pursuing music as a profession, I had to close myself off to my emotions and create a hard shell of protection. In teaching I have been able to open myself and have been able to reconnect to that part of who I am. I bring my compassion, sensitivity, intuition, humour, creativity and imagination to the classroom. In teaching, these qualities are strengths and they are not weaknesses. My desire to connect with people is a desirable quality that I bring with me to the classroom. Although I am still finding my way as a teacher, I am off to a great start. I have worked with people who have been identified as having special needs, adults, children in kindergarten, children in grades two, three and four, and students in high school. I know that regardless of age everybody wants the same three things for sure: to feel respected, to feel their voices are heard, and to be treated with kindness. My philosophy, as I have entered classrooms this year, remains the same. When I stand at the door to greet the children as they enter the classroom, the smiles on their faces warms my heart and I know that I am exactly where I am meant to be.

- Believe in yourself. Listening to my inner spirit has been a constant guide and source of strength for me.
- Learn how to forgive…it feels so good when you do.
- Embrace humour…try to see the humour in every situation if you can.
- Nothing is really that serious. Seriously! Unless it is a matter of life and death, stop taking it so seriously. Whether it is a mistake, or a deadline, or something someone said, try not to take it too seriously.
- Stop taking things personally. This one is difficult, but when you stop taking things personally you will realize a freedom and will feel a release of tension. Criticisms and negative comments say more about the people who make the comments than they ever will about you.
- Find people who make you feel good and enjoy their company. Don’t waste time with people who make you feel bad. You have a choice!
- Spend some time with nature. My inner voice is strongest when I am in nature. Taking time out of a hectic schedule to enjoy the sounds and sights of the natural world is pure bliss.
- Remember, you don’t know everything—be open to new experiences, knowledge and learning. I learn a lot every day just by listening and keeping an open mind.
- Be kind...kindness and compassion are gifts of humanity…use them!

MELANIE MARKIN

4. DANCING THROUGH LIFE, ONE STORY AT A TIME

INTRODUCTION

I am a single woman in her early thirties, still living in the city in which I was born. I have a slightly younger brother and wonderful parents who emigrated from England forty years ago. I am a French Immersion elementary school teacher, a dance teacher, sometimes a choreographer, and right now, a graduate student pursuing a Masters of Education. However, does that really tell you anything about me? Our interpretations of this information are likely different. Maybe I am just like you or perhaps we are worlds apart. In fact, even what that means to me and about me, is continually evolving in my own life. My current thinking is that my "selves" are dynamic, always dependent on my past experiences and my present situation, and I am still learning how each of them contributes to who I am, and to my outlook on the world. I would hope that if I describe myself as 'unique', this might suffice, but sometimes that is just code for 'different'. There have been many occasions when I have felt that I don't quite fit; my perspectives, perceptions and ways of doing things are somewhat different from the mainstream. It is not that I am wrong but I recognize that sometimes it feels as if I am trying to belong to a world with which I 'almost' connect. I think that it is this feeling that brought me to graduate studies. It is something to do with the search for people who think like me. However, along the way I am realizing that accepting my own 'unique', artistic and creative way of interacting with the world is what makes me, and makes me who I am. It is not my curse, but rather my gift.

Hopefully, this perspective will help me to mentor others who are searching to understand their place and the role of the arts in their lives. Maybe it will help me to find the connection that links me to my inner being, and to others and the world, in a meaningful way. As I was learning to write my personal narrative, I came to know and understand the arts as one of my significant means of connection. They act as the threads that link together various people, events and themes in my life. They unite who I am and what I do, to create my own inimitable perspective. Hi, my name is Melanie Markin. Welcome to my world.

Stories of Self – Narratives of Understanding

> It is easy to underestimate the power of storytelling because stories are ubiquitous. They permeate our daily conversation so much so they often pass unnoticed. The truth is that our most meaningful communication takes place when we share stories with each other. Although storytelling appears to be a

M. Beattie (Author/Ed.), The Quest for Meaning: Narratives of Teaching, Learning and the Arts, 93–105.

> very simple process, it is, in fact, a complex activity that profoundly shapes our psychologies – both individual and collective – and our experience of ourselves and other people....In essence, the stories we tell are the people we are. (This quote is from an article entitled: The poetics of storytelling [bibliographic data unknown])

In my view, part of the power of a story is in its ability to be both uniquely personal and entirely global in its interpretation. Stories seem to welcome us into a virtual world allowing us to create meaning and to reveal 'personhood'. Sometimes creating or re-visiting the story can help with the realities of living life. How would you tell your life story? I would dance mine! I think you would learn a lot more about me that way, for although I speak both English and French, movement is my first language.

Recently, in one of my graduate courses, I explored my journey to graduate studies through dance. My body re-visited the dichotomous sensation of being stuck in a comfortable yet disconcerting rut, the confusion of being torn and pulled between my familiar teaching environment and the unknown world of the graduate student, and the release of deciding to take the plunge and apply, feigning indifference of course. I embodied the aggravation of waiting 'patiently' for news, the frustration of others' hopeful inquiries and the clarity of realizing how much I wanted the change when I thought it wasn't happening. Finally, I evoked in my soul, both the pride in being accepted and the sadness and loss that came with leaving my classroom, students and colleagues to embark on this new journey. Along the way, I invited dance colleagues to engage in the same exploration of a meaningful moment, seeking to understand if our processes and experiences were similar. I worked with some of my dance students, eager to see how they would respond and was overjoyed when they started making connections to the ideas of 'freedom', 'expression', 'self' and 'others'. Personally, I found dancing an excerpt of my life was a challenging and affecting task, but strangely familiar and reassuring. I was surprised by how many emotive sensations remained hidden in the sinews of my being and how powerfully they rose to the surface. By dancing my experience I deepened my personal understanding of what my journey meant to me. I suppose I should not have been surprised really, because you see, before anything else, I am a dancer.

I am sure that I was born that way. It all began on Saturday, February the eighth, 1975. My parents were hosting a dinner party. The guests were on their way, the meal was in the oven and then my mother started spotting. When their friends arrived, my parents left them to entertain themselves and headed off to the hospital. My Dad came back for dinner and my Mum had a dry ham sandwich at the hospital. The next day my parents were supposed to be going to the ballet in Toronto to see Sleeping Beauty. Although not due for another six weeks, I had other plans – "labour"!

Perhaps I was trying to make the matinee or just make sure I was part of the fun. Even today it is said that I enjoy being the centre of attention and I love the theatre. Anyway, the ballet tickets went to friends as it appeared evident that my parents were in for another kind of show that afternoon! As the day progressed it seemed that perhaps I had changed my mind. I am still known to take forever to make a solid decision. So in the early hours of Monday morning the doctor said it was unlikely I would make my debut anytime soon. However, things began to move faster than anticipated and, as with all great stories, tensions began to rise. Shortly before 4:00 a.m. they began to lose my heartbeat and they had to put my Mum out. The rest is a blur for her and I was not even aware of all this, but I was born ...on Monday, February the tenth, 1975, six weeks premature, at four pounds and one ounce, a footling breach. Yes, that means I came out feet first, with one leg leading the way through the birth canal and one knee bent up, already in position to perform my first pirouette. Right away I was centre stage under the lights - not stage lights of course, but those of an incubator.

Dance therefore, is not simply something that I do, although I have danced for twenty seven years and been a dance teacher for the past sixteen years at the same studio. Dance is also a significant part of who I am. Dance is my sanity. It is my social outlet, an emotional release and can even be a physical test. Sometimes it is almost a habitual activity, but it makes sure I stop and take some time for myself. It is also one of the only ways I can switch off the other thoughts that float around my head. There are times when my body communicates more eloquently, authentically and profoundly than anything I could ever express verbally. This bond can be difficult to understand, even for myself. Sometimes it is more significant in the doing or in the watching.

Last year, I left a school that has teachers who taught me as an elementary student, colleagues with whom I attended school, and children whose families I have come to know well for over ten years. I left a building that felt like home and people that felt like family. I danced my goodbye! If I am honest, I wasn't sure I could even do that, but it felt like the best way to let them glimpse that little part of me I keep to myself. I wanted them to know the impact they made on my life. It was my only way to say thank-you! Although I am aware of my audience when I dance, sometimes I am lucky enough that my soul overpowers my brain and that awareness becomes peripheral. I must admit, the idea of performing turns me into a bundle of nerves, but often once I start it is almost indescribable. It is like being in two places at once; inside and outside myself in unison. When I was done, I was struck by a comment from one of my colleagues, my former teaching partner of five years. Steve said to me: "as you danced it was like watching the years fall away from you, almost like watching you become you". At the time I didn't quite understand, but felt it to be a compliment in the truest sense of the word. Upon reflection, I came to understand that perhaps Steve had, in fact, glimpsed "me". Not the "me" that gets presented to the outside world, the "self" that is responsive to those around me, but the "self" that is vulnerable and innocent and only appears when it is secure. My inner "artistic" self is the one that is accessed when it is safe. For me, it is most often artistic endeavours that seem to provide that sanctuary. Imagine, if everyone could access that well of security, if we all had a place where we could just 'be'.

Dancing my life would likely be the most authentic and personal window into who I am. Movement doesn't lie and I believe that it is often possible for the body to know truth before it is conscious in the mind. Sometimes the only way I know how I am feeling is to trust in the movement, the music and myself. The lyrics of a song can feel like they were written specifically with me in mind; capturing my thoughts, struggles, emotions or a particular experience. The beat itself can surreptitiously seep into my soul. Together they can manifest in my body and my mind when I least expect it and when I am most in need. Or, I can actively seek them out to help console, inspire, motivate and reminisce. In this respect, they are like secret friends or the imaginary best friends of childhood, always there when you need them.

Safe Spaces – Narratives of Enchantment

The idea of the arts as a safe space presents itself as a recurring theme in my reflections of both my personal and professional life, as I am a person who has been resistant to change. However, I am learning that because the arts are so much a part of me, I always have something familiar with me when venturing into the unknown. Armed with this ‘artistic companion’, change has suddenly become a way of getting reacquainted with myself in a different context. It is amazing that the ability afforded to me by various artistic endeavours, to vicariously experience the lives of others and even take on a different persona, helps me to connect with who I am and understand my perspective of the world. I am sometimes asked where I find my ideas. I don’t really know if I learned to see the world artistically or if I choose to interact creatively and imaginatively with my surroundings. Either way, the arts act as my connecting language.

My favourite childhood story, like that of many girls no doubt, is Cinderella. I loved the sense of magic, and possibility. I believed in the power of what-if and, of course, the sparkly dresses and glass slippers were the icing on the cake. Even as an adult, if “princess” could be my career, it might rival teaching as my chosen profession. I still remember the first time I came across this enchantment on stage. It was when I saw Andrew Lloyd Webber’s CATS at Hamilton Place.

I can recall the “orangeness” and the wood of the theatre in stark comparison to the “bigness” and darkness of the stage. The set featured a huge tire, a ladder, and half of a car. It looked like a magical indoor junk yard, and that was likely the point. There were giant things hanging down from the ceiling and along the curtains. Spirals of smoke would appear from time to time from the dark crevices on stage. I think it was the magnitude of it all that impacted me the most. It was safe because I was in these bright orange seats with my family, yet there was this mysterious, magical, daunting, but inviting place at a hop, skip and a jump away from me. Then I saw the eyes, flickers of red and orange from various nooks and crannies that would vanish in an instant, leaving me to question if I had seen them or imagined them. Then the music built to a crescendo, with its “dah dah dah dah!” and finally the movement began on the stage.

Although I delighted in the entire show, from the beginning I have always wanted to be the “white cat”. Victoria was the only cat that was dressed head to toe in white. Immediately she stood out from the others. She was unique, and of course, different. In Victoria's case however, different meant special. I knew she was a classy, elegant cat. She had both aloofness and finesse to her movements. She wasn't one of the leading cats. She didn't have a song about her and probably wasn't key to the action. However, I knew she was important. Why else would she be the only one completely in white? She did have a dance solo and it was beautiful; she seemed so long and strong and yet simultaneously graceful. She often leapt onto the stage and then passed the time with small, delicate, intricate movements. I knew that if I ever got to be a "cat" I would be her. Then, in grade seven it happened; I got my chance to be Victoria! What an amazing experience it was for me to combine imagination with reality. It was compelling reinforcement about the power of what-if! Now I can see many parallels between my own self conception and the persona I pulled from this feline character.

This 'willing suspension of disbelief' that is so vital in the theatrical experience seems to me essential in living an artful life. Going to the theatre is a regular occurrence in my family and I am thankful that my parents introduced me to the gifts of live theatre. On my 17th birthday I saw "*Aspects of Love*" in Toronto, an amazing show confronting the challenging issues of love, life and relationships. However, what I remember most vividly is the transformations I saw in the characters on stage that were reflected by costumes and set design. In the beginning everything was white, reflecting innocence, joy and hope. Gradually, as characters lost direction, black became the dominant theme only to be tempered by black and white as characters confronted issues that helped them understand the complexity of life itself and find a balance. The introduction to symbolism afforded by this play affected me deeply and seeps into my artistic works today. As an adult, I make time to go to the theatre with friends and family. I feel that many of these excursions bring us closer together as they frequently result in engaging conversations about the human condition, personal choices and the lives of others. It is amazing to me how much we can learn about ourselves through the lives of others.

It is this sense of enchantment that makes me envious of the children with whom I work. It is also one of the reasons I love being a teacher. In the same way that artistic endeavours have the capacity to attain my complete attention, it is also almost impossible for me to think of other things when I am working with children; especially if we are working in the land of imagination. Although I am their teacher, I learn so much about the magic of possibility from them. It is my belief that to be an effective adult you have to remember what it is like to be a child. You have to remember that sense of wonderment and awe. As a dance teacher, I try to bring that wonder into the studio. I find it easier to make a personal connection when I bring the sense of story to my choreography. In this way, dance continues to be a universal language with the power to communicate to others. I also learn effectively by making associations, therefore I use a lot of metaphors and visual imagery when teaching. As a student I used to create choreography to help me study for exams. Now, journeying with my students through a whirlpool, under a bridge, up a mountain and through the tall grass using only a ribbon and some music is my chance to recapture my childhood and one way that I can encourage my students to make connections to the world around them.

Sometimes those real world what-ifs can seem scary and easily turn into a fear of failure or a reason for not doing something. I am gifted at seeing the 'worst-case' scenario of any new situation and have had to talk myself, or be persuaded by others, into many a new opportunity. I have been told that we often see ourselves reflected in our students and teach to those needs. I see it as my childhood stories informing the new chapters that I co-author in my classroom. As a classroom teacher then, I strive to provide a safe space for students to confront and explore those what-ifs. Part of this is the realization that we are all meant to learn and we learn by making mistakes, me included. As a French Immersion teacher I ask my students to take a risk and step into an unfamiliar world everyday. The world of French is one that most of them only encounter at school. In many ways, although it is a familiar world, it is one that holds lots of unknowns and both the possibility of success and failure in a child's eyes. As I consider the arts and imagination my means of connection and my safe space, I try to fill this new French environment with many creative outlets, strongly believing that artistic endeavours are valuable both in general and in the acquisition of language. My classroom management strategies for transitions, listening and tidy-up are rooted in songs and my science and social studies explorations frequently involve role-play or movement to interpret meaning. In my classroom we have explored the water cycle using diamond dances. We have become scientists trying to uncover the identity of mystery liquids. We have held an animal council meeting to determine how to deal with a lazy sloth and we have also taught an alien about the meaning of family.

One of my first ever role-drama experiences in my own classroom was based on the book *Plumeneige* (Trans: Snowfeather), about a snowman that comes to life. The students were positioned in pairs all around the room. One partner had just finished sculpting the other into a snowman that was about to come alive with our classroom chant. One snowman sculpture in particular caught my attention; she was standing with her feet together and both hands over her ears. At that moment she sparked to life with her first excited snowman words; "Où sont mes oreilles? (Trans: "Where are my ears?"). She jumped up and down, took her hands off the side of her head into an 'I don't know' position and then returned to her original tableau. I was mesmerized; not only was it a clear French message but it made snowman sense. How many snowmen have you seen with ears? This might be a definite concern if they did come to life! The energy and desire that fuelled the students' next few classes as we explored the adventures of Plumeneige was inspiring and even motivated our first official piece of French writing. In that role-drama, and other experiences since, I have discovered the power of alternative realities to teach me even more about who my students are and what they need. I have also been able to recapture some of that childhood magic despite being an adult. Do you remember how it felt to put on a costume and become someone else for a change? Do you remember exploring someone else's life and making a connection to your own reality? In my own experience I think that playing with what-if can sometimes give us the courage to make it a reality.

The power of the arts to provide alternative opportunities for exploration and self-discovery should not therefore be limited to the sphere of childhood. Exploring issues of identity, isolation and belonging are important for young people as well. In my adolescence, it was many of my extra curricular arts experiences including dance classes, Performing Arts Camp and school musicals that let me explore different facets of my personality and work through social issues in a creative and safe manner. With a similar goal in mind, for the past five years I have used text sources including poems, books and personal anecdotes, to explore various issues with small groups of intermediate students at my school. Together we have created bilingual drama and movement pieces to share our understanding of these issues with audiences at our Board wide Drama/Dance festival "*Creating a Scene*". We have used a poem about Remembrance Day to explore peace, a rap to promote anti-bullying messages, and have created our own dramatic script about personal identity. We have also explored the cultural and emotional impact of the tsunami disaster, and the issues surrounding the rights of a child. The most rewarding outcomes of this process are not necessarily the amazing performances they create, but rather the sense of community that develops and the openness that ensues. The shared arts experience helps us to create new relationships, to uncover the layers of our personalities, and explore our individuality. People see themselves, each other and their relationships in a new light. I believe this shared story then opens up alternative channels of communication and understanding.

Awakening Secrets – Narratives of Revelation

Many kinds of stories have a way of illuminating the unknown about the self thereby resulting in greater self-understanding. In the same way that dance acts as a window to my soul, other art forms have resulted in personal epiphanies. One art form can also reveal the secrets of another. For me, one such art form is poetry. In high school, I wrote a poetry anthology about dance. It was the first and only time that I had written about the emotional side of dancing. Looking with today's eyes I see hidden meanings. In some of the poems, dance comes across as romanticized, almost a metaphor for a relationship presenting images of magic, attraction and trust. In others, dualisms are present; the freedom of dancing versus the confinement of rehearsal, the elegance of costumes versus the torn feet and tired muscles, and belonging versus isolation. A strong theme of perfection and sacrifice, though not necessarily in a negative light, also prevails. These poems allow me to re-experience one of my passions and yet gain new insight and fresh understanding of its complexity.

I was first introduced to the magic of poetry by my Dad who gave me Shel Silverstein's book, *A Light in the Attic*, for my tenth birthday. Inside the front cover he had written me a poem. That was the first time I can remember anyone writing something specifically for me. It made me feel very special. It also touched me in a way that made me want to understand others in that same manner. In university, I wrote a poem about a friend who seemed disconnected and reluctant to show any vulnerability or dependency on anyone.

DEAR ONE

Who are you dear anxious one?
Why do you cling to the periphery,
not quite willing to belong?
Taking three steps forward and two steps back.
Is there a reason why you dare not let down your guard?
Have you been disappointed?

Who are you dear unhappy one?
Why do you frown in the face of life's little miracles,
and seek solace in the realm of hopelessness?
Is there a reason why you no longer dare to dream?
Have you been frightened?

Who are you dear fearful one?
Why do you hide behind so many walls
and lock your heart away?
Is there a reason why you let no one quite near enough
to turn the key?
Have you been betrayed?

Who are you dear bitter one?
Why do you veil emotions in quick wit
and distant tones?
Is there a reason why you drown in false indifference?
Have you been forgotten?

Who are you dear lonely one?
Why do you suffer in silence,
hidden behind a mask of contrived emotion?
Shatter the darkness and
Silence the questions!

For though you may have been disappointed and frightened,
betrayed or forgotten.
You are not alone!

Open your eyes to the everyday wonders of the world.
Open your heart to the passion that soars around you.
Open your mind to the joys of emotion.
Open your hands to the endless possibilities.

Find the child that was lost in the journey.
Find out who you are,
Dear one.

(M.M., 1996)

Imagine my surprise when years later, upon reading the poem, the person I saw reflected was none other than myself. I wonder how many others might see themselves exposed in these words or what more I might come to see clearly in the years that follow. This revelation of self-knowledge and self-understanding over time has made a powerful impact on me. It reminds me that poetry, like most art forms also has the power to reveal what you need to know when you are ready to see and understand its meaning.

Stories of Others – Narratives of Inspiration

In many ways, thanks to some amazing elementary teachers, just as I consider dance a language so I consider teaching an art! When I consider the person and teacher I am today, I need to reflect on my past stories. I feel my memories of childhood experiences significantly shape the person I am becoming and I am only now beginning to understand their role and value in my life. Along the way I have learned about the importance of mentors and role-models. As a teacher, I often hope that I am making an impact. I am sure this question of influence haunts many educators and people in general, but if I am any indication the answer is yes. I would not be the person I am becoming today without the experiences provided to me by some amazing mentors along the way.

My first clear, conscious memory of speaking and hearing French is in grade four. Mme Begg, my classmates and I are singing *Rock and Roll Frère Jacques* (Trans: Rock and Roll Brother John) and *J'entends le Moulin* (Trans: I hear the mill wheel). I love to sing and move, so whenever I think of French and that memory comes to mind, I smile. Monsieur Legault and Mme Forth continued to make learning French fun, interactive and artistic. I was learning the language, but most of the time I was experiencing their passion and the joy of exploring another world. They taught me another way to see the world, in languages, just like dance. It is strange to me that although I was a shy and quiet child even in my first language, as evidenced in report card comments, I discovered my voice alongside teachers of a second language. In learning the language I began to re-envision myself. I found a confidence and uniqueness in the world of French. Like dance, French became a land of possibility. My eventual conceptualization of dance as a language and language as an art now shapes my own philosophy. I understood passion then as a student, but it has come to inform my own teaching. I learned that students will recognize passion, hear joy and feel encouragement before they learn content. Therefore, for me to make learning meaningful and fun for them, it is important that I draw from my own passions, inspiration and way of knowing the world. I believe teaching about and through the arts provides a joyful learning experience and honours what I know of myself thus far. There is however, much to be learned.

In further exploring my arts and language connection, this year I found myself writing about my transition into my career as a French Immersion teacher. I was surprised at the outcome. The story was easy to write and just seemed to flow out of me, but upon reading it, I learned something about myself and my professional identity. I know I hold myself up to high expectations in my career, but I don't think I ever realized why it was so important for me. In my first few years as a teacher, sometimes a wave of fear would wash over me. I would look around at a room filled with innocent, smiling faces and wonder who put me in charge of their development. The importance of the task of education would weigh heavily on my mind. I would put the image of the 'teacher police' discovering me as a 'fraud' out of my head and then refocus on the room of expectant faces. You see I have a secret, well I did until now! Although I came through the French Immersion program, took my French as a Second Language Additional Qualifications courses, passed the oral and written components of the board interview and was deemed 'qualified', my undergraduate degree is not in French.

In fact, when I was given my first full time position, teaching grade one French Immersion, I panicked! "What if my French wasn't good enough?" Reading and reflecting on this story allowed me to come to terms with some of my teaching behaviours and their origins. I settled on teaching as a career path very early in my life, but it seems as if my 'secret' is a catalyst for some of my professional outlook and behaviours. Firstly, I am often seeking opportunities to improve my French, be it a French Bursary program the summer before I started my first job, an immersion and culture summer program for French as a Second Language teachers, additional qualification courses or conversations with francophone colleagues. Secondly, I try to make sure that what I do, I do well. It is important to me to make a positive difference and a meaningful impact on the lives of my students. I don't want to give anyone the opportunity to say I shouldn't be a French teacher. I believe I can do that if I don't forget the significance of the 'call to teach' and the joy that learning can bring. Personally, this means not only asking my students for their 100%, but consistently giving my 100% as well! I guess people might say that I should just make it easier on myself and teach English, but the French language, like dance has become an integral part of who I am. Just as the arts allow for the exploration of alter egos, I am passionate about my French for the same reasons.

In Retrospect – Narratives of Connection

Another one of my mentors also taught me about the importance of being passionate about the artistry of teaching. She is my dance teacher of 27 years. Mrs B has an amazing gift as a choreographer. She seems able to find the essence of the music with her movements. She is able to draw out of her dancers a truly unique combination of movement, emotion and presentation. It is as if she is creating a reaction between the dancer's innermost thoughts and the movement itself, allowing a new and powerful story to be told through their dancing. I believe however, that she can do this because she connects herself, the dancers, the music and the movement in a harmonious way. In my own journey to become an artist and growing as a person, the connecting story takes on a greater voice. It has become increasingly important for me to explore these connections in my personal life, my teaching endeavours and my research as a graduate student. Arts, education and language all help me explore the other in greater depth and facilitate my understanding of who I am and how I got here. Both my arts and education mentors have had significant influence on my perception and choices.

Memories of some of those magical, meaningful moments, creating and inspiring with students, friends and mentors continually influences the decisions I make as a teacher and a person. In grade seven, I had the role of 'Kitty' in our school play "*Star Dreams*", which was all about students realizing their passions in the arts. Miss Blair made all the cat ears for my number and just before I went on stage she told me how special it had been to work together. After the show I remember speaking with or receiving a card from our Vice-Principal. Either way I discovered that we shared a secret, that her nickname growing up had been "Kitty". So, from then on we had this special bond. They are both small actions that revealed the person behind the teacher, but they made a significant impact. The longer I teach, I try to show my students that same humanity, even though there is a part of me that believes in setting and maintaining boundaries.

Similarly, one of my proudest moments as a dancer came from working on a duet entitled "*Double Vision*" with my friend Kari. It was the first time we had learned and performed a duet and the process taught us a lot about each other, dance itself and our relationship with our teacher, also her mother. The goal of a duet is to dance the same as each other, but this was also a lyrical style which means that expression is important. At one competition, dressed in our blue and silver dresses, we were awarded a trophy for best emotional execution. Of all the awards I have won as a dancer, this is the most meaningful. Sharing these experiences allowed me to learn something about others and myself that I would never have been able to know otherwise. Here lies the power of the arts for uniting and revealing the human connection. Maybe it is the memory of feeling known and understood, of seeing myself reflected in the eyes of someone I respected, which makes me want others to know that sensation. Accessing emotion is challenging in itself; bringing it to the surface and communicating it meaningfully to others is harder.

Artistic endeavours help me connect to the emotional side of myself and for that I am lucky. They not only ground me emotionally but also spiritually by allowing me to remember what came before. For example, when I listen to the song, *Scarlet Ribbons*, I think of my granddad. When we visited him in England he used to sing it to me as I sat on his knee. He had a deep husky voice, but breathy in the same vein. He would wrap his arms around me and I would feel protected and happy as he sang. In many facets of my life I search for those safe place sensations, such as this song provides. To this day, it can inspire me, comfort me or transport me to that time and place where worry subsides. Sometimes, with everything that is going on in the world and in my life, I think I forget to be grateful for the life I have lived thus far. It can be hard to make yourself vulnerable to the world around you, to admit that you are imperfect and fallible, to accept when you need help and guidance, and to acknowledge when you have done a job well and deserve to be proud of your abilities and accomplishments. I might not be able to say it, but I am getting better at feeling these emotions. They are present in that mind-body connection and reflection that are highlighted by artistic engagements.

I am a keeper of stories, my own stories and those of others. In reading, writing and dancing my own stories I have come to reflect on my life's journey so far. I have a greater understanding and appreciation of the person I am today and of the origins of some of my values, choices and decisions along the way. I am a unique work in progress. The more I learn about myself and the world, the more there is to seek and discover. In my world art is life and life, at its best, is artistic. I think it is important to find wonder in the everyday and part of that wonder can be found within. I am learning that it is alright to march to a different drum provided you enjoy the music that's playing. My Masters journey has rekindled my artistic energies and allowed me to understand their importance in my daily life. I can now revel in rather than fear my constantly evolving personal story. It is not meant to be about the book, a finished product, but rather it is the chapters that speak to the journey. Remember, the world will happily tell you who to be until you show them by drawing, painting, singing, writing, or even dancing who you really are.

Me, I am a dancer. I am a girl who tap dances when she's nervous and bops around the kitchen to synthesize the day. I am girl who loves anything that sparkles and can be inspired by the glittering of ice on the pavement and the glimmer of starlight. I am a teacher who is just a big kid at heart, one who loves to pretend and play and who is learning alongside her students. I am a graduate student who has changed and grown along a path of discovery and who now hopes to inspire other teachers and students to connect artistically to their classrooms and revisit their stories of self. I am a person whose mum gave her a pewter wishing wand that says 'imagine, enjoy, love, shine and create'. I believe it is paramount that every person has the chance to experience those concepts. I think that it is important to feel known. I believe that everyone needs to know that they are unique and special and to understand their place in the world.

In sharing my stories with others, both friends and strangers, I have seen myself reflected in their eyes and discovered aspects of myself and my relationships that were previously hidden from view. The relationship between arts and experience, story and self, and their impact on my personal, professional and academic life is notably complex and evolving. As I continue to grow, explore and experience new things, this connection will hopefully allow for continued insight and understanding into the person I am becoming. Still, knowing that relationship is part of what makes me uniquely me, is now comforting. To know me is to know my 'arts', and for me to know the 'arts' is to know myself. Let the dance of life begin!

AFTERWORD

Have you ever had one of those quiet, moonlit, melancholic evenings where you are overwhelmed by the desire to thumb through an old photo album or open the treasure chest of mementos from events passed? If so, you will understand how I felt as this artistic rendering of my journey emerged into this narrative. First came the joy of reconnecting with all of those wonderful experiences and opportunities, followed by the task of framing them in a lens of identity. In all honesty, and much to my surprise, the connections seemed to appear almost effortlessly. What I found most delightful was that once I began to see connections in one area of my life they came alive everywhere. It is truly remarkable how interconnected our lives are if we are open to see and learn from the associations. Furthermore, if you have been known to acquiesce to the aforementioned desire to while away a few hours reminiscing, you already know something of which I was reminded. In bringing my story to the surface I realized the importance and value of personal reflection. So often, likely in any career, but definitely in teaching, we spend so much time planning, delivering, assessing and evaluating in relation to others, that we seem to forget to take the time to see where we belong. I believe that the more we understand our journey the more likely we will come to know our authentic selves. For me, this process was re-energizing. I became re-connected with the passions that are innately part of the person I am. I gained understanding and appreciation for the path I have travelled thus far. I discovered new gifts, interests, desires and perhaps, most importantly, I started to find what I was looking for – me!

CARLY STASKO

5. THE POWER OF STORIES

Tracing the Creative Thread and Healing the Self Whole

PROLOGUE

The Art of Falling and The Dance of Life

When I was three my Dad would often call me "*Stumblelina*" because I was what many would call a clumsy child. He also gave me some wise advice, which I remember and continue to follow and share to this day.

"Carly", he said, "When you're dancing and you're going to fall, tumble so that you don't hurt yourself and **whatever you do - don't stop dancing**. Pretend like it was all a part of the dance. Do something on the floor, twist around, kick your legs, sway your arms, and find a 'dancey' way of getting back up." At the time this seemed like pure wisdom – the kind of advice that could actually help me rather than being told not to dance or not to fall – both of which were simply not options.

A few years ago I had a memorable dream during the weeks while I was waiting for biopsy results (these results would determine if there was a re-occurrence of cancer in my 27 year old body). I had already gone through a year of treatments for Hodgkin's Lymphoma and was bracing for an unknown future. Nightly I had my own personal dream-a-thons, as I struggled to make sense of the rapid changes and challenges I was undergoing. In this particular dream I am explaining to a friend how I'd been invited to participate in the Winter Olympics as a figure skater.

"I didn't know you could figure skate, let alone that you were a professional!" exclaimed the friend. To which I gave this odd explanation.

"Well", I explained confidently, *"I don't know how to figure skate, but I'm very good at getting back up after I've fallen, and that's why I've been invited to compete in the Olympics. There is a big audience that wants to see how I get up from falling. It's more about the recovery than the skating"*, I summarized.

At first this dream seemed strange, but I liked it. I appreciated my confidence and my ability to participate unconventionally in a very structured and hierarchical competition. I realized later that the dream was showing me that recovering from a fall is an art in itself and that it's something I've become very good at.

Sometimes during the months and months of bi-weekly chemotherapy treatments I had previously undergone, I would refer to the whole experience as the "Cancer Olympics". I felt like there were so many different challenges ranging from the endurance challenge of chemotherapy itself; overcoming nausea (to get a few meals in a day); dealing with losing my long hair; moving home to my parents

M. Beattie (Author/Ed.), The Quest for Meaning: Narratives of Teaching, Learning and the Arts, 107–118.

house; trying to get the best possible care from my doctors; making wise medical choices; overcoming fears, shame, and my need for absolute control; letting go of all my plans and being in the present; and of course the one challenge I hadn't anticipated, the roller-coaster ride of falling in love while undergoing cancer treatments.

My whole "Olympic career" was about falling with grace. I watched my white blood cell counts fall with every chemotherapy treatment, my hair fall off my head, the future and life I had expected fall away, and my own fragile heart fall in love. Trevor had said to me early on not to "fall" too hard. He felt the unbelievable pressure of the situation and chose to begin a romantic relationship with me anyway. Those cautionary words were for him just as much as they were for me. I took my Dad's early advice. Rather than deny the fact that I was falling which could likely lead to real pain and injury, I tried my best to accept the fact that I was falling and to fall with grace, so that I could dance my way back onto my feet again, fully aware that to do so put me at risk of falling again. What a worthwhile risk it is.

To Weave Oneself Whole: Narratives of Possibility

> She has repositioned herself as the conscious controller of the warp and weft of the imaginary life that she spins and weaves. (Mechem, 1998, p. 129)

I first began my studies in education in the midst of a deeply significant transition in my life. Previously, I had been teaching media literacy as an Imagitator (one who agitates imagination) with the Toronto Youth Media Literacy Project – an organization I had founded and run for over eight years. On a more urgent and personal note, I had just come through two difficult, yet ultimately triumphant and transformative years facing and overcoming cancer. I was in my late twenties with what felt like a new life, a "new normal" and a new emerging sense of self and purpose as a result of my recent life-altering challenges. It was a crucial time to reflect on my identity and to reconnect with my future goals. I had an intuitive sense that through my studies in education, I would continue to heal and formulate a more cohesive sense of my whole self. At the time my identity felt very fragmented. There was an uneasy division that existed between my *before* cancer self and my *after* cancer identity. This rupture had called other parts of my identity into question as well, and I felt a strong need to re-imagine future narratives for myself as a writer, artist, activist, educator, scholar, healer and citizen. For this reason I was drawn to begin my research with an investigation into a narrative, holistic, and arts-based approach to educational studies. Through biographical and creative reflective writing, I have been able to weave the vibrant threads of past experiences together in ways that allow me to imagine new and inspiring future narratives for my personal, professional and scholarly life.

Identity, Purpose and Creating Cohesion

> Telling our stories is an act of bringing order to our universe by making it clearer to us how we see the world, the universe around us, and our role and place within it. (Atkinson, 1995, p. 13)

I am very interested in the ways that stories form the foundation of our identity (Holstein & Gubrium, 1999), and that stories are our primary mode of understanding and interpreting experience (C. Carter, 1993; K. Carter & Doyle, 1996; Egan, 1986; King, 2003; Polkinghorne, 1988). Given that our lives are storied and narratively constructed (Eakin, 1999; McAdams, 1997), it makes sense that much healing and learning can happen during the story telling process. Not only does writing help to connect or relay events, but it also allows for new ways of envisioning and understanding oneself and one's life. (Anderson & Anderson, 2003, Atkinson, 1995)

In my creative and scholarly work I am inspired to explore what semiotician and qualitative researcher, Linda Rogers (1998) describes as the "often highly embattled process of meaning-making in order that teachers, educators, therapists, and cultural workers might re-fashion both the personal and public self in the interest of the healing and social transformation of the larger social order" (p. xiv). In my healing journeys I have explored the question ***"How do I create and re-create a whole and interconnected self?"***

The question: *"Who am I?"* is inextricably wrapped up in another important question: *"What is my purpose or place in the world?* Not only are these questions key in the healing process - they also open doors into the ways that I will teach, create and socially engage in my life. In *The Courage to Teach*, Parker Palmer says that "we teach who we are" (Palmer, 1998, p. 2). This is why the question of identity is both important on an interpersonal and intrapersonal level.

In his philosophical text *On Creativity*, David Bohm, a famous physicist and thinker argues that our creative tendencies derive from our need to "assimilate...experiences of a vast and awesome universe – a need to make sense of and relate to this universe rather than simply react to it" (Bohm, 1998, p. xi). My personal epistemological impulse corresponds deeply with Bohm's description of *relating* to the universe rather than simply *reacting* to it. This form of relational pedagogy is about seeking out connections, cohesion and resonance—some of the founding principles of Holistic Education (Miller, 2001).

It has been very important to be able to connect the story of my earlier life with the life I lead now. In the following narrative I explore the ways that my creative "culture jamming" and work as an Imagitator has helped me to overcome cancer and to transform my greatest challenges into a source of inspiration and guidance for the future. This collection of thoughts, poems, images, stories, ideas and questions is the synthesized result of a sustained multi-mediating meditation about my identity and interests as a creative catalyst for change and ever-evolving human being. This collage of ideas flows out of an intuitive, creative and inquisitive process guided by wonder and shaped by multiple disciplines including: Arts-Based Research, Semiotics, Psychology, Holistic Education and Cultural Studies. I have been advised that the best way to approach such a project is to "play" and as you will discover, play is at the root of much that I do – it is one of my favourite verbs.

Adventures of an Imagitator

> If you summon it by the right word, by its right name, it will come. This is the essence of magic, which does not create, but summons. (Kafka, 1988)

Several years ago, during a moment of brave and hopeful inspiration, I created my own dream job title and began calling myself an "Imagitator" – someone who agitates imagination. Since then I've been hired as an Imagitator by organizations ranging from local NGO's to the UNESCO World Urban Forum. The most rewarding work I've done as an Imagitator has been to agitate my own imagination – to light my creative spark during my darkest times. In dreaming up the name "Imagitator", I created more than a name, I created a new path in my life – one that continues to be enriching and inspiring.

Eight years ago I founded the Youth Media Literacy Project, through which I visit high schools across North America and teach workshops on self-publishing, media literacy, globalization and art for social change. As an Imagitator in the classroom, I strive to be a catalyst and to be catalyzed.

Cut N' Paste (R)Evolution

> It is only through creating and recreating perceptual worlds in a continuous interaction or communication between the bodily self and the environment that we achieve and maintain an identity of our own and are at home within our own uniqueness. (Cobb, 1977, p. 66)

My relationship with art and media began to shift in a very significant way at age fifteen when I started to cut up fashion magazines and create my own collages. It was then that I first learned to use art as a tool for dissent. I used to read teen fashion magazines in a form of trance. I would consume the images with a sense of curiosity and urgency, as though my teen survival depended on it. Once I'd finished devouring the magazine I tended to feel dissatisfied with my body, clothes, lifestyle and gender. The images and messages in the magazine reinforced my insecurities and introduced many new ones. Tampon ads would feature a woman from waist to knees wearing white pants showing no arms, face or feet. All that was shown was the contentious area where a woman might stain her clothes if her tampon leaked blood. Many of these ads showed me that it was embarrassing if anyone found out I had my period, and reinforced the idea that menstruation was dirty, unclean, and smelly. These were NOT the kinds of messages I needed as I entered womanhood. They filled me with shame, insecurity and fear.

Everything changed the day I took out my scissors and glue and started cutting up my teen magazines. I created a collage of a monster made up from bits and pieces of different models. Instead of looking beautiful, this Frankenstein-like model exposed what I believed to be the ugly underbelly of the modelling industry: eating disorders, dangerous plastic surgery, and self-loathing. Next I started to cut up a box of maxi-pads, changing the logo from "Always" to "Go away", with a slogan that read "Tell Manipulative Media to Go Away!" That is when the power first started to shift. I felt like I was revealing something. I showed it to friends who would laugh, nodding their heads in approval. Through this new kind of storytelling we were empowering ourselves.

I covered the walls of my bedroom in cut and paste creations. These were very personal because they attempted to piece together the few empowering voices and images I could find in the media. Then I got the courage to take my other collages, the ones that expressed my anger, critique and awareness, and began to publish them in a zine (a self-published magazine pronounced 'zeen'). In addition to sharing my zine with friends, I would leave copies in bookstores using a technique referred to as "drop-lifting" (the opposite of shoplifting), which involves leaving creative artefacts in stores in the hopes that someone will serendipitously stumble across them and feel curious. It was through publishing my own zine that I was able to find my voice as a writer and artist. I've come to believe that everyone has a zine in them once they've tapped into their unique truth.

Culture Jamming

Culture Collage.

Navigating through the world with my imagination,
trying not to drown in all the information.
The saturated self overwhelmed by stimulation.
The only way out is to follow inspiration.
The best defense against the barrage,
is to commence a culture collage.

(C.S. 2000)

Soon after publishing my first few zines, I started to take my collages and commentaries even further out into the world as I began pasting, sticking, painting, and performing them around the city. I began what is called Culture Jamming, which tries to challenge, subvert and reclaim mind-share and public space by playing with the symbols and slogans from commercial advertising. I frequently enjoyed jamming bus stop ads throughout the city by writing speech bubbles coming from the mouths of anorexic looking models that read "FEED ME". I was also inspired by a group called "*Pretty, Porky and Pissed-Off*" who posted stickers that read, "Be a Revolutionary and Love Your Body". The city became a playground. With a small troop of jammers I began climbing up onto billboards dressed in disguise as an employee of the billboard company. During these "billboard liberations" we would mount new banners that exposed the underlying and often insidious messages of the ads. Once we changed an ad for Target Cigarettes looming over a schoolyard to read, "The Target is Children – No More Death Ads". Our motto was "Don't Get Caught", but I always felt ready to defend and justify my actions. Culture jamming, activism and self-publishing opened up a whole new world for me, connecting me with a larger community as well as to my own strong voice. Through culture jamming I was able to express my own resistance and critical awareness so that as I travelled through my environment I could feel authentically engaged and empowered.

Spreading the Jam

The verb "to jam" has three meanings that help illustrate the distinctive elements of culture jamming. The first meaning of "jam" is to create in a spontaneous and improvisational way, as a jazz musician might jam. The culture jammer must improvise as they work within the restrictions of a pre-existing situation; a billboard, an idea, or a physical space. Jamming also means to disrupt as in to "jam the machinery". The culture jammer disrupts dominance and power by subverting meaning or reclaiming space. The third interpretation of jam refers to the production of a sweet preserve that can be spread on crackers or toast. In this third meaning, the culture jammer is involved with the preservation or even "cultivation of sweet things", such that new meaning and new culture is created. Thus, through improvisation and disruption something new can be created and shared. As I continue to culture jam, I've come to see it as more than just subverting consumer ads but as a whole way of approaching creative self-expression in the broadest sense.

Play is the Way

Open you eyes and demystify
the worlds that reside in your dreams where they hide.
Never mind if they're silly, bizarre or insane,
for you'll find that you're willing to explore just the same.
But remember my friend, the goal is to flow –
not to measure, to name, to own or to know.
So question your fears, leave them all at the door.
Embrace the unknown and prepare to explore...

(C.S. 2000)

Play is a key element of creative presence. I've come to appreciate the experience of creative *flow* and to see how "joyful and interesting complex symbolic activity is" in all aspects of my life – and particularly, in regard to the healing process (Csikszentmihalyi, 1996, p. 125). With enough courage we can channel our anger, fear, and pain into something as brave as play. Playfulness is ever present in all the various forms of creative expression I have participated in, from zine publishing, street art and performance, education, and even my own healing process. I've come to see my experiences as a healing journey. At first I began to heal my relationship with the media in my environment, whether it was advertising, education or public space itself. But these were all just a warm up, a gradual preparation for dramatic new challenges that lay ahead. More recently, it has been my relationship with my own body that has been healing. What connects these seemingly different experiences is the role of play and creativity as tools for transformation and invention.

Jamming Cancer

> I'm a girl with a positive vision; I'm going to laugh myself into remission! (Carly Stasko, 2005, announced this to friends and doctors in the hospital the day after a cancer diagnosis.)

At first my experiences with cancer and mortality were so frightening and traumatic that I could not integrate them with my earlier experiences, or even future possibilities. In "Healing: A Journey Forward After A Crisis", Sarah Rae Mechem (1998), describes the impact of trauma when she narrates her own experience with random violence.

> I had no idea how to handle the emotional, physical, mental, and spiritual upheaval in my life. Nothing in all my experiences has prepared me for the feeling of insecurity, helplessness, and terror. (p. 136)

Cancer felt like random violence perpetrated by an invisible assailant. In the echoes of shock it simply didn't occur to me that my acts of creative resistance—or rather, my approach to culture jamming—could help me through this terrible time. But slowly and with a courageous and playful spirit, I began to formulate a new way of envisioning such challenges.

Upon hearing the news of my diagnosis a friend encouraged me to say that I "was already healed", and not to call myself "sick". Something about this resonated with me. Yet I wondered if I would be trying to define my own reality in too radical a way. How could I reconcile the gravity of the moment with a playful and creative outlook? And how could I do so when everyone I cared for looked so distraught, and countless patients struggling with cancer surrounded me? I wanted to say "I am already healed" as a form of affirmation rather than denial, and in the end I decided to follow my courageous instincts and try it. I explained to my friends and family that I wanted to claim my power to redefine the situation, that I would refer to myself as "already healed", and that the chemotherapy and radiation treatments and the unknown path ahead of me was all part of the "The Dance of Life".

I began to notice that all of the metaphors available to me for describing the healing process relied on military imagery such as "a war in my body", mechanistic imagery such as "broken parts", and capitalistic frameworks in which the body is a "consumer of health services". These dominant metaphors remove power from the individual, and reduce the body to the site of civil war, a broken machine or a passive consumer. In the true spirit of a scholar/artist, I did my own research into the biological process occurring in my body and created new metaphors that were empowering. I began to visualize my immune system like a well-run and loving community, where everything is recycled and sustainable. I would not use the word "mine" to describe "the" cancer. It was just passing through. "It's not *my* cancer," I would say as I respectfully interrupted family, friends—and even doctors! Eventually they all began to adopt this new paradigm too!

I felt remarkably encouraged as I deconstructed the language about health and disease, using all of my creative abilities to jam the situation. On several occasions

I even dressed up in various costumes as the white blood cells in my immune system, and did theatrical dances to help me visualize what was happening in my body. As Shawn McKniff suggests, when we "envision ourselves as actors, we can try out new ways of being in the word". (McKniff, 1998, p. 81) My friend dressed up as a "Friendorphine" (a healing endorphin brought on by friendship), and my boyfriend dressed up as "Love"; supporting characters acting out the great drama that was taking place inside my body. Talk about Do-It-Yourself media! Today the dance continues. My doctors have declared me cancer-free, and though I remain under close observation, my healing continues.

I've come to believe that the power to imagine and heal rests within us all, and that healing has more to do with creating a meaningful life than it does with survival alone. It is through engaging with the arts and allowing our many narratives to interact that we can form a clear vision of our hopes enacted, giving them the power to become reality.

(R)Evolutionary Healing: The Spiral Journey

Healing is a vibrant dance of life. Healing is awe inspiring, powerful, subversive and is continuously happening holistically throughout all aspects of the body (physically, emotionally, spiritually and psychologically). I've come to see creative healing and transformation as a process that can be envisioned as a spiralling wheel. The cycle begins with a ***challenge***, something that has reached a crisis point and must be addressed. It could be an absence or silence in the mainstream narrative of history, education or media. It could be a social, economic or environmental injustice, an unsafe space, sadness, loss or a life threatening illness.

The next phase of this cycle requires individuals and communities to muster up their ***courage***. It takes courage to believe that we can make a difference, or that creativity, which is so often disregarded as trivial, could provide new solutions for resisting and transforming what is challenging us.

The third step isn't always obvious – it is to ***play***. Playfulness is ever present in all the various forms of creativity I have participated in such as zine publishing, performance art, education, and healing.

The final step in the cycle is ***love***, which takes the form of a new vision of the world and a new sense of purpose or place in that world. For example, this is demonstrated in culture jamming by increased media literacy and a stronger sense of belonging and participation in public space.

This transformational process is what I call (R)Evolutionary Healing. With each revolution around the wheel, we pass through *Challenge, Courage, Play* and then *Love*. Rather than travelling in a straight line or repetitive cycle, this (r)Evolution is a spiral – a process through which each time around we have the potential to move closer to the central goal of wellness and interconnection. This model doesn't limit us to the metaphor of a linear path; the occurrence of new challenges do not signal a failure, but instead indicates that there are still further opportunities to transform, lessons to learn, and connections to forge.

Interacting Narratives

> Humans are storytelling organisms who, individually and collectively, lead storied lives. Thus, the study of narrative is the study of the ways humans experience the world.
>
> (Connelly & Clandinin, 1990, p. 16)

My experiences with creativity and culture jamming can be understood through the concept of interacting narratives (Beattie, 1995a; Beattie, Dobson, Thornton, & Hegge, 2007, Dobson, 2008). The study of interacting narratives considers the storied nature of individual lives and the effect of such individual storied lives on each other when they interact. Recent work by these narrative scholars expands the notion of interacting narratives to include the inter and intrapersonal interaction of both lived and chosen narratives in an innovative manner that provides new models for the study of knowledge creation and re-creation.

My 'lived narratives' of commercial culture, sexism and illness interacted with the 'chosen narratives' of collage, resistance, healing and play. The result was the creation of a new narrative that helped me to better understand myself, and my place in the world. Through this imaginative and transformative process I was able to create and continue to recreate myself by weaving narratives from my inner and outer worlds into the ongoing 'text' of my evolving Self. My interest in interacting narratives is about how people connect both inter and intrapersonally, for as Beattie (1995b) explains, it is "within interacting narratives where lives come together, influence each other, and become increasingly more responsive to each other [that] professional development and change can take place, and individuals can re-form themselves and their communities". (Beattie, 1995a, p. 133)

Creativity, Interconnection, Healing and Wonder

> Eventually the cells in my body were brought back into a state of communication, communion and harmony. Now my vision of healing is one in which all the different parts of my self; spirit, body, mind, emotions, and the unknown continue to listen and learn from each other and to keep each other on their right paths. That is my vision of ongoing health: valuing all my different sides, but working together as an interconnected whole. (Carly Stasko, Journal, Feb 6th, 2008)

I breathe art. I am art. I feel connected to all things because we are created and eventually destroyed. I feel that I am part of a larger creative cycle, and so I see creativity as a means through which I connect with the sacred. Creativity is an integral part of my life, my identity and my blossoming spirituality. It is through seeing the world in a creative and playful way that I approach the art of living with reverence. When I make art and weave stories about my experiences with healing I am expressing reverence for the artfulness of the healing process.

Art is not only found in artefacts but is also found in play and transformation. I think that the ultimate piece of art is our own creative consciousness – the way that we see the world and create meaning from our lived experiences. As a child, I was taught that we could all live life as though we were the characters in our favourite books – we could be the main characters in the books that we ourselves wrote in the living of them. This idea resonated with me so much that it became fully integrated into the way that I lived. The idea that I could create my own life gave me courage to dream aloud and to overcome challenges.

When I was diagnosed with cancer I was determined that while this would likely be a "difficult chapter", it would only be one chapter in a long series of triumphantly joyful chapters to follow. Like the early collages that covered my bedroom wall and filled the pages of my zines, I have found a way of piecing together my own pain and fear into a larger image of hope and resilience. Collage is the art of weaving fragments together in order to tell a new story. Sometimes these fragments are sharp at the edges where they have been broken. I must handle them carefully and can't always keep my blood off the page. In the collage of life, we sometimes have no choice about which fragments to work with, because we can't control everything that happens to us. The power of the artist in all of us is evoked when we work with the pieces that we have in order to create the life we want.

Given that "the strongest form of power may well be the ability to define social reality, to impose visions of the world" (Gal, 1995, p. 178), it is important for teachers, students and for everyone to be actively and consciously engaged in the creation and recreation of such visions. I've come to believe that reclaiming the power and tools to tell our own stories (often defiantly piecing them together from fragments of popular culture, the arts and daily life), can be an act of social justice and cultural resistance.

Living artfully and seeking out the interwoven stories of my life through autobiographical narrative work has nurtured my sense of wonder and courage in the face of fear and uncertainty. From a position of wonder I am able to bring my whole self forward to the task of engaging with the unknown as a scholar, creator, healer and human being.

Wonder is an exciting alternative to fear that allows for a "response to the novelty of experience (although not to the totally unexpected, which tends to arouse anxiety)" (Cobb, 1977, p. 28). Edith Cobb argues that when "maintained as an attitude, or point of view, in later life, wonder permits a response of the nervous system to the universe that incites the mind to organize novelty of pattern and form out of incoming information" (Ibid, p. 27). The expansive nature of sustained wonder allows for play, fluidity, liminality and imagination (Hirshfield, 1997).

Wonder allows for what Zwicky (2003) refers to as an ethical position of awe. It is from this humble, inspired and authentic location that we can play at the edges of the known and the unknown. Play enables us to "rearrange our capacities and our very identity so that they can be pursued in unforeseen ways" (Nachmanovitch, 1990, p. 19). Reinterpreting reality and begetting novelty in turn sustains our dynamic fluidity.

In the journey of life I have had many inspiring adventures through the fields of art, education, social transformation and celebration. I have also faced great challenges, such as illness and loss – which have called me to summon up courage from hidden reserves and to re-*imagine* my life and identity. The process of weaving together stories, meaning and metaphor has been both healing and transformative for me. I am so happy to say that I can truly feel the positive effect that engaging in this process has had on me. I am pleased to share my story with you and to imagine what lies ahead!

LYRIC SELF PORTRAIT

The Imagitator agitates imagination.
The Culture Jammer plays with meaning and power.

The (r)Evolutionary Healer transforms with grace,
turning a fall into the spiral dance of life.

The Artist-Researcher explores the imagined-nation,
guided by parallax towards relational ways of knowing.

I am all of these and more.
More than a human-doer.
I am a human being – Heart, Spirit, Body, Mind – Combined,
Engaged, inspired and flowing.

With love, light and laughter…
Who I am is not fixed, nor ever broken.
Dynamic in a tale that is danced, collaged and spoken.
In between the beginnings and the ends,
The challenges and friends and most of all the bends
In the road that lead me home – only to know it (and love it!)
again for the first time….(C. S. 2009)

AFTERWORD: THE STORIED PATH OF LIFE

The process of weaving together a narrative that integrates my various experiences creating, teaching, learning, healing and transforming has been an important step in my journey, both personally and professionally. At times in this process I was frozen in my tracks and found it difficult to find my footing or take the next necessary step. At other times my feet surrendered to their natural rhythm and I could dance along the storied path of life. I've come to see living, loving and learning as a dance. In this dance of life I've learned some of my most profound lessons on those occasions when I've mustered up the courageous vulnerability to dance my way back up after a hard fall.

After overcoming several years healing from cancer in my late twenties I felt very fragmented and fearful. As a collage artist who cuts and pastes found and created images, fabrics and quotes into something new, I have experienced my narrative process as one of integration and discovery. I have had to (and continue to) use all my previously learned and emerging creative narrative abilities to piece together a new sense of self and purpose in life – so I can better understand and integrate my personal/professional/embodied/spiritual/emotional/intellectual self into a holistic and dynamic being.

As I continue on the journey I draw strength from my ability to weave healing narratives, knowing full well that living involves falling, unravelling and transforming. While I may not be able to always "hold it all together" or control all (or even most) aspects of my life's journey, I can always continue to nurture my creative and adaptive abilities to put the pieces together in new, inspiring and meaningful ways. Throughout this process I have been inspired by the connections between my personal and professional journeys. I hope to weave insights from all these aspects of my life into the teaching, creating, learning and passionate living that lies ahead on paths still yet to be discovered and explored.

BOB PHILLIPS

6. BEING SEEN

> If we are convinced that art is a transformative undertaking, and learning is a fluid, dynamic process, what we must do, I believe, is to act AS IF our lives are ongoing works of art.
>
> (Taylor, 1992)

> I guess I start from the premise that the possibilities for art are something that everybody has—in other words, everybody has something inherently creative and artistic in them. And it's in the nature of social life that there are ways to realize those possibilities; in fact, those possibilities are what make the world a habitable place.
>
> (Kirshenblatt-Gimblett, 1995)

> Teaching is an interpersonal affair, and as soon as you say "inter" you mean (or should mean) that teacher and student(s) seek to understand each other and it is the process of seeking that the qualities of the teacher as performing artist can be observed.
>
> (Sarason, 1999)

As a secondary school educator for nearly twenty-eight years, and one who is immersed in the arts, specifically the visual arts and drama, I have witnessed countless adolescents realize that learning through and about the arts can transform the quality of their lived lives in powerful, significant ways. In fact my dedication to teaching as a vocation has its origins in comparable types of qualitative, life-altering moments which were mediated by artistic engagement. This story—and the original academic study from which it is derived—begins with myself, someone I have come to know rather well, through these processes of inquiry and writing.

I am fifty-one, and have just moved to the city of Stratford, Ontario, a bona fide enclave of artists, actors, musicians, and home of the acclaimed Stratford Shakespeare Festival. Although we relocated here for eventual retirement, my partner and I were anxious to establish roots in a community that practiced and valued the arts. This creative hamlet has allowed me time and space to produce abstract drawings and relief print portraits, and attend assorted theatre performances, musical concerts, and art exhibitions. My life would be very different—most likely beige and arid—if not for my connections with the arts: I feel more alive and present as an artfully-distracted being. I also attempt to season the suburban high

M. Beattie (Author/Ed.), The Quest for Meaning: Narratives of Teaching, Learning and the Arts, 119–134.

school where I teach with this wide-awakeness to life as realized through artistic pursuits. Illustrations will follow.

This chapter is divided into two sections. "Beginnings…" introduces and locates the focus of this narrative self-study in the personal, my current sense of self as an arts educator, and goes on to propose general notions of living and being artful in one's lived life. The following section, "Inventions," involves some autobiographical self-disclosure and recommends examples of my own artful pedagogy for consideration.

Beginnings…

My previous research grew out of a once-overwhelming sense of guilt and regret. Such an admission probably doesn't inspire teeming confidence with respect to an author's intentions, but I firmly believe that any authentic transformation of teaching practice is provoked by the sensation of an inner imbalance, a recognition that one's personal journey directly influences professional identity and experience. In retrospect, I now see that I wasted a great deal of time and energy over a perception that was both fallacious and stifling. Yet, traces of this debilitating misperception continue to penetrate arts education literature, teacher dialogue and to stain public assumptions about teacher competence. Here, I am speaking about the contentious teacher-as-artist (or artist-as-teacher) conflict, a premise that visual arts teachers, along with being skilled, knowledgeable instructors, must also be practicing, exhibiting, artists. This view of "practicing artist" means someone who is maintaining a competent, evolving, and sustained level of production, creating one or more art forms, working regular hours as an artist, and, most importantly, exhibiting from time to time—putting one's art out there. Like teachers in the other disciplines, visual arts teachers focus on students' learning, and expend much of their own creative vitality on their students' artistic output which leaves little in the way of reserves for their own personal art making.

Banner and Cannon (1997) urge that a teacher "should know enough to be a thinker as well as an instructor" in their given field (p. 11). One would expect a significant degree of adroitness from teachers who are discipline specialists, and standards for professional growth insist that keeping abreast of new knowledge and forms of expression are necessary functions of one's job. English teachers are expected to read themselves and to be adept at writing; and math teachers should be capable of ciphering or devising algebraic problems with ease. The inability to realize one's own artistic potential, while art-making is happening all around you in the context of the classroom—compounded by an nagging public assumption of the teacher-as-artist producing and exhibiting artwork—is frequently frustrating and downright demoralizing for many visual arts educators.

While teaching the visual arts to preservice teacher candidates in a university setting, I encouraged them to develop as well-rounded a content background in the visual arts as possible, knowing that the breadth and depth of their knowledge would also mature with time and experience. However, many of the experienced visual arts teachers they met in schools, made them aware of the sad reality that allocating sufficient time, production space, and human energy, let alone the requisite inspiration, vision, and acute perception, to the creation of personal artwork is virtually impossible because of the normal (these days, superhuman) demands of teaching.

Too much of education can be passionless. This void in the visual arts teacher's indivisible personal-professional life must somehow be filled with artistry in order to make them whole and transform them, their pedagogy, and their students. An artless existence, here denoting the inability of teachers to create tangible artwork, can also mean that one's soul remains malnourished and can easily grow polluted by the secular malaise and mechanical, commonplace interactions of daily reality. Thomas Moore (1992) indicates the significance of art to transcend ego: "[t]he point of art is not simply to express ourselves, but to create an external, concrete form in which the soul of our lives can be evoked and contained" (p. 302). At the same time, how does this emptiness in the teacher affect the students? Jack Miller (2000) acknowledges that "[i]f the teacher's soul is contracted and impoverished, then there is little chance that the student's soul will be adequately cared for" (p. 121). I can relate innumerable cases as a teacher where not only the artistry, but the absolute life has been sucked out of my teaching: preparing grade 10 students for the mandatory provincial literacy exam; reviewing school-wide procedures or school board policies; negotiating with a particularly self-righteous individual over a mark or grade (while the experience remains uncounted).

I believe an exploration of artful pedagogy and teaching qualities, with its concomitant integration of a teacher's personal and professional selves, can reveal avenues for creative personal renewal and genuine educational reform. My investigation of artful pedagogy might sound trivial to other teachers who are facing a litany of accountability pressures, public perceptions about diminished literacy and numeracy skills, dissatisfaction among racial and ethnic communities, scientific data-mania and rampant technology-induced myopia, and the incomprehensibility of top-down, train-the-trainer, no time, just ends-in-mind government reforms. It is not. It is actually pivotal because it involves a teacher's identity, those aspects which define who we are and how we become, and those artful qualities that some teachers exhibit. Elliott Eisner (1991a) talks about "the meaning of those qualities and the value we assign to them" as a means of illuminating aspects of "intimate social relations," like in schools (p. 1).

Techne or Being?

I have always been convinced that the most influential and successful teachers (and other intriguing people) whom I have encountered are those who live their practice, who allow their passions to infuse every aspect of their daily existence. Those I have known who are artists, or connected to artistic practice, or who are simply open in their dealings with the world, seem to embody artfulness in their conversations, manner and attire, attitudes, personal spaces, and their very essence. They ignore the moribund, usual, isolated, technical ways of being in the world, prizing instead those actions which lead to contemplation, dialogue, and compassion.

If people consciously design their lives as works of art and embody all of its facets in their lived experiences, then artistic attributes such as creativity, appreciation of form and enhanced perception (aesthesis), intuition, contingency, and deep understanding will infuse everything that they do and are. This harmonized, artful existence also effaces the modernist credo of separating art from everyday being-in-the-world. Many believe that, as human beings, we all posses some innate artistic proclivities and that, philosophically, art is a unique quality of human experience which suffuses the everyday.

So why not regard teaching as an art? Pedagogical actions, when performed by someone who embodies artfulness, can assume artistic form and presence. By this I mean more than just technical mastery or the command of subject knowledge. While teachers can be adroit at communication or possess distinctive ways of doing things, versatility as a hallmark of superior performance—all observable and equally legitimate attributes—, I would contend that artful teaching is much more than mere style or a set of characteristics for assessing job performance. What I advocate here is a particular quality of being, a valuing of certain kinds of encounters with others in the world, within a context of formal education. These encounters, because they are guided by aspects of hope, vision, imagination, agency, pleasure, intuition, and compassion, also bring about a deepening of soul. Artful being/teaching can elicit soulfulness in both the practitioner and the recipients of that practice. As Parker Palmer (1998) reminds us, "[w]e teach who we are" (p. 2).

As a remedy for this artist-as-teacher malady, this inadequacy or lack which plagues visual arts educators, I propose a way of thinking differently, more completely about ourselves. Harold Pearse (1993), in noting the inextricable and reciprocal relationships among teacher, learner, and subject discipline, claims that "a real art teacher embodies art" (p. 63). It is the artful practice of teaching that can be understood as a performance, a creative, purposeful endeavour, and an intentional representation or making of meaning directed towards others. In advocating this merging of social practices, teaching and artistry, I hesitate to claim that teaching is a genuine substitute for or recourse—inferring a diminished sort of experience—from other forms of artistic expression. For instance, the quality of experience which painting provides—or quilt-making or ballroom dancing or acting or operatic singing—is a singular, nuanced form of transaction with the world; substituting one kind of experience for another—teaching for painting—is qualitatively impossible to do. Both teaching and painting have their own experiential value; one act is not empirically more essential or significant than the other. Simply, artful pedagogy or teaching artistry is another, different form of realizing one's creative voice, a means of sustaining spirit, and filling the creative void which exists in the frequently frenetic lived lives of many visual arts teachers. I contend that some educators achieve a degree of artistic satisfaction through their teaching practice, and come to realize what Michael Ignatieff (2000) calls their own "ideal of authenticity" (p. 99) as human beings.

My intention in pursuing this line of inquiry however, apart from an earlier divulged personal reason, is because I see this inquiry into artful pedagogy contributing to educational discourse in two interdependent ways: as social agency, by reinforcing the continuous improvement of teaching and, as personal renewal or truth, by reinvigorating the confidence, strengthening the competence, and challenging the hearts of classroom practitioners. (I believe that the ultimate consequence of both these purposes is the betterment of student achievement.) I'll discuss the latter contribution first. Teacher efficacy is vital to the on-going health of schools. As cultural workers in education, teachers who feel capable in their work are more willing to take risks, innovate, question misconceptions, resist complacency, and fortify their practice. The idea that teaching can originate from artistic locations within, offers the visual arts teacher aesthetic possibilities for re-visioning, reforming, and eventually transforming their ways of doing and being in classrooms. Understanding teaching as an artform consolidates our subjective, artistic lives and professional careers, allowing us "to act on our desires, to break through the obstacles, to become different, to be" (Greene, 1995, p. 112).

In addressing teaching improvement, an artful pedagogy offers latitude and agency for social change by pressing individuals to think differently about the world through what they teach—curriculum—and how they teach it—instruction and engagement. Artistry is informed by imagination and, in *Releasing the Imagination* (1995), Maxine Greene indicates the importance of imagination in making empathy possible. Artful pedagogy (and teaching performances) can enable empathic responses in students through the play of imagination in shaping sensations about identity and community. In the process of touching students' imaginations, artist-teachers can also spark interest and channel engagement, diverting students from the stereotypical, unquestioned, prescribed images and activities of their fixed reality, and make them more wide awake to contingent, open-ended, and ambiguous views of their world. As well, teaching artistry applies, and instigates in others, intuitive and tacit ways of knowing what we know; these subjective understandings attribute value to an individual's consciousness, while at the same time constructing a more expansive, meaningful collectivity. Finally, artful pedagogy is invested with creativity and, in turn, invites creative reactions from students; conversely, from a cultural perspective, creative ideas, actions or products rely on the values and meanings which audience, social influence, and dialogue bring to them and, therefore, must inherently be situated within a receptive, knowledgeable community. All of these factors can potentially improve teaching and learning by activating hope and humanity in people through artful practices and performances.

Inventions

The title for this chapter, "*Being Seen,*" was chosen for its ambiguous implications and its reference to visuality. (It was actually suggested by the title of Jerzy Kosinski's novel, and Hal Ashby's subsequent film, *Being There.*) Works of art, those which must be looked at in order to be understood, are always being seen by spectators, whether one talks about a sculpture, a photograph or video, a dance work or a play; teachers, as performers in classrooms, are always being seen (and heard) by their student audience; I, as educational researcher, am 'being seen,' in a sense, by those who will read these pages and formulate opinions about its content, but I am also a 'being' seen, as the person who exposes himself to the scrutiny of others, consenting to being 'looked at,' in relation to my artistic works, my pedagogy, and my educational inquiry. (This postmodern predilection for layering meanings, subverting the patent sense of a text or an image, is a strategy that I frequently employ in my artwork and my pedagogy.) Perhaps an impression of voyeurism sticks to this idea of being seen, where the subject remains unaware of the persistent and prurient onlooker. Quality artworks, if invested with presence and integrity, invariably reveal to the spectator, either intentionally or by chance, some truth about their maker. Artist-teachers, those who practice artful forms of pedagogy, also disclose aspects of themselves in their daily performances; their young spectators are desirous, not in any carnal way but, instead, for understanding and attention. How does this knotty title connect with this inquiry? It alludes to autobiography and personal disclosure, the sharing of instances from my personal-professional narrative. Wanda May (1993) indicates how we are able to distinguish artful teaching from that which is not: "[b]y feeling, remembering, naming ourselves" (p. 216), by locating instances of artful pedagogy in our lives.

At this point, I will describe examples of my own artful pedagogy and teaching performances to illustrate these theoretical claims. My autobiographical accounts will reveal selected pedagogical (inter)actions and exchanges which I feel have artistic qualities and can, therefore, be labelled as artful. Although I have not fully articulated the relationship between teaching performances and artful pedagogy, it can be presumed that performances, or performative actions, are also forms of artistry.

Imaginative Flights: Curriculum Artistry

As a teacher in Ontario, I am required to deliver particular curriculum expectations by the Ministry of Education, but the form these learning expectations take, and their delivery to students, are not prescribed. My creative energies are continuously engaged as I plan—frequently in collaboration with colleagues—tasks which will allow students to effectively demonstrate their perceptions, levels of skill, and comprehension of concepts. I believe that I demonstrate artistry in my curriculum planning. For instance, I use sample artefacts created by particular visual artists, as well as their ways of working, as a catalyst for student-generated artworks. My grade ten classes explore identity and biography through an extensive installation art project called "*Guess Who's Coming to Dinner?*" Students select a historical, sports, entertainment or pop culture celebrity to initially research and they produce written biographies of these individuals. Then students design and sculpt three dimensional clay objects to visually represent their celebrity, including a dinner plate and a drinking vessel (mug, cup and saucer, or goblet); these utilitarian objects must be presented as a portion of a larger installation artwork, which includes a place card, place mat, eating utensils, and any other bric-a-brac, images or symbolic items to complete their table setting. The original inspiration for this assignment came from feminist Judy Chicago's "*The Dinner Party*" project (1974–1979), (Bersson, 2004, pp. 617–618). I want students to explore the identities of others and the mingling of diverse artmaking traditions (so-called fine art, crafts, and installation) through an opportunity to work as a collective (a dinner party-like installation, installed in the school, is the culminating exhibition), and demonstrate effective and appropriate ceramic construction skills, while making imagery choices that will best communicate their celebrity's personality and life. It's the particularly imaginative framing of these sculptural, graphic design, painting, and biographical writing activities that I believe makes this an artful pedagogical encounter.

Another artful approach to curriculum involves a task entitled "*The Museum Mutant*." Here students are motivated by an imagination-stretching fictional narrative:

> This is the story of two paintings. Each was very different than the other, although they hung side by side in the museum. As the course of true love goes, these two works of art felt some kind of mutual attraction. One morning when the curator arrived, to her astonishment she noticed a new and rather unusual painting hanging on the museum wall, between the other two. After some research and stylistic investigation, she concluded that this "mystery" work was actually the offspring of the other two paintings, "a chip off the old canvas", so to speak!

Instructions to students problematize this visual investigation about concepts like appropriation, style, and synectic thinking: they are required to select two paintings by different artists—one from the Renaissance and one Modern work—and create a new artwork through a synthesis of these two artist's visual styles. The task is initially daunting, but the narrative premise, opportunity for choice, and open-ended fun of messing around with another artist's work easily preoccupies students' thoughts. The artistry involved with this learning task allows students to replicate real image-making strategies employed by contemporary artists, while simultaneously exploring art historical precedents and challenging their technical skills. The resulting works appear as strange hybrids, amalgams of images no longer inexorably fixed in space and time. How is visual meaning altered if Duane Hanson's stereotypical Americans from *Tourists* (1970) are abruptly relocated to the setting of Jan Van Eyck's *The Arnolfini Wedding* portrait of 1434? This seemingly absurd project forces students to think very differently about artistic intention, context, and interpretation; it also becomes a form of learning-by-copying, a practice full of contention for some educational purists. I see nothing wrong with it! Students are actually learning lessons from professional artists as they examine artworks in meticulous detail in order to understand their appeal. I learned to draw by copying images of superheroes and their foes from Marvel comics and from narrative situations on TV. I still discover so much by ransacking art books and magazines, and interrogating pictures or objects in exhibitions. Images are my blood—they sustain my transit through a frequently unremarkable world.

One memorable example of this artful approach to curriculum and skills acquisition happened very early in my career. I was searching for a more inventive means of reviewing essential hue relationships in colour theory, with a grade ten group. The standard twelve hue Munsell colour wheel had been slavishly duplicated by them the year before and it was necessary to revisit it. I devised a more patent exercise which included the requisite review, but allowed these teens the freedom to expand their imaginations about their various circumstances and play with non-art materials. They had to include all twelve hues, in their correct order, but they could use any media, materials, and settings to produce their "wheels" (which did not have to be circular, either). One student purchased twelve white painters caps, painted them with acrylics, and displayed them on a wooden coat tree; another young woman created a full-course meal in which all the foods were naturally or artificially coloured the proper hues; one ambitious youth constructed a 3D snowscape in his backyard, over which he poured twelve buckets of dyed water and documented the resulting winter wonderland in colour Polaroids. A truly amusing instance of this task involved a young girl who coerced her younger brother to act as her "canvas." She actually painted him from forehead to belly-button with the twelve hues, mixed in tempera paint and lanolin (so it wouldn't itch, she assured me). The resulting photographs revealed a grinning, multicoloured nine year-old, who also sported a garishly coloured (but accurate in hues) tea cosy on his head!

Windows & Mirrors: Artful Inquiry

I was determined to further apply my ideas about teaching artistry to the curriculum for preservice teacher education, while I was seconded to teach in the teacher education program at the Ontario Institute for Studies in Education at the University of Toronto from 1998 to 2002. During this time, I was eager to offer beginning teachers a venue for imaginative ways of regarding their world, and for testing alternate learning methods. The Intermediate/Senior Visual Arts methods course had for years organized a year-end art exhibition of the teacher candidate's personal artistic output, and this was not really connected in any way with the program. I decided to resurrect this tradition, but to integrate it with the methods course as one of the students' final research assignments. This form of arts-based qualitative research has gained recognition and validation as a bona fide approach among educational researchers, and it makes sense to me as an authentic and potentially transformative means of representation. It capitalizes on the tacit knowledge and intersubjective voice of the investigator, and dismantles the boundaries between artistic thinking and educational inquiry. Why not have these teacher/artists make art as tangible responses to their understandings and questions? Why are words and numbers trusted more as means of communication, while images are tolerated as mere illustrations?

The project I initiated was called "*Kidspeak: Portrait of the Adolescent Learner.*" It was meant to synthesize the assorted learnings that students had witnessed about adolescent psychology, youth cultures, and their interactions with learning in schools. Procedures asked these students to create a visual 'portrait' of the adolescent learner, a psychological or sociological statement that could take any form and employ any medium: collage and/or photo montage; a static narrative painting or image series; a video document; photo essay; computer-generated imaging; a mixed media piece; text & illustrations; textile or fibre work; sculpture in paper & cardboard or clay; performance art; or an installation or diorama. Ultimately, they had to communicate a clear image of contemporary adolescents, incorporating some aspects of both internal (physical, emotional, spiritual & psychological) and external (culture, community, family & school) developmental factors. The final portrait could even highlight a particular component of the adolescent world: a sub-culture; gender or sexual identity; values & morality; self-concept or identity. I was deliberately vague about the final product in order to allow for individual inclinations and maximum creative thought.

The resulting exhibition of artistic statements was always insightful, provocative, moving, and frequently 'in your face' about the lived lives of adolescents. Lengthy research essays of expository text would be inadequate at capturing the subtleties, complexities, and colours of personality that these artworks envisioned. Of the many works that were submitted during my tenure at OISE/UT, I will describe only a few: a digital video loop that presented a fictional narrative about bullying in urban high schools, featuring student actors; a sound installation that recounted young womens' singular stories about body image involving eating disorders; a patchwork quilt comprised of transferred drawings and photographs by students which told about their unique lives as variously ethnic Canadians; a photo mural which probed the lives of three teenaged girls, along with images of personal artefacts and intimate interior shots of their bedrooms; and a sixteen year-old boy's vacated clothing pinned to the wall, affixed with information cards that explained how each garment simultaneously displayed and camouflaged his identities. This conception of merging art-making with educational inquiry is analogous to my argument about the parallels between teaching and artistic practices; it has to do with creating transdisciplinary, more integrated and fluid ways of representing, interacting, and being.

One personal incident involving art making in the service of research happened in a grade 12 Chemistry course. In order to support me in learning chemical formulas and molecular structures, a forward thinking science teacher permitted me to paint molecular models of oxygen, hydrogen, helium, and such on the sides of this plain wooden box that he used to demonstrate a chemical unit of measure. Do I recall these chemical representations? No, but I did improve my comprehension of perspective drawing and ability to model forms in colour values. And... I got a B+ in the course!

Two other arts-based forms of teaching and learning that I used were equally successful in allowing participants to locate and reveal their artistic selves. One task involved non-arts specialist teachers in a related studies course I taught called "*Education and the Cultural Community.*" Following in-class discussions about extending learning opportunities beyond the classroom—in museums, galleries, historical sites, theatres, zoos, and community centres—and about acts of interpretation as meaning-making and demonstrations of personal understanding, the teacher candidates were required to seek out an unfamiliar experience in the local cultural community and respond to it using artistic means. That is, if they had never experienced a stage performance, see one; if they hadn't attended a symphony concert, go and listen; and if they weren't accustomed to visiting an art gallery, view an exhibition. I intended that this activity model the types of community-based cultural events to which these teachers could expose their students. The format of their responses could be entirely visual (i.e. a painting or complex drawing, a collage, photo-essay, video, small installation, fibre art work, illustrated book); written (i.e. narrative, poetry, dialogue, letters or postcards, a biographical journal); musical (i.e. audio recording, original composition, soundscape); a performance (i.e. role-playing, readers theatre, monologue, characterization, dance or movement piece); or some other hybrid form of creative expression or sensory experience, and this response had to communicate something about their subjective experience of this cultural event, a personal interpretation of meaning.

My artful intentions with this undertaking were not only to expose neophyte teachers to distinctive forms of cultural representation—namely, the arts—but to model for them a type of valid interpretative response which they could, in turn, use with their future students. Indeed, my teacher-candidates, though originally horrified and intimidated by the prospect of creating something artistic ("I haven't got an artistic bone in my body!"), came to appreciate just how much their personal learning could be reinvigorated and their skills challenged. I had science majors painting, geographers writing poetry, physical & health educators composing music and dancing! One memorable incident involved an elementary education candidate who had not drawn or painted since grade 8. She proudly contributed a booklet that she had written and illustrated about her visit to a local art gallery exhibit. She also admitted that this artful foray had changed her, and she assured me that her students would be offered similar opportunities.

Further along the continuum of teacher professional development, "*Windows, Mirrors, & Signposts: Self-Portrait as an Educator*" was a performance task that I devised to compliment a written personal philosophy of art education, for Visual Arts Honour Specialist candidates, in an OISE/UT Additional Qualifications summer course for teachers. My thinking was that if we truly believe "teaching is an art" [Eisner, 1979; May, 1993], and that artistic disclosure/expression is a valid means of knowing about someone and their place in the world, then visual arts educators should be able to use a visual medium to explore notions about themselves and their lives as professionals. These candidates could use any medium, exploit any form, and say anything that they fancied. However, these portraits had to inform a wider audience about who they were and what they believed as teacher-artists. Of course these self-portraits were displayed, along with artist reflections, during our final week of classes. The sophistication of visual responses which these variously experienced teachers presented helped to more than merely illustrate key ideas from their personal philosophies. I was rather moved by many of works: a poetic video presentation about a juvenile cousin's struggles with learning; children's garments hung from a clothesline that were embroidered with particular statements about teaching; graphic cardboard sculptures, painted with graffiti, that decried recent changes in provincial educational policy; and a series of engraved ceramic vessels, lovingly formed and partly destroyed in a visual declaration about the fragile nature of learning and morality. These artists freely admitted that their self-portrayals poignantly captured aspects of their personal-professional lives that writing was unable to effectively articulate. Their disclosures were triggered by reflexive inquiry and the integrity of voice which this artful license furnished them.

Activating Spaces: Installation Art(istry)

Artful pedagogy not only encompasses the choices one makes about curriculum content and delivery, it also concerns the definition and disposition of one's teaching environment. If one is truly living an artful life where artistry is involved with all facets of being, then it would be fair to expect that one's working context should reflect, even emanate artfulness. Art educator George Szekely characterizes the site of teaching: "The art room is... the teacher's canvas on which ideas are showcased, the curious are challenged, and responses are invited." (Hurwitz & Day, 2001, p. 379) We also know, through brain-based research that enriched learning environments can directly stimulate brain function and intellectual insight, thereby strengthening learning potential. As an arts educator and visual learner, I have always attempted to surround my students with artefacts and images that stimulate thoughts, memories, and feelings, or invite contemplation. Art reproductions, postcards, student artworks, found objects, sculpture and ceramics, colour charts, instructional posters, photographs, text or quotations or visual arts terminology cover every possible wall surface and fill shelves. I make available an extensive personal library of art related books, catalogues, comics, children's illustrated storybooks, and periodicals. Bulletin boards celebrate students' recent creations, and are accompanied by didactic panels to explain intentions. Digital, poster or postcard reproductions of artworks—as well as videos, animated shorts, and film segments—are routinely used to delineate a lesson or exemplify a concept. Publicity posters for recent films or local events, and news media articles help to enlarge student understandings about the arts infusing out broader culture, where significance is both individually and socially constructed.

I frequently bring into the classroom various artefacts from my personal collections in order to pose questions about interpretation, beauty, and cultural value using concrete materials. For instance, while attending *The International Society for Education through Art* conference in New York City, in August of 2002, I purchased a disposable camera and went out at 8:00 on a Sunday morning to capture my overwhelming sensations of Times Square. I stood on the boulevard, smack in the middle of this vibrant site, and shot the entire film in a 360 degree pan around the intersection. Once processed, I created a photomontage, similar to artist David Hockney's "joiners," using these Times Square images. I showed them to a grade 10 Non-Traditional Media class one day; as I spread out the 4 x 6 and panoramic images on a table, the students poured over them with varying degrees of interest. When I explained that these were impressions of my Times Square experience, and that I intended to put them together as a single image because I thought that it was an appropriate presentational format, I asked them what they thought about my artistic decision. An animated discussion ensued. Some thought that I should select only "the best" shots and edit out the others; a few students quizzed me about my reasons for creating the composite; others asked about how I felt at the time I made the photos; while still others wanted to know exactly what it might look like. We spent twenty minutes arranging and repositioning the photos like a large jigsaw puzzle, all the while proposing individual visual decisions which were validated or rejected by the collective group. In the end, we came up with a collaborative compositional solution, partially based on aesthetic compromise, for this representation of my memorable experience. We then deconstructed the activity in order to make the creative and interpretive processes obvious. This strategy directly engaged students in the kinds of procedural thinking that artists use to pose and solve visual problems. Students were able to reflect on this to understand the significance of the experience. When creating personal artworks, my typical planning process is not extensive—I prefer to capture spontaneous, unlaboured impressions or visualize imagery while contemplating rough drawings or examples of other artists' works. This collaborative approach to art making pushes me to remain open to the responses of others.

Extending the teaching environment beyond the physical walls of the classroom helps students to recognize the persistent and authentic nature of learning. One can infuse communities with artful practice. While working with teacher candidates at OISE/UT, I arranged a field trip to the Art Gallery of Ontario; again, many of these people were not frequent gallery visitors, so I endeavoured to make this excursion as unintimidating and student-responsive as possible, as I hoped they would one day do with their own classes. However, I also wanted to dispel the stereotypes and preconceptions they harboured about being spectators in a gallery or museum: don't talk above a whisper; follow the chronology of display as dictated by the curators; don't look and make meaning for yourself—read others' interpretations about what you see; don't interact or dialogue with friends so as not to disturb other patrons; and so on. I usually find museums and galleries stifling, cold, authoritarian, and exclusive, not the least bit conducive to open-ended, collaborative, experiential learning. This seems ironic when one considers that galleries and museums were originally founded as sites for educational edification. With the assistance and institutional mediation of some gallery educators, I arranged for quite an unorthodox, interventionist sort of visit between my students and the gallery's holdings.

Using the galleries as performance spaces and adapting dramatic arts activities, participants were divided into groups of four and assigned one of the following tasks: choose four or five works and create a relationship among them, across the gallery space using dramatic forms or conventions, e.g. mime, dialogue transfer, character monologues, role-playing, interview; create a soundtrack for an artwork and use realistic or stylized sounds to accompany the action depicted or extend the visible scene; using tableaux, narration, and transformations, create a continuous narrative using three artworks as your settings; represent an important role or significant character in a painting using an invented monologue that recounts their personal history, but other group members must take over this same role so that it becomes a collective representation. Not only did the resulting performances furnish these novice actors with interactive and culturally collaborative ways of attending to and extracting ideas from their chosen artworks, but the presentations became spontaneous artworks in their own right. During these performances, ordinary gallery patrons would usually stop to take in our antics and ask various questions about our activities. I dare say we disturbed a few folks, including one shocked gallery attendant who had not been informed about our presence and was determined to have us removed from the building. Many bystanders were impressed by these teachers and their intervening antics. Ultimately this method of artful interrogation provided agency as a form of performance art and transformed the art gallery into a more interactive, hospitable space.

Histrionics in the Classroom: Performance Art

Arguably, the concept of establishing stimulating settings or enriched environments for artful practice can be located in both the traditional disciplines of theatre and visual arts. Another example from my artful pedagogy exploits this inter-disciplinary approach. I borrowed a postmodern unit of study from a couple of former student/teacher candidates; it went by the intriguing title "A Paradigm of Prisons," and essentially presented the idea of prisons, as social institutions of confinement, as a metaphor for contemporary artistic agency. In order to place my grade 12 class in a confined mindset, as none of them could personally identify with incarceration, I chose to launch the unit by creating a tangible sense of restriction and confinement using their classroom. When these students arrived for class that day, they found the entrance locked, with a sign posted which instructed them to line up along the adjacent corridor wall and wait to be admitted. After a prolonged period of time, I opened the door and confronted them fully attired in black, carrying a policemen's baton, and stoic in expression. Of course, having no prior knowledge of this eccentric performative introduction, these adolescents responded with incredulity and guffaws. An uncharacteristic bellow from me of "shut up" soon quelled the unruly bunch and convinced them that this was serious stuff. I distributed to each a photocopy of "rules and restrictions" to be adhered to for the duration of the class: you must sit in your assigned seat; no communication with anyone else is permitted; leave all your personal belongings in the hallway; avoid physical contact with anyone else, nor touch anything once you have entered the room; interruptions and questions will not be entertained; infractions will mean immediate isolation from the group; etc. On entering the dimly lit classroom, they saw that the tables and stools had been removed except for a cramped square arrangement of tables, with bunched stools inside, situated in the middle of the room. This configuration was further separated with blank portable bulletin and chalk boards as temporary walls. Two large, intense photo floods became the only sources of illumination; these were raised on tall tripods to shine down on the centred stools. As the students shuffled into the enclosed pen, they were directed to numbers on each stool which corresponded to the red numeral on their handout of rules. Once all were accommodated, I, as their silent keeper, stood up on one of the tables and peered down at them. Almost indiscernible in the background was an audio recording of a ticking clock which they soon became very aware of. I simply stood over them and regarded them coldly.

I waited for about four minutes, until they were suitably anxious and extremely unnerved. I then broke character and asked them how they felt about this experience. Their reactions were predictable—imprisoned, restricted, punished, degraded and humiliated, controlled, submissive. I asked them why they weren't comfortable in this type of socially accepted circumstance. Their explanations and interpretations generated a fruitful conversation about confining places, human relationships, and psychological conditioning. As a performance, my role and its fabricated context allowed students to gain some direct knowledge about confinement through dramatic simulation; this enactment was also intended to elicit prior knowledge and personal associations that would enrich the ensuing unit. As a motivational "hook," I stimulated curiosity and engaged students as co-learners through imaginative role-play and improvisation, highly effective and artful ways of teaching. For me, the artist-teacher, this became a performance art piece, a means of creative agency and form of cultural production. I was invigorated by this playing!

I have used moments of performance to create dramatic situations, forms of teaching artistry, for other purposes, most effectively to enliven aspects of art historical studies. For a glimpse into the anarchic hi-jinks of early modernist DADA anti-artists, and their reliance on performance art as an anti-bourgeois artform, I have staged a DADA happening in my senior visual arts classes on a number of occasions. These involved myself as the poet-artist reading from a found script—usually a page torn randomly from the phone directory or help-wanted ads from a morning newspaper—and dressed in a hodgepodge of garments, swim goggles, a Balaclava, one skin diver's flipper, a bare foot, and a kilt leaning askew. I recall once cradling a cow's skull and carrying an old miner's lamp. I arranged for ambience, too: one spotlight in the back corner; two audio cassette players, each blaring music or sounds from unrelated traditions; two student confidants armed with water pistols; and a large oscillating fan to provide some air movement. My colleague ushered the unsuspecting class into the darkened room. On entering, I mounted a table and proceeded with my poetry reading, all the while attempting to dance an awkward soft shoe to imaginary music. With light circling, water flying in my face, and a cacophony of sounds, music, and ambient noise, I completed the four minute diatribe, bowed low to my startled and amused teenaged spectators, and exited unceremoniously. The absurdity of this extravagant performance assisted in releasing the imaginations of the class so that they could better comprehend the motives of these early twentieth-century creators.

An introduction to art of the Middle Ages, inspired me to rent a monk's habit from a Toronto costumers, play Gregorian chants as background music, line the front of the classroom with votive candles (unbeknownst to the fire marshal), borrow a large leather bound Bible from a colleague's place of worship, and cover the outside windows with coloured cellophane to approximate the lighting effects of stained glass. The grade eleven class for which I performed was baffled, but genuinely courteous, then intrigued as I preached about some of the ground rules of Medieval Christian liturgy and its impact on daily life. I'll admit that these performances have added exhilaration to my teaching experiences and allowed me to cultivate my love for theatre; I'll also acknowledge that secondary school audiences are among the toughest... and the most rewarding!

I see these forays into dramatic (re)presentation as deliberate ways of enlivening often distant historical content for students and engaging disaffected or diffident learners. As an advanced organizer or 'hook' for grabbing student attention, these happenings outfit serious learning in playful garb, and allow students to view their teacher as someone who is willing to take a risk and be slightly silly.

On Stage: Performing Self

A final remark about my performing activities as a teacher connects with the assorted role playing and performance art instances revealed above, but addresses more the regular happenings, convolutions, and anecdotes of classroom interaction. It is the notion of teacher-as-actor, an analogy that places the teacher on the classroom 'stage,' performing for their student 'audience.' Yet, I have come to understand that most 'acting' in the classroom emanates from the personality and creative ingenuity of the teacher, from within the individual being, not from any formal actor training. Admittedly, I have dramatic arts experience in my background, but nothing as disciplined as acting classes; my theatre knowledge comes from an intermingling of high school classes, co-curricular high school directing, and audience pleasure; however, I do regard my past theatrical exposures as critical in developing greater self-esteem and social fortitude. Countless incidents of playing, behaving, and acting with my students (note the interactive emphasis) come back to me.

Once I've become familiar with students, I tend to become more playful and overtly expressive in speech. I have a powerful "teacher" voice and I'm not afraid to use it! Lesson introductions take on a vibrancy and air of excitement when I combine my responsive voice with hand gestures and the odd foray into pantomime. My students frequently muse that I wouldn't be able to teach if my hands were tied behind my back! I always throw out ideas packaged as questions, even when answers appear self-evident—playing 'dumb' is often a very effective form of pedagogical acting business. I thrive on ambiguity and complexity, qualities which induce curiosity, inquiry, and, every so often, genuine wonder. Emotional expression is rarely disguised; my students notice that I can be a very effusive person, but I also encourage them to share their feeling selves, particularly through the medium of their art. I've resorted to exaggeration and histrionics in order to elicit student reactions: describing an unbelievable incident that happened on my way home yesterday or explaining what the word "grotesque" means—with suitable sound effects—or faking incredulity during an aesthetics discussion about which displayed artefact is most beautiful. Things remain hidden until that all important moment of revelation—I have a black cloth that resembles a magician's prop. I use others' voices for emphasis and mimic characters when viewing artworks. Trading quips and jokes with students happens a lot; it's a great ice-breaker when I hear a trite response to a question or recognize a detached individual. I perform as a visual artist when I do demonstrations of techniques or introduce new materials; this type of 'playing around,' so important to the overall creative process, assumes an air of significance and validity when the only adult in the room is doing it. The messiness, the mistakes, the frustrations, the joys, and the adventure all come across during these acts of artistic generosity.

Louis J. Rubin (1985) claims that "[t]eaching as acting, consequently, has to do, among other things, with encouraging teachers to allow a bit more of their personality to show (p. 135)." More than injecting personality into the classroom, these teaching actions help me to grow as an artful educator and, with retirement looming larger, these assumed characters and roles sustain me by injecting a bit of playfulness into pedagogy. My performances affirm my being-in-the-world and exist as aesthetic occasions of teaching.

AFTERWORD: W\RITES OF PASSAGE

This inquiry was a pilgrimage of sorts, but to a place that was simultaneously tangible and indistinct. In writing about my teaching as a form of artistic practice, I was hesitant to articulate something that I thought others might not be able to recognize or, instead, would label as soft justification for years of unproductive artistry. However, this self-narrative has fortified my sense of purpose. It has revealed those aesthetic qualities and nuances in my teaching with greater clarity, and made me feel more positive about my professional contributions during this time of scepticism about schooling. Through this writing I have articulated what was unspoken and have excavated grounds that were already mined. My artful ways of being as a teacher were always already present, but it required this writing as public admission to authenticate these practices. An apt analogy for this thinking would be the aesthetic question that I frequently ask senior students: if an artist creates an artwork, but locks it in a closet so that no one can see it, is it still a work of art? Perhaps exhibition is requisite for artistry—being seen for understanding.

The writing has given me permission to cultivate my authentic self amidst the frequently arid and sometimes obscured landscape that is educational research. On this journey, I have heeded the directions of Maxine Greene, by allowing imagination to create openings to the unpredictable, and Parker Palmer, by re-inviting my undivided self back into the classroom to form a learning community of truth around that great, transcendent subject that is the arts". Elliott Eisner (2002) acknowledges that "there is the potential for an aesthetic experience in every encounter an individual has with the world. (p. 232)" We must continually look for the artistry in our daily lives.

PART THREE: THE DIALOGUE WITH OTHERS: HEARING NEW VOICES, PERSPECTIVES AND INTERPRETATIONS

The dialogues we have with others provide us with contexts for the interaction of our narratives, for lives to meet lives, and to influence, inform and inspire each other. Through these interacting narratives, we can experience the interplay of diverse ideas, perspectives, and understandings, and learn that our ways of knowing and being are not universally shared. We can learn to create new connections, new possibilities, new forms, and new narratives for our future lives.

- Chapter 7: Between the Laments and the Lullabies: *Angélique Davies*
- Chapter 8: Autobiography as Genesis: Linking the Student, Writer and Teacher in us all: *Carol Lipszyc*
- Chapter 9: One Lens: The Role of the Arts: Beginning with Myself: *Catherine Dowling*
- Chapter 10: Learning from my Experiences: The Role of the Arts: *Masayuki Hachiya*

ANGÉLIQUE DAVIES

7. BETWEEN THE LAMENTS AND THE LULLABIES

As I write my narrative I am a forty-two year old woman with several years of experience in the field of early childhood education and care. Most of my jobs have centred on the needs and interests of young children. I have also had additional work and volunteer experiences in museum education, teaching music in early childhood, developing curriculum materials and web content for a charity for children, teacher training and recently hospice care. I have long believed that many who make a career of working with young children wish to provide care, protection and learning experiences that they may not have received in childhood, and by doing so, to heal some part of themselves. To some degree this has been true in my own case. For much of my life I have felt separate from others, and have tried to resolve this by seeking a sense of belonging – a sense of *family* - through my work.

Writing my narrative has enabled me to see the influence of my early experiences on my work as an educator and on my creative expression as an amateur musician. It has allowed me to reflect on the extent to which music has been my heart *and* my voice, on what it has given to me throughout my life and what it has inspired me to give in return. By connecting me to the child within, music has helped me to connect with others. Writing my narrative has let me see meaning in feeling separate, and realize that through sharing my story I become a part of those who hear it. Then I am not so alone. My story has both somber and sweet refrains, but through its telling I am bridging the distance between the laments and the lullabies. I invite anyone interested in my song to listen and perhaps through listening, to hear the opening bars of their own song.

"Music is Like the Sun. Its Rays can Touch all Areas of Development."

Donna Wood wrote these words in 1982, in an influential book entitled, *Move, Sing, Listen, Play*, which she published for teachers, to convey the holistic nature of early childhood music education. A true arts advocate, Donna believed that a comprehensive music program for children should include physical movement, opportunities to sing, listen to music, and explore instruments, so that they could to be expressive in different ways. I met Donna only a few times, and read her book while studying to be a music educator. Her words have resonated with me because my own musical education was far from holistic. It did not make me feel *whole*. Although I have expressed myself through music since childhood, I often felt separate from this music. It was as though I had something to communicate but no one could truly hear me. Those who mattered most to me did not listen. Music

M. Beattie (Author/Ed.), The Quest for Meaning: Narratives of Teaching, Learning and the Arts, 137–147.

making became a solitary experience rather than a special part of myself to share. After working in the child care field for several years, I experienced a strong impulse to create, that had been resting for years in the margins of my work and of my life. Watching hired music educators in action in my work place inspired me to take on that role, to embrace the artist within the teacher and to somehow make my musical voice heard. But as I moved in that direction, I found myself simultaneously travelling back, engaging in conversations with the child in me whose creative path had been altered, whose voice had been silenced. I first needed to wander through the darkness of my childhood before music could light the way for me, and lead me home.

Music is at the heart of my story, although I have never thought of it as my vocation. This story is not as much about my calling as it is about the voices that have called to me in its telling. I think that trying to express myself musically was also about straining to hear a voice of love. I was born to be able to do something special and spent a lifetime waiting for this to be acknowledged. From a very young age I was able to learn melodies and songs easily, and to sing them, or play them on an instrument, even without knowing the names of notes or anything about theory. At age seven I composed a simple song on harmonica, which my mother named *Little French Town*, and I played many more by ear. This music kept calling out, and listening for the encouragement it needed in order to hear itself. Many voices would speak to me as I studied music and played various instruments, voices both positive and negative, and even one "celestial" voice that would guide me to eventually trust my own. Finding my voice when I did helped me to realize that I was in a unique position to try to help children and other teachers to find theirs.

Since that time I have taught music, edited a newsletter for a professional association for music educators, presented workshops to early childhood practitioners and conducted graduate research related to early childhood music education. Interacting with other music educators, reading about their work and conducting my own research have all helped me to see how music has influenced my life and work, and the value of sharing what I have learned. Developing a model of music curriculum and implementing it in my own classroom showed me ways to respond to children's interests while exploring my own. Studying the issues surrounding arts education in the early years gave me a more clear understanding of how early childhood practitioners might influence the delivery of arts programs in day care settings. Hearing my own voice was empowering, but sharing what I had learned – with adults and children alike - gave me a deeper connection to music and to others. My journey as a teacher artist began when the child within me heard music as if for the first time and learned to share that music with children and their teachers. It is a song that is far from over and one that hopes to echo in many early childhood classrooms.

Music Box Ballerina

When I was little, I had a small white music box. Each time I turned the key and lifted the lid, it played *Brahms' Lullaby,* and the tiny plastic ballerina would pop up and spin until the music came to an end. I had the power to make the music play and to cause the ballerina to dance. I was much like my ballerina – living under the spell of the music and waiting for the magic key to turn. Each of my parents responded in different ways to my musical nature. In his quiet way, my father supported me by supplying the means of music making – a harmonica, a guitar, a flute. But he was very absorbed in is work, and often not available to notice any music I played. My mother was more involved in my life but by contrast was quite negative and critical. Even as an adult I found our relationship difficult and stressful. The truth is that years after her death I have continued to try to win her approval. She often referred to the sounds emanating from my bedroom in a disparaging way. *"What's that noise?"* I simply did not receive the kind of praise and attention that I believe all children need in order to feel confident about their capabilities. I envied the attention my brother received as he learned to play the drums.

Still, the negative attention I got was a very strong reinforcement, better than receiving none at all. I persevered with my playing, secretly hoping that my father would one day make time to listen, stubbornly trying to force my mother to acknowledge that what she referred to as noise was in fact music. *Music made by her child.* I think that without the voice of love that I really needed, I was not able to love my own music and accept it as a lovable part of my self. I would spend years relating to music in this way until I found myself one day teaching young children. I would need to dance between the present and the past, and between feeling rejected and accepted, to learn to hear and appreciate my own song and to be set free by it. Like my music box ballerina, the beauty I had locked within me simply waited for the key to be turned and the lid to be lifted, so I could spin and spin, liberated by my own lullaby.

The Siren's Song of the Past

There were some wonderful moments in school that gave me joy in music making. In fourth grade, I had a very creative teacher who taught everyone in the class to play the ukulele. I remember forming my own ensemble, performing *The Entertainer* at an assembly and being applauded by the whole school. This was a time in my life that has loomed large in my memory. I even wrote about it for a creative writing course – a few chapters for a juvenile novel about two musical siblings competing for the love of their parents – a project that waits to be finished. Ironically, during this time, I felt a greater sense of belonging at school than I felt in my own family. School provided a place where my music was noticed and valued, which was perhaps just enough attention and praise to build the esteem I needed. But that ended when my family moved and I was forced to change schools. This was part of a pattern of feeling like an estranged member of my family and later, my community, the same way my music was an estranged part of me. Until I felt rooted in the music within me, no matter where I was, I knew that I would never really feel at home.

I played flute throughout high school, participating in concert band and occasionally in pit bands for school plays like *HMS Pinafore*. This experience connected me with others and gave me a sense of belonging. After I graduated I did very little music making through university and later, college. It was not until I had been an early childhood educator for a few years that I began to yearn for the creative fulfillment that my work was not giving me. As a remedy, I joined an adult recreational band and resumed playing flute, eventually playing in small ensembles. But this didn't satisfy me as much as it made me doubt my ability to play. One of my teachers was very negative and made participation in her lessons a truly joyless experience. My mother's voice echoed in hers – this is a voice I don't actively seek, and yet I find myself drawn to it. *This was the voice that motivated me to keep going, the voice I kept trying to please even after my mother had died.* Although the impulse to prove I could play was strong, all flute playing eventually stopped. I later explored violin lessons after ending a long-term relationship, thinking that playing a challenging instrument would distract me from my sorrows. Once again, I had a critical teacher, but I enjoyed playing, and even started to become skilful. Unfortunately, after two years I had to give up the violin because I entrapped a nerve. I had injured my neck and left arm from excessive practice, from pushing myself too hard to win that elusive approval. While trying to find the path back to music, I nearly allowed the Siren's song of the past to damage my ability to pursue any further music making.

I was referred to a holistic health practitioner who prescribed several cures, among them yoga, massage therapy, increased protein in my diet and reading Julia Cameron's *The Artist's Way*. He also conducted numerous tests as I played the violin, to measure the muscle tension I was experiencing. Computer readings indicated that my physical tension was so extreme that it could not have been caused by violin playing alone. My doctor surmised that I had been retaining a lifetime of tension, that my muscles were holding on to hurts and frustrations that I was unable to release – perhaps because I had never been permitted to speak about them, or to openly express any kind of negative feelings. I was raised in a home where children were *seen but not heard.* I began the process of letting go as I spent the next twelve weeks writing what Julia Cameron called 'morning pages', slowly acknowledging the anger I felt towards my family.

Each journal entry was an opportunity to dialogue with those who had made me feel discouraged and negative about myself, to understand their reasons for doing this and to feel forgiveness towards them. The pages enabled me to see my family as human and to empathize, and eventually make my peace with them. Because the pages also involved setting creative goals for myself, they led me to two realizations about what was important to me, things that I had loved when I was young but was not pursuing in a meaningful way. One was writing, the other music … *soundless words, wordless feelings*. I see now the purpose that such non-verbal communication had served for me when I was a child, how my voice had found other forms. Writing and making music had made self-expression possible for me. Indeed, they had given me a "self" to express.

The morning pages also helped me to see that the music that had been my heart and voice was something I had kept separate from my work with children. The music I was making by and for myself, was keeping me as separate from the children that I taught, as it had kept me from my own family. Once I found myself in a care-giving role, I did exactly what my parents had done – I had failed to pay attention to the children I watched over every day and withheld something from them, something that had always been within me to give. Meanwhile, the musical child inside that so wanted to be heard, sought music making opportunities in other places. *On reflection, these places were not safer than my own classroom.* As a teacher and musician had I become so convinced that my gift was inadequate? What was holding me back? After all, it was my role as a teacher to create a safe community where children could express themselves. I could scarcely expect that to just happen if I was not prepared to take artistic risks there myself. Surely, teaching music would enable the musical child within me to feel a real connection to the children I cared for, and to at last begin to sing. I soon enrolled in a certificate program to study early childhood music education. With the decision to take this chance, my journey as a teacher artist began. The music box key had started to turn. The lullaby would soon be released.

Standing in the Light of Marguerite d'Youville

Long after the completion of my field placement I would see new meaning in my efforts to transform from early childhood practitioner to music educator. Once enrolled as a graduate student I was introduced to narrative inquiry. Professor Mary Beattie encouraged me to explore the role of the arts in my life. As I told and re-told my story from the points of view of the child, teacher and musician that I was, I could see the themes that kept emerging even as the landscapes of my life and work changed, and friends and family members came and went. *The need for approval, the sense of always feeling separate from others, the desire to find my voice and make it heard.* I want to share what narrative inquiry helped me to understand about the voice of music that has struggled to find expression in a way that was uniquely mine, and how this helped me begin to listen to the voices of others.

My narrative started with a recollection of a child in my care, a little girl who had trouble expressing herself creatively because her mother had instilled in her a fear of being untidy and getting dirty. One day we had planned a pretzel making activity and each child received a portion of bread dough that could be shaped into anything the children wished. The little girl held and looked at her dough for a long time but it seemed that her hands did not know what to do with it. They were not able to give the dough some shape or form. Instead, her hands parted and the dough fell to the floor. She stood for a moment and then just wept, tears quietly streaming down her cheeks. Her hands had betrayed her, almost mocking her as the chance to create slipped away. I understood very well how much she suffered from being unable to express herself, from not hearing that voice of love and approval. The child in me wept in solidarity for that little girl, and for my own unsung songs. In the end, another child, without hesitation, tore her own portion of dough in two pieces and shared it with the little girl. Through this innocent act of redemption someone had given her a second chance. In time I would see that I had received one too.

The need for acceptance and the desire to give something of myself motivated me to pursue music studies. If my gift of music found acceptance, the children I taught might then discover the music within them. Expecting to learn how to teach music in a day care setting, I was introduced to the methods of Dalcroze, Orff and Kodály. I learned to sight sing musical notation, to imagine the sound of written melodies and to compose music using solfa. I played children's songs on recorder and glockenspiel. Experiencing music in this way, I was a child again, hearing music as if for the first time. I watched true music teachers in action in the conservatory setting and eagerly tried what I learned in my own classroom, taking more artistic risks, and enjoying the feelings this evoked.

But I soon realized the distance between theory and practice. Many ideas could be imitated easily, but not everything that worked at the conservatory was so successful in the day care setting. Simply copying my teacher was a strategy with serious limitations and not a substitute for feeling truly grounded in what I was teaching or for adapting music experiences to the realities of my classroom. I observed that the sequential lesson plans that worked so beautifully at the conservatory – with a skilled music teacher, separate age groupings and students to assist – did not reflect the needs of day care teachers. The challenges I faced included inadequate support from my colleagues, coping with unpredictable behaviours, planning musical experiences that met the individual needs of children, and relating those experiences to the rest of the curriculum. Music simply could not be taught as a subject separate from the rest of the life of the classroom, as it was at the conservatory. Music had to be part of the total learning experience, and part of the total child, a problem not addressed at the time by this certificate program. My focus slowly began to shift from cultivating my own musicianship to considering practical solutions to this problem.

There is a chasm between music pedagogy and day care curriculum and I had internalized it. I wanted to be both an early childhood educator and music teacher, but I struggled to make music pedagogy fit where I worked. My practices as an early childhood educator did not fit well in the conservatory setting because of the limitations of my musical skills. I was emulous of those true music educators, and the desire for their approval distracted me from the goals I hoped to achieve in my classroom. Despite trying to blend what I had learned from both fields, I worried that my approach would not be considered *pedagogical* when the time came for my capabilities as a music educator to be evaluated. As the voice of love eluded me yet again, I began to have terrible doubts about whether or not my work would be worthy, about whether or not I would find acceptance as a music teacher. But the field placement was rapidly approaching and I needed to feel more certain of what it was I truly wished to achieve. For a while, I abandoned my books, instruments and voices and fled to Montréal.

While there, my husband and I paid a visit to the Church of the Grey Nuns, where I first learned about Marguerite d'Youville, a saint who lived in the 1700's and devoted her life to helping those in need. After the tour, visitors were invited to sit at the historic bedside of the saint and take a moment for quiet contemplation. I am not a particularly religious person but I prayed for guidance, for some sort of sign, and for the successful completion of my field placement. As we left the church, we were each given a small, plastic, glow-in-the-dark statue of the saint. I laughed! This was not quite the sign that I was looking for, but then I suppose we don't always find the meanings we seek where we expect to find them. Still, as I examined the statue, I could see that Marguerite was reaching out to me. She carried a food basket over her left arm and held out a piece of bread with her right hand. *What did this mean? What could this possibly have to do with the field placement?*

Clearly the statue represented generosity. But I realized that it addressed much deeper reasons for studying music in early childhood. Was the experience supposed to be about proving some point about my own musicianship and about emulating teachers who were more skilled and knowledgeable than I was? I realized that I wanted to enrich what I knew already, share what I could, and try to broaden the creative experiences of children in my care by broadening my own. Seeing this meaning in the statue helped me to take satisfaction in the act of giving music away without worrying about external approval. This feeling of peace and certainty would carry me through my field placement, as I created musical experiences that reflected who I was and what I believed as a teacher, and that worked best for my children.

The field placement itself enabled me to see a new interpretation, not just of the hand reaching out, but of the bread. As I created weekly lesson plans, integrating what I knew as an early childhood practitioner with all I had learned about teaching music, implementing the lessons and watching the children thrive, I realized that this experience was about change and transformation. I pictured the bread dough falling from the frightened, open hands of that little girl. I could see her friend, so sensitively and so generously sharing her portion, putting dough back into the little girl's hands. I could see hands transforming ingredients into dough, then transforming dough into some imagined thing that did not exist before, children being transformed themselves through the act of creation. I saw myself, transformed as a person and as a teacher, changed by shared experiences with the children, changed by how their creativity interacted with my own, changed by learning all that I did to make those changes I wanted to make in my classroom and in myself. I saw the statue of Marguerite d'Youville, extending her hand to me, passing me bread to break with others, so that we could all be nourished by the experience. And I found myself asking how I came to see all of this in a small, plastic, glow-in-the-dark statue.

Marguerite replied, *"I am not just a plastic statue. I am the voice of love you needed at a time when you felt uncertain. And I do not glow in the dark. The light in which I have been standing has enabled you to see me."*

And through her, I could see the separate parts of myself - artist, teacher and person – united at last

Last Goodnights

With the start of my graduate studies came what would be significant endings. After twelve years, I left my job in day care to pursue graduate research in early childhood music education. To that point, my music studies had prompted me to develop and deliver a workshop to encourage non-musical educators to bring music into their classrooms. This experience revealed broader issues in arts education that I wanted to explore. The dough I had been shaping with young children was changing hands now, and being re-formed by teachers. I would no longer be making music with my own children, in the safety of my classroom but aiding other teachers in creating music in the safety of their own. I was exhilarated to move forward but sad to let go of what had at last become a safe place for me. But an even greater loss was yet to come.

Soon after I left my job, my father was diagnosed with terminal spinal cancer. *One, perhaps two years to live.* Separated from children, and preparing for the final separation from my father, voices that had accompanied me on my path started to become more and more faint. My father would not live to see me graduate. And although there were many stories he had never told me that he now wanted to share, there was not enough time. As I studied, my father and I lived parallel lives – with me trying to conduct my research and to write and publish my paper, and my father trying, without any success, to publish poems he had been writing. We were each trying to share and preserve something precious to us: our voices. My voice had waited for so long to be heard, and Dad was using his remaining time to make his voice heard. *And remembered.* As the newsletter editor of a professional journal for music educators, I invited my father to write a lullaby for the back page, with the guarantee that he would be published. This seemed such a simple gift to give him, a creative experience I hoped we could enjoy this together – a union of our voices. But instead it would reveal the distance between us.

As he worked away on the lullaby, I conducted my research project. My music studies had prompted me to develop and deliver a workshop designed with the needs of early childhood educators in mind. In order to explore the efficacy of the workshop, I presented it to educators at their day care centre. In addition, I taught music to the infants, toddlers and preschoolers there, in collaboration with their teachers. In my absence, the teachers were to explore music with their children, using lesson plans I provided for them (if they wished), to keep journals for me, describing what happened, and to answer various questions for reflection. Eventually I interviewed each participant, and constructed from the collected data a narrative of their experiences.

I wanted this research to portray the stories of early childhood practitioners learning to teach music, and I wanted it to be published in a trade journal they would likely read. In every way I tried to apply all I had learned about narrative inquiry and to be respectful of their voices. On reflection, I was not able to treat my father's voice with the same respect. *Somehow my academic life had remained separate from my personal life.* Music had brought me closer to other people but had come back to remind me of how separate I felt from my own family.

Making music with my father involved a different kind of transformation than the experience of making music with young children. He had written a very charming poem about little animals, and I spent days composing the melody for it. The first two stanzas spoke of wishes and dreams. In the third stanza a little mouse protected himself against a bitter winter, while the fourth described a little bird flying and performing all kinds of acrobatic stunts. I found these stanzas odd and lacking the tenderness that had been established at the start of the poem. The melody I wrote was meant to communicate a parent's love for their child and I found myself changing the words to reflect the mood of the music. Now, in the third and fourth stanzas a mouse was lovingly being tucked in by his mother, while the bird soared ever upward, filling the air with its lullaby.

At the time I didn't really think about what my father's words might have meant, only what I felt they should be communicating. I had even convinced myself that making the changes that I did was a reflection of my solid editing skills. I see now that in his dreams my father was afraid of what was happening to him, and longing for when he was still free to do everything for himself. I had taken on a parental role as my father began to need more and more help and was preparing myself for his eventual ascent to heaven. But he wasn't ready to let go. When I didn't hear my father's affection in the lullaby, I inserted this. Perhaps I never really wanted the composition for the newsletter. I wanted it for myself. I wanted one last chance to hear my father's voice of love, but he was not singing to me.

I remember the last good night of my childhood. I had tucked myself into bed and then called out to my parents repeatedly. *"Good night, Mom! Good night, Dad!"* I could hear my parents speaking in hushed tones before my father came into the room and sat on my bed. He asked if I thought that perhaps I had become too old to be kissed good night. I didn't know what else to do except agree. The next night I went straight to bed without a word, to show them that I understood. *My parents no longer wished to say good night to me.* I was told that I was to continue to say good night, though I could no longer expect this formality from them. It is strange that this memory should surface as I write about a conflicted lullaby written by a dying father and his daughter. My father was frequently absent as I was growing up and because my relationship with my mother had been so conflicted, I may have wished for my father to be more openly affectionate than he actually was able to be. For their own reasons, my parents hurried me to abandon my childhood. But I wasn't ready to let go. There I was, my father's child, *soon to be an orphan*, and never to hear my father's voice again. But somehow we had brought into existence a lullaby that would allow me to remember my father's last good night as it should be remembered, and to hear his voice of love.

I cannot claim to have truly sung to my father in a voice that was mine. I merely composed a melody and re-wrote part of his poem. *Wordless feelings, soundless words.* Unable to sing or perform the piece myself – finding on this occasion that my own voice was inadequate - I borrowed the voice of my friend Penelope, a lyric coloratura, and the piano skills of her husband Richard. They created a gorgeous recording of the lullaby for me, which I gave to my father for Christmas, and which he listened to only once before he died, one month later. There is a deafening silence in the beautiful song that contains the best parts of each of us. There is a melody revealing feelings that my own words could not, and a poem concealing feelings that my father could never express. The most precious gifts we possessed we could not give to each other, even knowing we were on borrowed time. I played the lullaby at my father's funeral, the lid of the music box opening and our song of sorrow – my father's and mine – rising upward as the lid of his casket closed. I have wished my father his last good night. Now only in dreams can I hear his voice of love.

But the lullaby lingers.

Donna's Lullaby

> With every gain I've made on my musical journey, something was also lost along the way. My mother died before I completed my certificate in early childhood music education. I left my job as an early childhood educator in order to pursue graduate studies, and could no longer apply my learning in a classroom I had long called my own. I lost my father to spinal cancer before I earned my Master of Education degree. It seems that as I got closer to finding my voice – *my song* – I found myself moving farther and farther away from those voices that had influenced me throughout my life. Although my parents have gone their silent way, the echoes of their voices still beckon me. After working in an office for three years as a curriculum developer and web content writer, I have longed to return to singing and making music with children. I continue to contribute to the field of early childhood music education as much as I can, editing a newsletter, delivering my workshop, teaching, and even occasionally composing simple children's songs. My favourites are lullabies. Perhaps this is because I am still trying to put those voices to rest, through a pure music that speaks with love and tenderness to those who have gone before me, and whose voices have guided me.

Donna Wood passed away in October of 2007, leaving behind a dream of music education for the very young that she had made real. As a graduate of her certificate program and editor of the newsletter of her professional association, I wanted to compose in her memory, a lullaby that captured the main themes of her book, "*Move, Sing, Listen, Play*". I found as I wrote the lyrics and composed the melody that I felt a terrible sense of sadness and loss. I had only recently lost my father and was now regretting the changes I had made to his poem, to the expression of his voice. I wept as I wrote *Donna's Lullaby*, thinking about how we all yearn to be heard and to know that somehow our voices will resonate after we have gone. The song was as much for me and for my father as it was for Donna Wood. Still, I wanted to capture the spirit of all that Donna had accomplished, and the music and creativity that she had inspired in so many children and their teachers. I wanted to communicate how we live on ourselves through touching the lives of others in some meaningful way.

I have discovered that in every life, in every experience, there is a story. There is a song that wants to be heard. Finding my own voice has been a struggle. I have been brought face to face with each aspect of myself – *child, artist and teacher* – and come to an understanding of what separates me from others, and what gives me a sense of belonging. And the experience has brought me closer to feeling more whole. Learning to teach music alerted me to the challenges this involved and made me a more creative teacher. Trying to communicate all I have learned to other early childhood practitioners through studying music, presenting workshops, writing articles and conducting qualitative research encouraged me to try to make a difference in the child care field, where arts policy has been static for years. *Did my research positively influence anyone's teaching practices at all? Have I helped teachers to hear their own voices and to pursue their own creative dreams?* Without knowing these things, I sometimes find myself wondering if my experiences – personal, professional and academic, both good and bad – have made a difference only to me.

But from time to time I hear about children I taught years back that went on to study music because they were inspired by their childhood memories of music making. I receive e-mails from workshop participants who loved the ideas I shared with them and are hungry for more ways to bring music into their classrooms. Those who read the newsletter occasionally would tell me that they learned something valuable from it. I have lived my song for a reason and I know now, that between the laments and the lullabies, my voice can sing out in a music that is truly mine, and mine alone. Although I may not always know who is listening to my song, or being touched by it, or what it might awaken in them, I know that sometimes someone *hears*.

CAROL LIPSZYC

8. AUTOBIOGRAPHY AS GENESIS: LINKING THE STUDENT, WRITER AND TEACHER IN US ALL

INTRODUCTION

As a remembering adult, I journey backward and inward in order to reconstruct my early felt experiences, to extract from them their meanings, and to story them narratively in the light of later experiences and feelings (Beattie, 1995a, p. 12)

My father's hands.
when my dark-skinned father
died of melanoma

after labouring
on high-rises
that scar Toronto's skyline

his shirtless back
branded by the August sun

my mother handed down two possessions
these are for *you,* she said

I lay the items in a paper vault
of rose and violet
behind the glass pane
of my bedroom t.v. stand

and since that time
eight years ago
I have rarely opened the box

barring memory
from the screen-lit dark

M. Beattie (Author/Ed.), The Quest for Meaning: Narratives of Teaching, Learning and the Arts, 149–160.

until today
when I recover his
stainless steel watch
band of brushed metal
links like fish scale

on its seafaring face
a glass dome
that keeps the hour

engraved on the back
in old English font
I read:

Torino
8–15–46

he would have been eighteen
when he first saw the watch
in a storefront window

Hebraica, the Italians called the smuggled Jews
granting him free streetcar rides for his losses

from a burrow
in the Berashtan forest

the hands of the watch pointed
to a city of kindness

he would wind the watch and listen
for the soft assurance of its *tick*..

I open with an excerpt of a recent, yet unpublished poem I penned to ally myself with my prospective students, to do in my life what I ask my students to do. In the fall of 2009, I am scheduled to teach *Introduction to Writing Poetry* in a liberal arts college that is part of the State University of New York (SUNY) network. One of the choices students will have is to commemorate a parent or family member using a concrete object. After an in-class activity where students will share stories and write briefly about their chosen artefact, models of published poets will play an integral role in the pre-writing, percolating stage. Like me, these poets have mined familial memories through possessions they can touch to convey what is most important. My objective is to show students how, in an elegy, poets enact an image of the one who has departed by blending the concrete with the abstract—by working with the inanimate objects left behind to suggest the emotional connection that once existed. In this way, the reader can participate more actively in the meaning-making process. I want as a poetry teacher to veer students away, at this introductory phase, from writing poetry whose meaning is opaque. I am, likely, anticipating that students may err as I have erred. Will I read the poem about my father in whole to my students? I may decide not to bring the writing into class. Nonetheless, my having shaped and reshaped that poem about a subject that is tender, raw and unsettling, makes me all the more cognizant and empathic of the process my students will undergo. That is a good place for educators to be as we guide, conference and assess students on writing that strikes a personal chord.

The timeline of my life has collapsed at the very outset of this narrative; I have moved from the here-and-now, eyed the future before steering backwards. And over time, I have come to understand how systemic living and teaching the arts can be, and how teaching and writing feed into one another. And so, I return again to this quest with a renewed, resituated curiosity. Investing energy and belief in the potential of arts-based qualitative research, I chart and follow a reflective path in this chapter, compose a narrative vignette of my graduate student days that reads like a historical site, and analyze as authentic data, my past Grade 12 students' and my own creative writing in prose and poetry. This study, therefore, is auto-ethnographic in nature, that is, autobiographical in genre yet inclusive of other voices including: my own lyrical/scholarly voice, the scholars I cite, and most importantly, the writing voices of my former high school students who enrich the inquiry. With this chorus of voices, I move away from solely a self-portraiture.

I choose this methodology to ascertain how *interdependent* my plural identities of teacher, writer and scholar are, and to further examine how these identities cross timelines and spatial boundaries in a complex yet integral way. It is my hope that in reading this brief chapter, students will affirm the belief that their personal, professional and scholarly lives can intertwine and that they may more fully realize their potential to make those connections.

Excavating Memory in First-Person Voice: Autobiography as Genesis and Teaching Heuristic

This story of my storied life begins with autobiographical writing. Speaking both as a student and teacher, writing in the "I" voice is an informed place to start any writing/research course in order to discover origins and weave storyline together with narrative unity. While enrolled in a graduate class, *Holistic Perspectives to Teacher Education and Teacher Learning,* with Mary Beattie, I was asked to write an autobiography and scholarly essay on my professional development, and to explore how I constructed and reconstructed my professional knowledge. The task seemed onerous at the outset after decades of work-related history. However, insights surfaced as I travelled back in time to an early literacy lesson whose imprint remains vivid. The listening/reading event that I will re-enact in the following paragraph served as the genesis for that autobiographical writing, for the subsequent creation of a lyrical poem, and for the design of a writing assignment that set seventeen-year old writers on a path of self-discovery about the craft and mystery of writing.

In elementary school, storytelling from children's Western European literary canon planted a formative seed in my future personal practice of writing and teaching. As a child, my strengths primarily lay in music and language arts. I could replicate, with reasonably good pitch, melody lines I heard on the radio, singing for anyone who would listen on our neighbourhood streets. I had a predilection too for dramatizing the written word. Believing, like many children, that the imagined realm was immediate and real, I was often haunted and spellbound by the larger-than-life characters I encountered in a story. That year, I entered the accelerated Grade 2 & 3 class at McMurrich Public School in downtown Toronto, a pre-WWI monolithic building within short walking distance from my home. My teacher was Ms. Granger, who, strangely enough, shared the surname of a character in the future Harry Potter series. Above all other memories of my primary school days, I recollect a supplement to the curriculum I now suspect Ms. Granger included to heighten our appreciation of the written word and engage us imaginatively (Dewey, 1902).

On Friday afternoons, Ms. Granger put aside our daily primary readers and mathematic tables, our crudely coloured maps and handwriting journals, and read aloud to us C. S. Lewis's *The Lion, the Witch and the Wardrobe*. Sitting atop her desk near the window, illuminated by the afternoon sun, she held the book's spine firmly, her slim figure dwarfed by sky-high ceilings. I remember a lavender sweater she wore and a close-fitting plaid skirt, her flesh-covered nylons and flat shoes. From the moment her reading began, she held the children captive. Never flagging in her vocal expression, Mrs. Granger ushered us in to the magical world of Narnia starring: the children sibling adventurers, the evil White Witch Queen, and the judicious and regal lion, Aslan, whom I worshipped as a godly creature. How I loved the idea of walking unaware into a clothing wardrobe and entering into another world. I wanted to be one of the children who could temporarily escape my world, restrictive and insular as it appeared compared to the world found in the book. Initially, stepping from the boundary of child in conventional world to child in imaginative world appeared easy enough for the sibling characters in WWII London. As the narrative unfolded, I learned that the children's fictionalized experiences were fraught with mystery, terror and delight.

From a professional teaching and writing craft standpoint, there are pedagogical steps and resources we employ as teachers to launch students into reading and writing and to hook them for good to the written word. Just as Mrs. Granger awakened and nurtured our love for reading, the professor modelled ways that students might trigger memory for autobiographies in graduate school. After reading her own autobiographical chapter about her early experiences with reading and writing, about her innate love and talent for music, I recall that students brought in artefacts as impetus for their first piece, presenting short, revealing explanations about the significance of those objects. This concrete pre-writing activity actively engaged us. Over the course of a few weeks, as we delved into the process of writing, the autobiography promoted our self-reflection and more as teachers, scholars and writers. Composing the autobiography some six years ago for the class, ignited the memory of Ms. Granger and the C.S. Lewis tale, in particular, which would incubate and serve as a model for my Grade 12 Writer's Craft assignment, and which would later evolve into a lyrical, autobiographical poem.

The magical C.S. Lewis wardrobe I first encountered in that tale so many years ago has also come to symbolize the genesis of writing for me now; it is, in fact, a metaphor I often employ when speaking to students about writing. One of the daunting challenges in writing is first stepping foot into the landscape of a poem, a narrative, an autobiography. To help students put aside their anxiety and fear of failure, and to encourage them to start writing, I call upon the image of a wardrobe, reminding them, from my personal experience and scholarship, that this often elusive entry point is highly individual and situational. For a number of scholars and writers with whom I share experiential knowledge, writing can be spurred on by a variety of variables: it can play out like a recurring image or a powerful feeling that wells up and must be released; it can emanate from reading texts that stand side-by side those we create, from interacting in response to a reality, and from the random events of coincidence (Capra, 2002; Bawarshi, 2003; Frost, 1964). Any combination of these variables has either propelled the initial writing of a piece or helped me through a period of critical instability when I searched for an answer to a writing challenge.

Over the years, as their introduction to me, I have asked my Grade 12 students in *Writer's Craft* to remember a text that stands side-by-side for them, that magically drew them into story land and nudges at them still. I further ask them to re-enact, as I did in graduate school, the scene when they first interacted with that text as either reader or listener, reflecting on the promise those transitional moments have held.

Students Write an Autobiographical Piece

> Ever since I was first read to, then started reading to myself, there has never been a line that I didn't hear…It is human, but inward, and it is inwardly that I listen to it. It is to me the voice of the story or the poem itself. The cadence, whatever it is that asks you to believe, the feeling that resides in the printed word, reaches me through the reader-voice…The sound of what falls on the page begins the process of testing it for truth, for me (Welty, 2004, p. 52).

After a few introductory narrative group activities, in my year-long goal to build a community of writers, I ask students in Grade 12 *Writer's Craft* to read an excerpt from "Listening," a chapter from Eudora Welty's eloquent autobiography, *One Writer's Beginnings* (1984). The piece reinforces the benefits of attuning one's ears to the symbiotic acts of reading and writing. Welty ties her early reading with the development of her ear to hear the written word and the music of language. She attributes her love of reading to her mother whom she credits with nurturing a love of words, though, in essence, both parents helped Welty construct her perception of her future vocation and art. In the chapter, the great Southern writer recreates her sense of auditory and visual wonder when first familiarizing herself with the alphabet and gradually discovering what happens when letters are joined together in meaningful and musical ways.

Writing models we choose as teachers are important authentic tools in expanding students' consciousness about reading and writing and about the arts in general. The models we select alert students to "see, hear, appraise and interpret through experience with a more finely-tuned sensibility" (Eisner, 1997). By prominently situating Eudora Welty as my first writer/student model, I begin to create a context that supports thinking processes and values that will engender development in students just as these processes and values have become part of my experiential and professional knowledge (Flower, 1990). As students enrolled in *Writer's Craft* have an interest in writing, I want them to reflect on and flesh out their early interaction with storyline and the oral relaying of story. Reading Welty's text will hopefully trigger a memory of a literacy experience and, thereby, generate an autobiography. In the assignment below, I try to inject enthusiasm in my students about their first piece of writing in the 'I' voice, which will serve as their introduction to me. The prompts help foster a means of writing and provide a checklist for elements I am looking for.

Assignment:

After reading Eudora Welty's autobiographical piece "Listening," recall, narrate and reflect upon an early experience *(one=1),* the first perhaps, when you knew you were excited about the written word. Maybe one evening, while you were tucked under the covers, a story was read aloud to you by your parents. Maybe you wrote your first composition in a Grade 4 class and found that experience rewarding, sustaining and memorable. Or maybe it was the first novel you read, the one you knew belonged to you, the one where the writing voice was so inviting that you felt at home in a new place. Recount that experience for me – make it as vivid and lifelike as you can for yourself and it will play that way for me. Length: approximately two pages double-spaced. Here are a few guidelines or tips:

A. Recreate briefly a sense of place and time through some description. When either you or a peer re-reads your draft, see if you have drawn the reader in to the here-and-now of the scene.
B. Welty cites her mother as a central influence. Who or what influenced you to read more seriously?
C. If you are referring to a particular story or book you once read, cite it. Feel free to integrate a passage if that part of the text will add texture and meaning to the piece as a whole.
D. Acknowledge the author if there is a commonality of experience or if he/she provided an insight for you, writing, for example, "Like Eudora Welty…" (If your experience was different, state that too).

Since this journal is autobiographical, write in first-person voice.

Excerpts of Student Responses

A) Natalie: Rediscovering a Love for Words

The following passage presents Natalie's transitional moment:

> I tiptoed to my bedroom and opened up the first page of my copy of "Harry Potter and the Philosopher's Stone." I was instantly transported to a world I'd never seen before. My head dizzied with details of the sights, sounds, and smells of the world that JK Rowling had created, seemingly just for me. Just as the character Hermione had recited a magical spell to open a door, so JK Rowling had opened the lock in my heart. I devoured the book, rereading and rereading, drinking in every single word like a thirsty dog back from a run in the park (Cooper, 2007).

To provide the back story for my first student's excerpt, Natalie writes of her early love of the written word, her "philologos," which she describes as being with her "at tender times like bedtime, and at times where I thought I would expire, like endless Hebrew classes....It shielded me, became my ultimate weapon, and my best friend." (Cooper, Unpublished Autobiography, September, 2007). With turn-of-phrases distinct in their irreverence, Natalie succinctly relays an incident where a Grade 3 teacher critically disapproved of her composition on chocolate, a piece she had carefully and privately laboured over. This early rejection by a teacher caused Natalie to temporarily reject reading and writing. As the reader can infer from the sophisticated quality of the above autobiographical excerpt, Natalie's early passion is restored when she reads the first in a series of J.K. Rowling's literary hits.

Reading Natalie's piece, I was uncomfortably reminded of the power a teacher holds as reader/assessor of student's writing and of the vulnerability students feel. It is the same vulnerability a writer at any age feels with every submission in and out of the classroom. No writer is exempt of rejections or criticism, and so I empathically related to Natalie, even as I took in to account her youth, and the urgency with which she calls attention to herself as an emergent writer. Students eventually learn that assuming ownership of their text brings both rewards and challenges. I have aimed to create a Grade 12 writing class whose culture provides a safe place for students to assume that ownership, experience agency, and test the timbre and range of their writing voices, as they stand at the threshold of young manhood or womanhood.

B) Hannah: Appraising Self as Child Reader

> I can remember the reason I favoured *The Lion King* over all other Disney stories: I felt that it was the most realistic. The other stories seemed too far-fetched, just a figment of some writer's imagination, created to enchant thoughtless children. But *The Lion King* was definitely no sugar-coated fairy tale, I figured, since one of the main characters is killed halfway through the story. Looking back, I realize that I was cynical for a child, and also quite

> inaccurate – as if talking lions are any more realistic than a flying carpet or an enchanted palace! Nonetheless, *The Lion King* was my favourite, the only book I would request, the only movie I owned, and the source of my dreams. Even after I had moved past the large print and colourful pictures, *The Lion King* set me on a path of love of animal stories: *Black Beauty*, *Mr. Popper's Penguins*, *Stuart Little*, and my favourite, *The Trumpet of the Swan.*
>
> Despite its seemingly childish style, *The Lion King* is a story I have yet to outgrow. I know it's embarrassing, but a month doesn't go by where I don't sit down, open the book, and relive all the fantasies I experienced as a child. And though I can no longer call it my favourite book, *The Lion King* turned me into an animal lover, a dreamer, and an avid reader who, when I am captivated by a book, will still read it over and over again, as I did so many years ago with *The Lion King* (Cohen, 2007).

The animal inhabitants of the lush and varied African landscape in *The Lion King* became Hannah's friends and playmates. Transported to the sweltering heat of the Pride Lands, she "soared with the gazelles and traipsed with the elephants" (Cohen, Unpublished Autobiography, September, 2007). In an objective voice unusual in one so young, Hannah rethinks her child's reading of the text, concluding with gratitude that the book's influence lingers still.

C) Becca: Power of the Spoken Word

Like Welty, Becca links her evolution as listener, reader and writer in an elegant passage:

> I am grateful for the English ear I cultivated during this crucial time. This special understanding of the language has benefited me. When I read, I still hear that young child sounding out each unique syllable. When I write, that voice guides my hand across the page as I masterfully string together those simple sounds that make beautiful stories of lands far far away with heroic knights and dazzling princesses (Bookman, 207).

In her autobiography, Becca writes of a different kind of learning experience, reflecting on the impact her voice therapy lessons have had on her young life to date. From the age of three, up to middle school, Becca made weekly visits to the North York General Hospital in Toronto to improve her enunciation and oral communication. Her thoughts came so quickly as a child that her words jumbled together and jarred the listener's ears. As she explains in her introduction: "In my eagerness to use my voice, it may have developed too quickly and needed to be calmed" (Bookman, Unpublished Autobiography, September, 2007). Every week, she climbed up a non-winding set of stairs to reach her speech therapist's office. Becca illustrates a highlight of one such lesson, integrating the past and present: "Probably the most crucial part of my learning came when we dealt with the words *ship, chip, wash* and *watch.* 'The captain of the *SH*-ip really enjoys eating potato *CH*-ips'" (Bookman, 2007).

And up there, in that room, paradoxically, as she painstakingly worked her way through the sounds of the alphabet, Becca's love for the English language flourished. Struggling with enunciation, contorting the shape of her mouth, tongue, teeth and lips, propelled the words' clarity, which in turn made Becca more cognizant of the language, and of the sounds she emitted as she worked towards her goal – to render a charming sound to her words.

The students' excerpts remind me as an educator how reciprocal learning can be as I note with pride and an element of surprise the self-assertion in their writing voices. As was true for me with the Lewis creation, imaginative works were enlightening for my students. In our collective dialogue about these respective texts, we forge a community of readers and writers.

Writing a Poem – Memory Re-Enacted In Poetic Form

I can imagine no better way for teachers to become "natural allies" of our writing students than to set similar tasks for ourselves, to undergo some of the challenges our students face, albeit with a well-stocked arsenal of writing strategies (Bloom, 1998, 123). Consequently, last year, I revisited that early memory with Ms. Granger, reshaping it into a lyrical, autobiographical poem that tells a story about storytelling. There was another motivation too – the need to converse with the all-important constituent of audience – an essential part of the rhetorical equation. I find it increasingly difficult to write for only myself and for no tangible purpose other than my own self-enrichment, though my audience consists of an ideal reader who shares similar tastes and life experiences to my own. Fortunately, in the spring of 2008, OISE co-sponsored a celebration of writing via the Toronto Reading Council. An opportunity arose to share my writing when Shelley Stagg-Peterson invited poetry writers of all ages to contribute to this event. I jumped at the chance to move from the personal and autobiographical to what Carr refers to as "we subjects," a collective of readers and writers who might recognize themselves in the poem and in their relation to the world (as cited by Conle, 2000). I quote this phrase to illustrate how succinctly scholarship can reinforce, legitimize and buoy my desire to write and extend my readership.

Let me respectfully direct my readers' attention to said poem that follows entitled "Narnia" and to my writing voice in a figurative style.

Narnia

Friday afternoon
school books stashed
in dungeon drawers

Crayon fingers trace epithets
carved on yellow wood
desk tops

Perched above us
Mrs. Granger wears glasses to read
on her rims
a gold-purple crocus budding east and west

Storybook in hand
her voice glides
over clouds of chalk dust
circling round our
unrepentant day dreams

Pages flip like tapering wings
as Lucy enters
the wardrobe of running imagination

steps into crystal cakes of snow
the numb slumbering winter of Narnia

On the second Friday,
cubes of turkish delight
stain our pink tongues

On Friday the good
King Aslan splayed on a stone table,
heart spliced by the witch's knife

Can sacrifice come from a promise?

* * *

Wardrobes tempt me still
I wade through
dark suffocating fur

resist the burn and chafe of wool
to land breathless
nascent
at the open border of a story

an uncrowned queen
in the realm of invention (C.L, 2007)

Valuing The Writing Process

It may well be that even as I wrote the autobiographical segment about Ms. Granger as a graduate student, I apprehended innately that I could imaginatively flesh out its details later, ultimately making way for the poem that would surface sometime in the future (Hillman, 1996). The intuitive and spiritual parts of the writing puzzle cannot be dismissed or undervalued as they intensified the wondrous emotions I first felt when hearing the novel read, and reactivated and expanded those emotions through writing the narrative vignette decades later. Emotion invited me to write the poem too. In composing the poem, I translated my emotion into imagistic words.

As a scholar, I have a keen interest in decoding the composition process, delineating highlights of what has transpired. The rationale for my interest in process and for engaging in this meta-cognitive activity is as follows:

- by better understanding the complex process of writing, I can better teach that process to students;
- by examining highlights of that process, I particularize its complexity;
- by examining what I do for what reasons, I heighten my awareness of the strategic knowledge I possess and have built over time, knowledge which I aim to build in my students. I access this strategic knowledge to meet the situational needs of writing. Building on that repository of knowledge empowers and promotes greater autonomy in student writers as has been the case for me.

In setting out to write this poem, I had a handful of specific writing goals in mind, which were incentives for me. Firstly, I wanted to engage the reader in the sensory detail of the formative event: in the tactile, the visual, the auditory, and sense of taste, and this universal element of craft directed my diction choices. My teaching of expressive writing over the years has only reinforced this central tenet of writing. Secondly, I wanted to weave a surreal or dreamlike quality with real detail together in the poem to foreground the power of imagination. The imagistic phrase "clouds of chalk dust" emerged, as Hague describes, like a "seedbed of images" from my unconscious psyche (2003, 67), while I purposefully and cognitively drew descriptive detail like the gold-purpose crocus from the original text.

The last three stanzas, which are perhaps the most memorable, echo my teaching practice of using wardrobe as a metaphoric or symbolic entry point for writing. In the poem, I go on to extend that metaphor, acknowledging the paradoxes and problem-solving inherent in writing with phrases like "dark suffocating fur", the "chafe and burn of wool" juxtaposed against the "open nascent" border of a story that lies waiting to be written. Often, the choices open to writers seem too numerous to make; we rub against words and listen closely for the ones that breathe most naturally and fittingly to the writing as a whole.

Characterizing myself as the "uncrowned queen/in the realm of invention," I acknowledge the insecurity writers face with each blank place just as I celebrate the act of writing. A teacher who writes understands this dichotomy experientially, which only heightens such an individual's empathy towards his or her learners.

CONCLUSION

I see multiple feedback loops in motion here, with one causally connected element having an effect on the next in the complex practices of writing and teaching (Capra, 2002, 1996). Imaginatively, I reconfigured the reading experience which once gave me so much pleasure as a child into a poem that, in turn, has been read aloud to children on a CD by Judy and David Gershon, children performers and songwriters in their own right. This exemplifies the cumulative power of the arts in my teaching and writing life and the "continuity of experience" Dewey prophetically wrote about so long ago (1938, 35).

Engaging in this brief autoethnographic study has imbued a certain dignity and authority to my practice and teaching of the arts. Such a brief inquiry has helped illustrate and more clearly articulate for me the circular, reciprocal nature of my personal/professional practices in the arts. Autobiography, I am more fully convinced, can be a fertile site for reflection and a dynamic vehicle for self-expression. The process of writing through an autobiographical lens for myself as graduate student/teacher/writer/musician and for my student writers has been one of discovery and re-discovery. Through narrative and figurative devices, we both explored our love of language and reaffirmed our pre-existing affinity with it. This past fall, I asked my students in our concurrent English education program to write autobiographies about a singular or formative educational experience so that they too could harness lessons learned to their current lives and future professional/personal goals. That segment of the course was mutually and beneficially valuable. I came, as did my participants, to be better acquainted with their writing voices, their past selves, their rationales for teaching, and their aspirations as prospective teachers.

Turning to the past in the present does not slow our tracks but enhances the journey of our evolution. And while the private dimension is necessary when writing, thinking and reading, we reap unexpected rewards when our autobiographical work shapes or influences the work of our students, who continue along their own experiential paths.

AFTERWORD

Having long been interested in the interconnectedness between writing and teaching, I approached the writing of this chapter as an important step in the continuum of learning about the arts. It seemed perfectly natural to think systemically throughout, and to discover by writing, a link between past and present in my multiple roles as graduate student, teacher of expressive writing, and poet. Ultimately, I refined the writing across expressive genres and for diverse professional purposes. In exploring the past, I examined a trigger and origin for writing, namely, a love for the written word as first read to me by an elementary teacher who left a deeper impression than she could have known. I am especially grateful to my Grade 12 students who shared excerpts of their writing in this article, and in some ways, I ended where I began: in a grade 2 and 3 classroom listening to a beloved book. Yet, as this plural self, and through the dual practices of writing and teaching, I emerged a more deeply connected whole, a more fully realized self.

CATHERINE DOWLING

9. ONE LENS

The Role of the Arts: Beginning with Myself

INTRODUCTION

Before I can know and share my current understanding of art in my life, I need to journey back to reflect on the role and significance of art throughout my life. The story of that journey follows.

It is a luxury for me to explore my personal relationship with art, and at this time in my life I understand art to have a limitless definition. I believe that it is realized and defined by individuals, and by their unique ability to choose, connect, create and live with what they in turn perceive and believe to be art. As young children we naturally learn and judge visually. This changes once we can speak and comprehend an oral and then a written language. Speech and words begin to dominate our world, refocus our lens, and subdue our earlier innate sensory experiences.

Earliest Memories

As a child I understood art by definition to be something that was accomplished in its precision and something you liked well enough to hang on a wall. It was created by an 'artist', specifically a painter, and was distinct from sculpture, music or literature. Both public school and after school art classes reinforced this limited understanding of art. It was often presented as something you were either good at or not.

Painting

In my childhood home, Sunday night family dinners were a weekly ritual that began well before the eating of the meal. The intoxicating aroma of beef as it slowly roasted on those long, quiet afternoons in the kitchen, sensually prepared our family for an evening of excellent food and interesting discussion in the most elegantly decorated room of the house. My seat in the dining room looked over to an opposite wall where one of my mother's oil paintings hung above the dining room buffet. The 'art' piece had been chosen for its pleasing subject of flowers in a vase and because of its colours that complemented the overall décor of the room. This would have been a decision made by my mother. I can also remember enjoying the pleasure that this art brought to our dinner each Sunday evening.

M. Beattie (Author/Ed.), The Quest for Meaning: Narratives of Teaching, Learning and the Arts, 161–171.

When I was young my mother painted original and copies of existing oil paintings. Today the smell of varnishes, oils and turpentine still evoke strong memories associated with the happiness of childhood and the busyness of my mother's hours spent painting. Some of the work was copies of favourite local artists while others were inspired from slides my father had taken on our various family travels. My father was the family photographer and responsible for frequent evening family slide shows. The painting in our dining room was one of my mother's many 'oils' (as she referred to them) that hung on the walls of our home.

Nature

From an early age I spent whatever time possible in the 'natural' or outside world. When my family travelled on summer camping holidays to nearby provincial parks in southern Ontario I had the chance to explore 'wilderness' places that were very different from the subdivision I lived in. I would spend hours imagining myself as a 'native Indian' from long ago who could glide silently through the woods. The sounds, smell, colours and light were like nothing I could experience at home. The forest seemed clean in comparison to the man-made world I knew. I could breathe and imagine in an entirely different way in those woods.

Building

Camping holidays gave me an opportunity to build things with my hands. My parents still reminisce about the twigs I would gather near our campsites, and which I would then fasten onto two closely growing trees. These connected trees and twigs would form the support for our plastic 'sink', making an outside washing area. Once the sink location was established, a place for a towel and mirror could then be made. Years later these innate design projects would fuel significant architectural research.

At home during summer vacations I spent endless hours making things mostly from materials available on hand. I would invent and craft the environments for my four inch Peewees (dolls) and Trolls who also would enjoy the pleasures I knew. Corrugated cardboard was used to build everything from a scaled miniature tent-trailer to a 'modern' family round house. The modern round house model was inspired by an unusual home my uncle had built for his family. My aunt and uncle were warm hosts who lived nearby and they had a strong interest in innovative design. I shared their intrigue and studied the difference between their home and the only one I would ever know before leaving home for university. I was fascinated at how differently people could organize their living spaces. I remember being equally surprised with the simple difference in the curtains used for bedroom doors at my grandparent's cottage.

Music

In grade four, at the age of eight, I became swept up in the celebration of Canada's 100th birthday and the anticipation of Expo '67, an international exhibition held in Montreal during the summer months. Singing in the school's centennial choir became a large part of my life as the school and community prepared for local festivities. I had a similar experience during summer camp stays at this age. During every meal in the huge dining hall the entire camp would sing together. Hearing my own voice blend and dissolve with so many others was a unique experience of connection with a larger whole.

Music was always present in my life and home. My father was active in a barbershop chorus and quartet, and our home stereo was always warm from the various musical tastes of my family. At public school and church I enthusiastically sang in choirs. As a teenager I dreamt of being the next Joni Mitchell as I learned basic acoustic guitar and dabbled in song writing. I started to 'read' music, composed a few songs and recomposed lyrics for some existing popular melodies. Playing guitar and singing on my own in front of others was one of the few things that made me uncomfortably shy. In high school I also wrote many poems and had one published in grade 11 which I have included here.

Sewing

During my teen years a lot of my time was spent sewing articles of clothing for myself. It was a 'hobby' that provided hours of pleasure. The ability to take something like a length of fabric in a raw form and be responsible for its conversion into another form was something that amazed and instilled a feeling of accomplishment and pride. It was to be many years later before hand-building would be understood as an art.

All of these early and pleasurable memories now make sense to me as natural beginnings to a way I saw and understood my world. Observations, resulting in inspirations, resulted in new creations of my own. My curiosity seemed constantly fed with a sense of wonder, desire to understand and to create that continues to this day.

SIGNIFICANT MEMORIES

Culture

Attending Expo '67 was a life changing experience for me. Immersion into its' foreign worlds of geography, languages, buildings, sounds, and colours fostered my innate love of variety, complexity and difference. My family spent a week in Montreal that summer, and each day we were transported by the futuristic monorail to fantastic discoveries. It was often a three hour wait to gain admission to a country's pavilion,but nothing was to be missed in this peaceful global celebration.

Drawing

At about the same age I remember making the only 'real' piece of art I would consider myself to make as a child. It was a detailed drawing, a copy of a 'Holly Hobby' greeting card, which was common at the time. I was home from school and sick in bed, finding it difficult to pass the hours, so my mother suggested I do some drawing. It took me a long time to do a black and white version of the coloured card. I used a soft lead pencil on ordinary paper. I was surprised by the sensation I experienced while focusing on this one object in order to make another. The quiet concentration required for each mark on the page was similar to the careful placement of my footsteps on the forest floor, focused writing or hand building projects. Time seemed to disappear and stand still until I 'resurfaced'. I surprised myself with my drawing's likeness of the original card.

With the exception of this one drawing I never considered any of the other experiences to be art. In senior elementary and high school it was generally understood that art offered no 'value' as a subject for future university study. It was known as a 'bird' course, something you took if you wanted an easy class, not a valued option for the university bound. For this reason I never took the available art electives. Instead I chose the two available spoken languages, French and German, and the visual language of technical hand drafting.

Language

In secondary school I was able to participate in French language exchange programs to Quebec. It was during the second summer that a fascinating transition occurred; I began to think in French! I no longer made mental translations. I reached a different thought process that I would not realize again until I tried watercolour painting for the first time during a university school term spent years later in Italy. What is interesting to me now is whether I had already experienced this level of focus and alternate level of consciousness much earlier in my summer days of building, singing, sewing and exploring the outside and man-made world.

LATER UNDERSTANDINGS

Stories and the Everyday

These past musings bring me closer to an understanding of how art has evolved and been under recognized in my personal life. In order for this writing to truly be a reflection of the art I knew in my childhood, it needs to include a brief reflection on the art of living. People who informed my understanding of the everyday either made 'art' or inspired something in me that became an ideal, an example of something beautiful in terms of how it could help me better perceive myself and survive in the world. The one person who stands out was also one of the best storytellers I have ever known. Annie Sykes was a family friend who stayed with my two sisters and I whenever my parents went away for brief holidays. Her bedtime stories were endless and always took my imagination to a world I had not known before. I was embraced in a secure world of warmth and love with Annie's tales.

In grade nine English classes I was introduced to a story that still resonates today. *Where Nests the Water Hen,* by Gabrielle Roy was a small novel that a thirteen year old student could read relative to that point in her life. What I understood then was the romance of a remote home, isolated in the wilderness of Northern Manitoba, and how a large French speaking family was able to realize their mother's dream to receive a 'proper' education from the English speaking government. My recent immersion in teaching and learning rekindled a desire to reacquaint myself with this story. My understanding of the ways this family lived in a self sufficient way grew and evolved through education, and travel has a new resonance for me today.

My early childhood interests developed into a number of interests and connections, and I understand that there is so much that I have not yet discovered. I cannot separate the arts as an entity from the world as I see and understand it. Art gets its life from the humans that make and use it. The layering of these multiple lenses is like a painting of many thin glazes of watercolour paint or layers of tracing paper. Only when combined can they reveal the whole. Without these many parts the richness necessary in art and life cannot exist.

PROFESSIONAL REALITIES

Studying

My years in university framed many new lenses of art as I entered the creative fields of Interior Design and Architecture. At this time, I was still not an artist in my own eyes. The art I posted in my residence room were these words by Robert Frost. They still provide inspiration:

> The woods are lovely, dark and deep.
> But I have promises to keep,
> And miles to go before I sleep,
> And miles to go before I sleep.
> (Frost 1964 page 27)

During my studies in architecture school, I spent a four-month fall term in Italy. During one class we were given the assignment that asked for a visual analysis of Hadrian's Roman Villa. No further specific instruction was given. We toured the remains of this emperor's oasis, a dwelling framed by fountains and great halls that once enclosed the welcomed public of the day. My final submission for the project was a recognizable floor plan but the earthly creation was re-presented with celestial proportion. I arranged a series of white (constellation) points on black card to create an abstract memory (plan) of the indoor and outdoor spaces. The resulting pattern of stars invited a broader understanding of this place while suggesting infinite connections.

> When all the involved calculations prove false, and the philosophers themselves have nothing more to tell us, it is excusable to turn to the random twitter of birds or toward the distant mechanism of the stars.
>
> (Yourcenar, 1974 p. 26)

Painting

I was inspired by the water running through, beneath and around Hadrian's Villa, and its ability to unite the fragments of the dwelling. I explored additional representation with watercolour paints. The medium was totally new to me but it permitted a letting go of any preconceptions I may have made with more familiar drawing tools. That sense of being lost in time returned – a feeling I had only known a few times earlier in my life. It was an experience that I recognized as liberating, enabling another part of myself to be present at the same time allowing discovery. It is something I have since learned to strive for in my work.

Culture

Through iconographic studies, the music, sculpture, literature and architecture of past cultures, I began to comprehend the relevance of individual wonder and perception that can inform understanding and beliefs that equally sustain a civilization at any one point in time. Twenty years after building the campsite washstand in the trees, the same intuitive and functional planning methodologies would be used for my architectural thesis, *Settling a Landscape in the Canadian Arctic* at the University of Waterloo. It was a time when I could use personal architectural pre-occupations to create a personally designed solution. The focus was to create a quintessentially Canadian design about what it means to inhabit a place. I can understand now how many earlier sensibilities about art, culture and the everyday were present in the journey of discovery that resulted in the creation of that project.

Learning and Building

As I teach, so I am again a student. I have started another pottery class and open studio at the DVSA (Dundas Valley School of Art). Art classes still are an unclear journey where I need to trust myself more, value and make my own decisions, because there can not be a clear or predetermined outcome. The written passage *Finite and Infinite Games* by Carse (1986) which I have included at the end of the chapter, brings me a confidence at these times of self-doubt. It is a piece that I share with my own students. For me the making of things usually is tempered by the usefulness of those things. I rarely make something for pure visual enjoyment, but it is not simply for a utilitarian purpose either.

The Everyday

I am reminded of the integral beauty the Shakers brought to their hand crafted tools and storage boxes. As a culture, the Shakers no longer exist, but their legacy lives on within their hand creations which are still produced and sold in the United States. I too enjoy and value the everyday quality and purpose from the things I make. Perhaps this excludes them from art, but I don't think so. Many pieces I enjoy are not the things of everyday life. This presumes that there is a hierarchy that exists in art forms that reflects our needs, like the art in a gallery compared with a cherry Shaker sewing box. Often seeing or hearing a special creation I am reminded of the everyday, the 'unspecial' and its equal ability to inspire. At the same time I am in awe of the 'master', someone who has perfected something, an ability I do not seem to have, and yet I know others do not see me this way. I think we see, feel, and think based on our needs at the time. This means that we all equally have something to offer, just at different times and places.

Poetry

I need to look out my 'memory box' to reread the poetry I wrote in my teens. This was a very insightful time for me. I experienced a lot of the transitions that are natural to that age, and redirected that energy by building a level of independence in myself. I see it now with my son. I am busy with teaching and studying and not looking after the things I used to do at home, so he is becoming more self sufficient than I did at that age. This has been good for both of us because at fifteen it gives him a time for his own inner 'tapping'. He is writing and playing music as I wrote poetry. It is wonderful to see and hear. I think art is synonymous with invention for me. It is story telling of one kind. The key is the change that it can inspire.

Nature

This fall at a friend's cottage I had a lovely long canoe ride with my husband. I found myself saying how I would love to live for one year, in one place, like the rocks, shore and woods we were gliding past, to really enable an understanding and observation of the change in a smaller microcosm, one I could totally take in. This is probably related to my desire for a slower life, more focus, and the ability to capture the gradual change in nature and life.

This is perhaps why I so enjoy watercolour painting, working with clay, digging in the soil. The doing is just as revitalizing and meaningful as the absorbing – the speaking as the listening, the teaching as the learning.

Concluding Thoughts

What is my connection with the arts if not an opportunity for knowing myself differently? I realize I am a person comfortable with adaptation, complexity, change and 're'presentation. I have always perceived my surroundings acutely – this includes people, animals, sounds, colours, smells, form.... I have seen through my writing journey how strongly I am inspired by nature and the everyday. I think I have known this at another level, for a long time.

From my travels I understand how the energy of different places invites a different person within me to emerge. If asked to pack a bag of artefacts that would define my idea of art, I know I could compose a different bag for each day! Sometimes I feel surrounded by the art of life without any specific direction, just a feeling of awe from with the infinite possibilities of life.

As I now shift my life from designer to teacher, I turn again to Robert Frost for my inspiration. Frost once said, “I am not a teacher, but an awakener”.

The idea of this life’s journey, one life for discovery, each new day bringing not new things, but new knowledge from different people and different places – this can only be taken in if the senses are waiting in anticipation. Each evening I am reminded of these infinite possibilities when I arrive home and I am greeted by an orchestra of crickets and a veil of stars overhead.

Ongoing Inspiration

I wrote a poem about Nature when I was fifteen which was selected for publication in our local newspaper. I still have a clear memory of the day, and of the place in which I wrote it.

Inspiration

Inspiration comes through a silent breeze
greeted by the few leaves that remain here.
I like this place
though most wouldn’t find it private at all.
The trees never ask why of my presence
as they stretch their branches to welcome the sun.
He himself silently watches each word I create,
And though no one else may know my thoughts here
I feel around me an understanding with the ways of nature.
Placed in this world where their beauty rests unknown
they only know a wish to live in a forest,
far away from the concrete horizons,
here where people only seem to know confusion
as their lives slip away.
I want to go with the trees
to know the harmony and peace of mind
I know I can find in a forest,
For there are so many beautiful things in the world,
even this place where the trees let me write awhile,
Giving me inspiration.

The poem still inspires me, as also does this piece of writing by Carse (1986), which I share with my students at Ryerson University in Toronto. I first encountered this piece when I was teaching part time at the University of Waterloo in Ontario, where it was given out to all first year architecture students.

> There are at least two kinds of games. One could be called finite, the other infinite.
>
> A finite game is played for the purpose of winning, an infinite game for the purpose of continuing the play.
>
> Surprise is a crucial element in most finite games. If we are not prepared to meet each of the possible moves of an opponent, our chances of losing are most certainly increased.
>
> It is therefore by surprising our opponent that we are most likely to win. Surprise in finite play is the triumph of the past over the future. The Master Player who already knows what moves are to be made has a decisive advantage over the unprepared player who does not know what moves will be made.
>
> A finite player is trained not only to anticipate every future possibility, but to control the future, to prevent it from altering the past. This is the finite player in the mode of seriousness with its dread of unpredictable consequence.
>
> Infinite players, on the other hand, continue their play in the expectation of being surprised. If surprise is no longer possible, all play ceases.
>
> Surprise causes finite play to end, it is the reason for infinite play to continue.
>
> Surprise in infinite play is the triumph of the future over the past. Since infinite players do not regard the past as having an outcome, they have no way of knowing what has been begun there. With each surprise, the past reveals a new beginning in itself. Inasmuch as the future is always surprising, the past is always changing.
>
> Because finite players are trained to prevent the future from altering the past, they must hide their future moves. The unprepared opponent must be kept unprepared. Finite players must appear to be something other than what they are. Everything about their appearance must be concealing. To appear is not to appear. All the moves of a finite player must be deceptive: feints, distractions, falsifications, misdirections, mystifications.
>
> Because infinite players prepare themselves to be surprised by the future, they play in complete openness. It is not an openness as in candor, but an openness as in vulnerability. It is not a matter of exposing one's unchanging identity, the true self that has always been, but a way of exposing one's ceaseless growth, the dynamic self that has yet to be. The infinite player does not expect only to be amused by surprise, but to be transformed by it, for surprise does not alter some abstract past, but one's own personal past.

> To be prepared against surprise is to be trained. To be prepared for surprise is to be educated.
>
> Education discovers an increasing richness in the past, because it sees what is unfinished there. Training regards the past as finished and the future as to be finished. Education leads toward a continuing self-discovery; training leads toward a final self-definition.
>
> Training repeats a completed past in the future. Education continues an unfinished past into the future. (Carse, J. 1986)

AFTERWORD

I believe in serendipity.

Three years ago, while investigating current design education programs offered at Canadian post secondary institutions, I saw an opening for a contract position as an Interior Design instructor at Ryerson University in Toronto. My first reaction was, "I could do that and study education at OISE!'At that time, I had been teaching on a part-time basis at Waterloo University for five years, and had become captivated with the opportunity to connect with and inspire architecture students. I openly admitted to colleagues that it was a willing experiment to teach full time on contract so that I could at last begin work on my Masters degree.

My initial questions about design and education that led me to the Master of Education, permitted not only a shift in my thinking but also in my career. I wanted to better understand the potential for society to have a deep appreciation for beauty, a second sense or innate respect for the natural world and 'good design'. I knew I had been privileged to study Design at the university level, but I was equally inspired by the unfettered curiosity of my own son and the elementary children I had worked with during architectural workshops I had given many years earlier. I felt that the education and experiences of a society must hold an essential clue to building a cultural demand for the quality of design I had witnessed in places such as the American Hancock Shaker Village, and in Italy and Scandinavia. The respect for local materials, and for working with one's hands, were consistent elements that were present in these places.

I was teaching in this contract position, and enrolled in the course, *Research and Inquiry in the Arts* at OISE, when I wrote my narrative. During this time I experienced a feeling of "coming home" at the Ryerson School of Interior Design, and I began to comfortably imagine myself as a full time teacher. The Master of Education provided me with an introduction to the language of education that varied but often connected to the language of design. It enriched my research questions within context, history, curriculum theories and social philosophies of education. I saw that teachers are designers when they embrace teaching and learning as artistic endeavours.

Today, as a tenure track faculty member with a mandated research agenda, I find myself in a fertile setting for continued investigations in design literacy and in the role of education to foster a cultural awareness of design. During the next couple of years, my research will be focused on Japanese and Scandinavian culture, education and design. Tours will include visits and interviews with designers, artisans and educators, and observations and explorations of these cultures in general. I will take language lessons as part of the extensive preparations for these itineraries.

I have experienced a delightful reconnection between the person I knew I once was, and who I now strive to be. I am now writing, making pottery and designing spaces that influence more people than would have ever been possible, if I had simply remained a design practitioner. The recounting of my earlier passion for art in my life has revealed to me a strong foundation for my future discoveries in learning and teaching.

As wished for in my narrative, I took the time over this past year to reread the writings I had done as a teenager. On a dateless scrap of paper I found the most significant message written in my handwriting:"the ultimate form of art is the conduct of one's life".

MASAYUKI HACHIYA

10. LEARNING FROM MY EXPERIENCES: THE ROLE OF THE ARTS

INTRODUCTION

This chapter explores the role of the arts in education and their powerful connections to my own life. It reveals how my involvement with the arts has illuminated my own personal and professional stories, and has strengthened my understanding of the special place arts education can hold for others, both inside and outside school.

Now in my mid-thirty's, the opportunity to write this chapter has caused me to recall and reflect upon my life in the arts, and the process of writing has allowed me to recognize and rethink my partnership with the arts throughout the last three decades of my life, in Japan and in Canada. I grew up in Japan and lived there until my graduate study years in Canada. I then returned to my home country to continue my career in the arts and education. In this reflective account, I reminisce about and reflect on my encounters with many people engaged in arts activities, and I celebrate the power of the arts as a transformative agent in our lives.

Remembering my Childhood

When I was a young boy, the seeds for my love of the arts began to germinate. Most experiences and events that occurred in my early years eventually had some connection with the arts later with my adult life. Now, as I reminisce about my early childhood, I realize that artwork was my favourite pastime. The first experience I can recall took place during my year in kindergarten. As part of the curriculum, I enjoyed playing the violin, drawing pictures, acting in plays, and singing songs along with the other children. I remember feeling shy when playing and acting in front of others, but the teachers seemed pleased with my efforts and encouraged me to participate.

I was also eager to enjoy some kind of art making at home. I repeatedly drew trains and buses, and I searched for details on actual vehicles by carefully watching them, so that each time I could develop my drawing more precisely. I think this began my learning process for solving problems. Also, I realize my mother was a great influence; she opened up a new world of imagery for me by often reading from children's storybooks and encouraging me to read. I particularly liked seeing the coloured pictures in these books, and enjoyed this much more than trying to understand the stories.

M. Beattie (Author/Ed.), The Quest for Meaning: Narratives of Teaching, Learning and the Arts, 173–183.

In elementary school, my involvement in several arts activities opened the door to exciting opportunities. At school, from Grade 1 to Grade 6, I usually had a weekly 90-minute lesson in visual arts, and two 45-minute lessons for music. These were my favourite lessons. I was happy to make my own artwork, and sing songs and play musical pieces on various instruments. At the end of each class, I looked forward to the next one. Even though I was a young boy, I felt the lack of time in art and music classes, and wished for more classroom time in the arts. Every year, students received free textbooks for most of the curriculum subjects, including art. These art textbooks were interesting enough to arouse my curiosity and spark inspiration; they were almost like small art catalogues containing pictures of paintings and sculptures, as well as various types of designs and crafts created by artists and students of my age.

In the early years of my school life, I remember that I kept a diary with illustrations as part of the homework assignments. I enjoyed drawing a picture and filling it with colours, along with a short story I had written. I also appreciated the calligraphy lessons that were part of the Japanese language curriculum. The teacher's words have remained in my memory: "When you grind an ink-cake, you begin writing." This phrase provided focus as I concentrated on the grinding. I would then begin the art of brushing. I felt a spiritual commitment from this teacher's words, as I represented my thoughts and feelings through grinding and brushing a letter into life. I recall these beginnings of crafting letters, the beauty of calligraphy, the sensation of graphic representation, as an entry point into the aesthetic and living power of art.

Although I enjoyed the art classes where I was allowed to draw, paint and model, I did not appreciate the moments when the teacher would just stand behind me without giving any comments. I always hoped that he would continue with his encouragement or offer suggestions. I remember that my hands would tremble as my insecurity or anxiety grew whenever the teacher walked away from me without a word. Did he examine my silent thoughts as well as my artwork? At times, I was pleased when he would remark, "This is so wonderful!" However, I felt discouraged when the teacher would ask me to correct something that I really felt reluctant to change.

I believe that nature and the environment have had a significant impact on my growth. I loved the beautiful scenery surrounding the city in a suburb of Tokyo where I lived. In the spring, the teachers brought their classes to a hill nearby to enjoy the blossoming of flowers, and to breathe in the season's air. In the fall, every student filled a plastic bag with fallen leaves lying in the forest. During those days, perhaps I did not notice how nature and all its beauty gave me pleasure, but it helped to sharpen my imagination and increase my appreciation of nature's creations. Although my father was usually busy working, during his leisure time he enjoyed sharing in the delights of nature, taking me and my two sisters to a neighbourhood park or into the country side, to Japan's mountains, seas, rivers and lakes at least once during the school summer vacation. I often drew and painted these scenes, and they remain in my mind's gallery.

Some people develop interests in the arts early on; others as they mature and become old enough to discover where their interests lie. By taking lessons outside school, I also had the opportunity to explore the arts when I was very young. At the age of six, I began taking lessons in classical ballet after my school hours. I attended these classes twice a week for almost five years, along with my older sister, who had started ballet lessons when she was only three years old. However, I soon felt inhibited because I was the only boy among fifty girls at the studio. I finally disbanded these lessons when my elementary school classmates started teasing me about this ‘girlish’ activity. I was always interested in my sister’s progress, and she continued with dance until she graduated from university in the fine arts. I believe that my sister’s enthusiasm and progress in ballet were a great influence in broadening my interest in the arts. I should point out that my mother’s care and support helped my sister to continue her daily practice.

When I started weekly piano lessons after school hours in Grade 1, I felt a passion for music. My mother believed the arts, especially music, would inspire emotional maturity and self-discipline. She tried her best to encourage me, and sincerely hoped I would learn piano, because she had missed her own chance during her impoverished childhood after World War II. My piano teacher was patient and kind, although she believed music had to be played with disciplined rules. Although I learned performance technique and music theory from her, I simply did not enjoy practising piano at home; rather, I preferred riding my bicycle and playing baseball with my friends. But, my mother was persistent and kept encouraging me. A few years later, I refused to continue with piano lessons, and quit. Nevertheless, I believe they helped me to acquire an appreciation and to gain valuable personal insight into music. I also realize now that my mother’s ambition for me was a driving force in shaping my interest in the arts.

From One Encounter

While I was growing up, arts activities continued to illuminate my thoughts and desires. As my tireless curiosity in the arts continued to develop, I still excelled at visual arts and music, even in my junior-high school years. Junior-high school provided me with academic stimulation as well as many enjoyable extra-curricular music activities. I played brass instruments in the wind orchestra; my favourites were the euphonium and trumpet. I also acted as a conductor of the orchestra. I still remember the city festivals that took place in the summer; I felt thrilled to participate as the students from the city marched in a parade along the main street. In the autumn, there were annual choral festivals in which all the classes participated as a choir. I was excited as a conductor of my class chorus, since my classmates all admitted the long practice sessions were worth the effort.

At school, my encounter with an inspiring teacher further stimulated me in the arts. He was my music and homeroom teacher, and I remember his telling me that the arts suited my personality; he recognized and praised my dedication to the arts, especially music. When he met my mother, he told her I had certain sensitivity for music. Perhaps he wanted me to become more engaged in a school activity that related to my ability in the arts. He helped nurture each student's talent, regardless of whether the student possessed any deep potential or not. I was fortunate to meet him as there were not many who were able to recognize the students' strengths and able to engage them in active, participatory learning. This was an effective teaching skill that perpetuated a legacy and pedagogical vision for education students to follow.

In junior-high school, my classes in visual arts became more advanced. While making progress in my artwork in the class, I was always anxious to receive the teacher's evaluation of my work. When my artwork was displayed on the wall of the school corridor along with some other students' artwork, I felt proud of my accomplishments. By this time, some of my classmates seemed to have difficulty with their artwork. Perhaps their efforts were stifled by the teacher's comments, as many of their decisions were based on his subjective judgements. In addition, there were final art exams held at the end of each semester in the school and these were assessed on the report cards. The questions were generally based on art history, and they made art seem to be an exam-based subject. I began to wonder whether or not it was necessary to have written exams for this subject. What was the purpose of a written test in the arts?

In Grade 9, while the students were studying for the senior-high school entrance exams, a guidance teacher told me to forego my favourite music activities in order to prepare for these exams, but I was not willing to do this. I hoped to continue with my music practice; perhaps, I wished to challenge myself and, I suppose, I knew that music gave me the necessary concentration that I needed. I continued spending time in the wind orchestra sessions, although at the same time I managed to concentrate on the exam subjects. It was a challenge for me to continue my musical activities while most of my classmates simply 'crammed' for exams.

From Music to Visual Arts

When I was in senior-high school, my program did not include any visual arts lessons. I was allowed only one credit course in the arts from visual arts, music, and calligraphy. That seemed to me unfair, but I chose music because I was more enthusiastic about it than visual arts. I then continued the wind orchestra at senior-high school. My school life was still focussed around music.

By the time I reached university though, my interest began to shift back to visual arts. I now recall that I had enough learning from studying music, and I thought I could go back to music anytime, not necessarily playing the instrument, but enjoying other involvement in the music world. My thoughts shifted from active to passive in my attitude towards music. I remembered that visual arts inspired me to use my creative energies on various occasions in school and beyond, and I hoped to begin studying visual arts more earnestly in university.

When I was in Grade 12, I went to an art institution after school and took a university preparation course. I wanted to be an architect who specialized in art design and its environment. During the course, however, I found that my objectives changed. As a result of working on water colouring architecture and constructing objects at this school, I came to know the limitations of my competence and talent in these art forms. The students who attended the course were all excellent artists, capable of being gifted university students in fine arts. In the preparation school, I knew that I needed to know much more about art. Perhaps I did not have a strong enough passion for becoming a professional architect while I was, like most college students, trying to find my identity.

I then began spending my time on plaster drawings in a dark art room, hoping to acquire the ability to see an object and to represent it on a white piece of paper. It was the intensive, independent learning in the after-school hours that became an essential landmark of art and education. While doing plaster drawings, many thoughts came to my mind: What kind of reality can I understand in art? What is the role and meaning of art in my life – an expression of ideas, or feelings, or a sense of self-achievement?

A Passion for Art and Teaching

My life began to change after entering the art education program at university in 1992. I spent the next four years furthering my academic studies, and at the same time concentrating on visual arts. I decided to choose a path leading to a career as an art teacher and to pursue studies in arts education.

My four-year Bachelor of Education program at university in Tokyo included teacher qualification courses as a generalist and specialist dealing with pedagogy, educational theory, practice, and formal art training. These courses also included creating paintings and sculptures, making prints, graphic and product designs, doing metal and wooden arts, and studying art history. Several art professors whose works were well-known and appreciated in Japan taught this program. Students were learning craftsmanship as they apprenticed and grew from each instructor's art-making and criticism.

Being involved in the courses at university made me aware of issues that had been creating problems for the implementation of arts education, especially in visual arts. Because I was interested in children's art, I hoped to learn an effective way of teaching art through communicating with young students. We all know that students need support and encouragement in order to develop their artistic skills, and they need to feel uninhibited when they are creating artwork. But, in what ways can teachers help students with their artwork? The issue of teaching and assessing students' artwork became of major interest to me later in my life, eventually propelling me to write a thesis on the subject.

At university, besides visual arts activities, I gained experience in theatre productions, calligraphy, and music, by taking courses that gave me further insight into the world of the arts and made me aware of how the arts play an important role in human growth. Being a student who had the freedom to spend time in one of the cultural centres in the world, I was constantly busy in arts-related activities – visiting art galleries and museums, and attending performances of dance, music, and plays. My involvement with these art courses and activities gave me opportunities to meet new friends, many of whom shared a vision of the arts, causing me to think about the nature of the arts and their unique contributions to a larger society. It was my great pleasure to listen to their diverse range of opinions regarding the arts and other subjects. Working in different areas of the fine arts program broadened my knowledge and taught me similarities and differences within individual viewpoints.

At university, I was swamped with doing artwork. Although it required self-discipline and patience, I was obsessed with my art productions. In the beginning, since I was eager to be successful at sketching, I practised endlessly. But at the end of the day, I often felt that work still needed to be done on my drawing. One day, I saw a sketch by Leonardo Da Vinci in an art gallery. Gazing into an authentic piece of his work, feeling the power emanating from the marks left on paper, made me aware of his amazing talent. These thoughts and feelings that emerged while I struggled with my art have been truly important for me as a student of teaching. Good artists are not always good art teachers. I do not need to be an artist; rather, I may want to have many experiences in the arts, and want to be familiar with the forms, the materials and the processes. Artwork requires patience, apprenticeship, time and energy, as does the process of teaching art to students.

During the third year of my studies, I taught visual arts to a Grade 5 class at school and I learned something important about students' attitudes. This was my first teaching practicum, and I remember one particular incident when I asked the students to make a coloured drawing depicting how they imagined their future lives would be. The students drew various pictures of their dreams for the future, but one girl did not draw anything. I was anxious to know why her paper was blank. Although I encouraged her, she seemed reticent; perhaps she was afraid of being criticized. However, after a while, she drew a picture of a mountain and a figure falling down from the mountain top. When I asked the meaning of her drawing, she answered, "Too much pressure for studying subjects makes me feel I am falling down!" I felt upset that a student experienced this type of distress in her artwork and even in her school life. Also, I was concerned – "Did I create pressure for her while in class?" I knew in theory that teachers should be patient and should encourage students to express their artwork in an uninhibited yet meaningful way, but the actual practice of teaching art was much more complex and responsive than what was told in books and lectures.

As my interest in teaching art increased, I became interested in issues in the school curriculum and art education. When I was in university, the arts in the curriculum were generally regarded as low priority subjects, and it seemed the arts might eventually be excluded from the curriculum. To increase public awareness of the importance of art education, I thought I should know more about the role of art in education. I spoke with my supervisor about my future education, and he encouraged me to go abroad to continue further studies in arts education. After completing my studies analyzing children's artwork for my thesis, a requirement for the degree of Bachelor of Education, I went to Canada to study English and arts education at the Ontario Institute for Studies in Education (OISE) of the University of Toronto.

Life in Canada

In 1998, I started my graduate studies in the Department of Curriculum, Teaching, and Learning at OISE, and during my first year in Canada, my personal life was quite difficult. I struggled with my first two courses in the Master of Arts program, not only because of the language barrier, but I also had to overcome the cultural differences between my Japanese background and the Canadian way of life. I became passive in Canada as I was not able to use the language fluently. I often felt, especially when I needed to talk in graduate classes, that I would prefer to speak fluently in my mother tongue. Then, while struggling, I came to realize, through experiencing the arts by visiting museums, art galleries, theatres or concerts, that there were not as many differences between us as I thought there were, and that I was not a stranger but a person like those who surrounded me. My graduate life became more positive. Fortunately, there was a multicultural environment in the graduate classes at OISE where the students and professors made me feel comfortable and welcome. During this complex time, the professors and my classmates helped to find creative ways to integrate me with the people around me. This was my first step forward as a new student in Canada.

In the first course I took in arts education, the instructor David Booth asked the students to give the definition of 'art.' I was startled by the question, and asked myself, "Why haven't I questioned this seriously before?" My classmates were also surprised. Through research, I found a statement by Herbert Read, who wrote:

> In any case, it is always possible to improve on the definition of a category like art, which is one of the most elusive concepts in the history of human thought (1958, p. 14).

In our daily conversations, although we often use the word 'art' with no particular intentions or specific definitions, I realized we should carefully examine the meaning of this word 'art' as it is used in different contexts.

In the context of my research, I visited a number of elementary and secondary schools in Canada. These schools gave me the opportunity to learn how important the arts were for students. I tried assiduously to learn to write about my interest in arts education in academic forms. My arts activities had been transformed from art-making and art-viewing to writing research papers and to observing students' artwork.

From my years of being an arts student, I learned how the quality of the teacher's instruction in art was important for the students' artwork. An art teacher candidate is often asked to provide a portfolio of his or her artwork in a job interview. What does this imply? Through my experience as a student and novice researcher in arts education, I came to wonder whether the degree of one's artistry should be regarded as a qualification for teaching art. Of course, the process of participating in artwork should help in the teaching of art, but it is probably more important to experiment with the world of art expression as well as knowing about the materials, styles and tools. However, first should come an awareness of the potential for human development and the developmental stages for young people in art.

During my graduate school years, I also learned how difficult it is for many elementary school teachers to cope with teaching art. They feel that "I don't teach art well because I'm not good at art." Teaching art is not dependent on what one has created, but how one instructs students in art, and responds to their processes of creating artwork. It is the communication between a teacher and a student in the context of art making that we must recognize as the heart of art education.

Teachers also revealed certain frailties in their methods of teaching art. Some admitted that they were not confident about teaching art as they had not been given enough instruction during their years at teachers' college. Others emphasized that teachers need to be careful not to interfere too much when students are involved in their artwork, since this might hinder creative expression. How much guidance and support should the teacher offer? When should feedback be given? How does the teacher motivate and encourage, while responding to, and instructing students in order to help them understand the processes involved in learning and creating in art? I felt I needed to explore the range of instructional strategies of a dedicated art teacher who can: "respond intelligently, sympathetically, and purposefully to the children's creative efforts [and] communicate with the students both knowledgably and honestly regarding their progress in art" (Wachowiak & Clements, 2006, p. 26).

On my thesis Journey

My thesis work was about art teaching and assessment, and I conducted a case study of an experienced art teacher. For the research, I was motivated by the understanding that teachers may find difficulties in teaching art because of the nature of art itself, since it deals with feelings, senses, creativity and freedom of interpretation, all of which cannot be evaluated by a simple measurement. These qualities cannot be easily guided nor assessed. There do not seem to be any standardized methods of teaching or assessment in art education. How then do we justify art in any educational curricula?

In my observations of classrooms, I learned that a teacher's comments like 'wonderful' and 'excellent' have often been used to praise students' work as teachers try to encourage them. But, by hearing this somewhat limited form of feedback repeatedly, how can students ascertain if their work is progressing? I wonder whether this praise is really effective. I was determined to examine the theories and practices in teaching art that might illuminate the pedagogy. I was especially interested in learning about an experienced and skilled art teacher's practice through ongoing observation and conversations.

I drew on my earlier work in Japan as a research assistant, and it provided me with valuable motivation. In my graduate school years, I had the opportunity to work with a professor who was conducting research on children's artwork collected in an elementary school in Japan. The collection included 15,000 student pictures of 100 years of Grade 6 students. This work provided an authentic picture of Japanese art education by portraying the changes in trends in the student artwork and teacher instruction in a century. Over time, the images have changed, because of the context of the times, but, more importantly, because of the instructional methods. These teaching methods in Japanese art education have continued to develop, and today, students are not encouraged to copy from books as they were in the past. Recently, students have been allowed much more freedom. It is probably true that those student pieces reflected teacher expectations of what adults wanted students to accomplish in art education. As a matter of fact, in the early decades, art instruction demanded skills of depiction, including perspective, composition, shading, and colouring, but after the Second World War, a child-centred approach has become pedagogically accepted. Through this research project, I became interested in teaching art in terms of navigating the creation and the production of student artwork. How do we help children to grow within the art field without destroying their delight and satisfaction from expressing their own thoughts and reflections? Simply put, how do we teach art?

When visiting art classrooms in Canada, I met an art teacher in an elementary school whose interactions with students, I found to be unique. In my field notes, I noted that her class was filled with inspiration and exploration; she expanded the students' ideas and extended their activities through her sensitive instruction as she gave encouragement and support during the classroom art time. A number of resources were always available for students, and she often said, "Use different materials," or "How about this new resource?" All this stimulated the students to explore different materials in positive ways. She also respected the students' ideas, offering comments, but the ideas of individual students were secure, and sometimes sacred. She accepted and welcomed a different way of creating art, letting them make their own informed decisions. When she provided suggestions, many times she added, "If you want," or "You don't have to." She repeated these phrases quite often. During the student artwork activities, she showed them how to do things themselves, with very few words. She sometimes provided a concrete example giving several choices such as, "You can do it this way," or "You can also do it another way." In this manner, she led her students into developing their own significant artwork. I had found a teacher who embodied the very essence of my beliefs in the value of arts education.

The teaching of art is a complicated process, and I thought somehow through this teacher, I would be able to understand and explain the task of an art teacher in the process of understanding and supporting students' artwork. In my study, I considered the techniques and strategies that can help an art teacher to stimulate and motivate ideas with children without putting a brake on their creativity. The circular relationship of helping students to both experience art and learn about art became the focus of my investigation (Hachiya, 2006).

During my thesis study I developed a schema of interaction, one that may provide teachers with a way of examining their own behaviours with their students during art classes, and perhaps in other areas. I now challenge myself to put my continuum of interaction into my own teaching, to examine my own ways of working alongside students, to ensure learning with, through, and about the arts in education.

Understanding Teaching and Learning in the Arts

As a post-doctoral research fellow, I worked at the Research Center for Children's Art Education, Tohoku University of Art and Design, Yamagata, Japan. A nursery school is attached to the center where the three- to five-year old children participate in education through the arts. My work there was to support a government-funded research project that proposed a concept of early childhood education through the arts. As I observed the children and took notes about their experiences and behaviours, I was reminded of my thesis where I came to value the importance of instruction and interaction in an art classroom, with a sequence of projects that took into account the learning development of the children involved. Indeed, having watched the case study teacher in my thesis research, and having read and researched the major authorities on arts education, I was aware of what I should discuss as we began constructing the shape of a new perspective for our art program, and as we developed a conceptual framework for the arts in early childhood education.

After two years of experience at the research center, I became a faculty member in the Department of Human Development at St. Thomas University, Hyogo, Japan. It is always difficult to become accustomed to a new position and a new city, and I proceeded bit by bit. I am now talking to my students in Hyogo about the arts, and about my life in Tokyo, in Toronto, and in Yamagata, which all relate to my ongoing explorations of the arts in education. I am teaching students who wish to become teachers in elementary school and kindergarten, as well as offering a teaching qualification program in the arts in education in the curriculum. Besides expanding the nature and practice of arts education, my life experiences, I believe, will help them better understand the arts, the children they teach, and education in a powerful, more effective and personal way. I hope that all my students, in their four years of undergraduate life, will become dedicated, passionate teachers who will communicate with their children through and about the arts in education, while understanding the characteristics and personalities of these children. I trust that they will constantly encourage children to deepen and express their thoughts, expand their students' knowledge, and believe in the unique and creative gifts all children possess. Dedicated and committed teachers can help students to explore and navigate the oceans so that they will learn more than they ever thought possible.

AFTERWORD

I realize how much my association with the arts has enriched my personal life, and to a great extent, directed and influenced my professional life. My involvement in the arts in my early childhood, my parents' encouragement, combined with my teachers' support during my academic studies, have all given me immeasurable pleasure, experience and background. The arts activities in Japan, as well as in Canada, have also broadened my knowledge and understanding of the role of the arts in education. Although I am not entirely sure of the true meaning of 'the arts,' I believe they tell me "how to be alive" (Eisner 1972, p. 281). Certainly, through the arts, I have encountered many people who have given me so much satisfaction personally and professionally. Intuitively, I must have known from my early childhood appreciation of the arts, that this would lead me to follow a career path as an arts educator who is 'living through' his theory and his dreams of arts education.

The arts have enabled me to transform myself and my ways of knowing and of being. They have helped me to make connections between the intellectual, emotional, spiritual, and aesthetic dimensions of my life. I feel that an arts education for me is a means of becoming part of a greater community where we alter our perceptions and increase our options as interpreters of our lives. Art in school is not just about drawing or painting or design: it is a process of human development.

At the present time, when world peace is so fragile and dissonance pervades our lives, we look to the ideals and thoughts within the arts world and with hope, question who we can become. The arts have been, and will always be, an integral and integrating aspect of my personal and professional lives, and I share my enthusiasm for the arts with my education students. I value continuing to learn and explore modes of arts expression; I search for new strategies and practices for strengthening arts programs; I support the sociocultural, academic and aesthetic needs of my students, and encourage them to do the same for theirs. I read the research and resources, both on screen and in print, written by professional educators in my field. I draw upon my life narratives to inform my present attitudes and behaviours, so that I can approach my teaching and my writing as holistically as possible. I continue to participate in the arts as an arts maker, an arts participant, and an arts lover.

As I reflect back on the process of doing narrative inquiry and writing a narrative, I recall that as a graduate student taking an academic course, *Research and Inquiry in the Arts*, and learning about narrative inquiry, I could not even imagine what it might include. Gradually, I came to understand how my former experiences in the arts had influenced and informed my work as an art educator. I came to realize that through narrative inquiry, I could explore and expand the meaning and value of my personal and professional lives and use my understandings as an important learning tool for integrating the two selves.

In the writing of my narrative, it seemed that scattered pieces of my memories from the past were rearranged into a stream of meaning that shows me what has led me to the here and now. Writing the narrative gave me an opportunity to look deeply into myself, to discover meanings that I had never considered, to re-examine my encounters with people, and to re-evaluate the significance of events that I had experienced throughout my life.

As I narrate my artistic experiences in the future, the meaning and value of my past events will have changed, even as the fascination of discovering the new meanings that are hidden in my life events goes on. It is like canoeing on a never-ending river towards a sun that never sets.

PART FOUR: THE DIALOGUE BETWEEN THE DIALOGUES: CREATING A NEW NARRATIVE THROUGH INTERACTION AND INTEGRATION

When we create new narratives for our lives, we weave the disparate threads of our past and future lives together into new and more meaningful wholes. As we do so, we make connections between what animates and moves us as individuals, and that which will allow us to live more connected, integrated and meaningful lives. The dialogue between the dialogues provides a context for the interactions, the integration, and the creation of the narratives which will enable us, in the words of the poet Seamus Heaney, to "be here for good in both senses of the word".

- Chapter 11: A Recursive Path: *Winifred Hunsburger*
- Chapter 12: The Artful Body: A Narrative of an Embodied Relationship with the Arts: *Rae Johnson*
- Chapter 13: Voices: *Benjamin Bolden*
- Chapter 14: Hearing my Voice While Listening to the Choir: *Carole Richardson*

WINIFRED HUNSBURGER

11. A RECURSIVE PATH

This chapter tells a story of rediscovering and reclaiming the arts, and coming to recognize the influence and role of the arts in my practice as a teacher and as a researcher. It describes my first encounters with narrative inquiry and arts-based research and how these compelled me to examine my assumptions about research and to revisit my evolving relationship with the arts. It also explains how new understandings that grew out of this inquiry helped me define a research question and method for graduate research, and how my appreciation and understanding for this new paradigm and my role within it continued to develop as I conducted my research and wrote my doctoral thesis.

As I recount this journey I uncover themes of tension and transformation in my participation in the arts. I expose my struggle to reconcile long held views about research with new ways of working aesthetically as a teacher and researcher. I reflect on what I have learned about how we come to teach and how our practice evolves. I offer narrative inquiry as a path to transforming our practice as teachers and researchers through reclaiming, re-integrating and re-imagining the stories of our lives.

Starting Point

I write this chapter as a newly minted "doctor" of education, having recently finished the final oral examination of my thesis. I write also as an experienced elementary and middle school teacher, program leader and teacher resource. My thesis, *Inquiry learning: A narrative inquiry into the experiences of three teachers,* is the culmination of my inquiry into how teachers construct and enact their understanding of inquiry learning, as well as a deeply personal inquiry into how the arts have influenced and shaped me in the roles I embrace as teacher, leader and researcher. I share the journey of that inquiry to show how the arts and learning through them influenced my practice. I reveal how the act of coming to understand this influence through narrative research has transformed the way I understand myself, how I understand research, and how I now work with teachers and students alike.

Setting Out

My journey began on a warm, humid July evening, four years ago. My husband Dave and I sat reading in our back garden. He was absorbed in some fiction while I tackled reading an article for a graduate research course which I had

M. Beattie (Author/Ed.), The Quest for Meaning: Narratives of Teaching, Learning and the Arts, 187–197.

recently begun. When I applied to graduate school I had intended to study global education. However, that focus had vanished when the professor with whom I had hoped to work accepted a position at another university, and the courses I had been looking forward to taking disappeared. I had wandered through my first year of study choosing courses haphazardly, hoping something would excite and inspire me. The reading I held in my hands that evening was for the fifth course I had taken, and I still had no clear sense of direction.

We sat for some time, both of us lost in the worlds of our texts. Eventually Dave looked up from his novel to see my shoulders shaking and my face drenched with tears. He looked at me perplexed.

"It's this article," was all I could manage to say.

"What in the world sort of research course are you taking?" he asked, apparently annoyed. I had no response.

New Ground

The course was called, *Research and Inquiry in the Arts* and the article, "*Beginning with Myself,*" was by Mary Beattie (1995a). It told the author's story of teaching and learning, and revealed the power of story to help us reflect on, reinterpret, and re-imagine our lives. It revealed how reclaiming our stories – most especially those deeply buried in our memories – could help us reconcile apparent divisions and contradictions in our lives and come to understand ourselves wholly. But what made this article so compelling to me was the way in which its message was delivered. The writing was graceful and lyrical; the text infused with music, poetry and literature. The stories told were honest and open. Never had I encountered writing that was so informative, so artful and so deeply personal at the same time. Never had academic writing moved me the way this piece had.

I could not have articulated this at that time. All that I knew or could tell then was that this article was telling me something very important about myself, and I needed to listen. The author's stories were calling out to "the untold stories bottled up inside me" (p. 2) and were shaking me deeply. That disquieting moment in the garden was my first step into a new land. It led me into narrative inquiry and arts-informed research, where the way of viewing the world, the way of interacting with others, the way of understanding knowledge and what it is to know were completely different from anything I was accustomed to or expecting. Although I could never have imagined such a place existed until that moment, once I entered it I felt as if I had found a new home.

Most of my previous experience with research had been with quantitative methods. I had worked for ten years in peri natal health research where methodologies such as randomized controlled trials were prized for their objectivity and potential to deliver definitive answers to questions about treatments and interventions. I had come to believe that the only way to study something was to measure it. Because personal experience is so difficult to quantify, it seemed to me, and to my colleagues, that it could only be researched in the most general and superficial ways and was barely worth considering. For the researcher to bring his or her own personal experiences or beliefs to research was to dispense with all credibility and validity. I held firmly to the belief that there could be nothing personal, let alone artful, about healthcare research. When I changed careers and arrived in elementary education, I assumed the same must be true of educational research.

As I made my way through the course readings my assumptions were deeply challenged. The next reading was Lawrence-Lightfoot's "View of the whole" (1997a). In it, the author explained that research could blend art or aesthetic expression with systematic and empirical description to convey the richness and complexity of human experience. This seemed improbable but exciting. Next, Eisner (1991b ,1997, 2005) called for research founded on literary and artistic principles. He insisted that such research would not only be engaging to read, but could express truth better than the prescriptive, controlled and "objective" prose of traditional research reports. Then Connelly and Clandinin (1985) contended that stories could be at once a way for understanding personal, human experience and for communicating it. These notions that research could be deeply personal *and* scientific, aesthetic and truthful, method and expression conflicted with everything that I understood about research, but I was intrigued.

Other readings contributed to my growing appreciation that educational research could be aesthetic, grounded in personal experience, and be valid, honest and valuable at the same time. Qualitative research no longer seemed to be a poor cousin to quantitative research, and personal experience was no longer out of bounds as an area to investigate and learn from. I began to understand how through narrative and arts-based methods, personal experience could be researched and such research could contribute constructively and profoundly to educational discourse.

However, Eisner's appealing theories about researching and writing aesthetically and Clandinin and Connelly's lofty notions about "living storied lives" and writing "narrative(s) of experience" (1994, p. 416) were still just that to me: ideas to be pondered, challenges to long-held assumptions. I needed to do more than read about how such research could really work; I needed to experience it myself. It was only when I began to work with these ideas, to conduct some research into my own practice and the influences on it and to do so in a narrative way, that I began to appreciate the truth and merit in these methods. And more importantly, I began to understand why I was so captivated by them.

Striding Ahead – Looking Back

The first assignment for the course was to write a personal narrative outlining how the arts had influenced my practice. I started the assignment wondering how I would be able to do this. Certainly I had loved and participated in the arts from the time I was a young child until I graduated with a bachelor's degree in drama. Indeed that was what had attracted me to the course. However, singing in school choirs and working in the theatre were activities in which I was fully engaged, when I entered the fields of peri natal research and education. I could see no connection between those experiences in the arts, and how I went about teaching math, science, language and social studies to grade six students.

The work on the assignment began with a taped interview with a classmate. My classmate started by asking me to reflect on "the arts" in general terms. What did the arts mean to me? How did I understand them? Why were the arts important in education? Later, as I listened to the tape, my answers seemed predictable and sounded empty. I said that the arts were a way of understanding and expressing ideas. I knew that many children and adults learned better through the arts than through traditional means, In fact, my own children had attended and blossomed in arts-based elementary and secondary schools. But these were intellectual understandings based on my understanding of educational theory and observing others.

However, when my classmate asked me to talk about a time when my own students had learned through the arts, I heard the energy in my voice change and a sense of excitement infuse my response. As I listened to the tape I began to glimpse how very integral the arts were (and are) to my teaching, and to suspect that this was based on more than an intellectual understanding.

I told the story of a math inquiry that began as a simple lesson in angle recognition and evolved into an integrated, student directed project where geometry, visual arts and language came together in the most surprising and elegant ways. We had started a geometry unit using manipulatives to compare angle sizes and types. The students seemed to enjoy this activity very much and were soon chatting with each other about their findings. One student commented to the group at her table, "Look, did you notice, if you put the points of enough manipulatives together, you get a circle?"

Another student considered this for a moment and then commented, "And, look, if you add up all those angles, you get 360!"

A third student asked, "Is that why they say a circle has 360 degrees?" There was a collective gasp of recognition at the table.

"Does it always work?" Suddenly the students were earnestly trying different combinations to test out their theory. Their idea spread around the room and soon all the students were engaged in creating intricate circular patterns. I was delighted how the students seemed to be developing a very concrete understanding of this mathematical principle.

As they continued with this self-generated task they became more and more absorbed in it and the circular patterns they created showed increased intricacy and elaboration. Their designs reminded me of the symmetrical patterns used in some meditation and religious practices. I displayed a few examples of mandalas I found on the internet. The students were excited.

"Wow, those are like the patterns we are making!"

"What are they? What are they for?"

"Can we keep doing this?"

"Well," I asked them, "is there mathematics in these designs?" I found the expectations for grade six geometry and shared them with the class. "Do you think you can show that you understand these concepts through making designs like this?"

Together we defined the assessment criteria for an art-based portfolio that would show the students' understanding of essential geometry principles. The students spent the next two weeks creating and photographing mandalas, and writing about the expectations each one demonstrated. It was a dream project for all of us, and one that seemed to spring organically from the students' fascination, questions and theories.

Once the students had launched the project it felt like I had little to do as a teacher beyond ensuring there were plenty of manipulatives and other supplies and observing and listening to their growing understanding of geometry concepts. I was pleased not only with how they had been able to grasp and enhance their understanding of geometry through art – but also with how much ownership they had taken for the process.

As I retold and listened to the story of the mandala project through a lens of how the arts affected my practice I began to wonder just how my own experiences with the arts had contributed to this inquiry project. I needed to find out.

Getting My Bearings

I had written narratives for other graduate courses. They had been opportunities to recount interesting stories from my life to justify what I thought I knew, where I thought I stood. This narrative was different. I was no longer sure what it was I knew, I was writing to find out.

I began by laying out for myself all my experiences with the arts. I created annals and chronicles listing moments and events that stood out in my mind. I wrote vignettes about nearly forgotten experiences. I kept a notebook for significant memories that started to arise. And as I did so recollections of a childhood love of music and art, and a passion for theatre resurfaced. I remembered how much I had loved gathering around the piano with my kindergarten classmates to sing with Mrs. Bull. I recalled the pleasure and satisfaction of singing in the high school choir. I remembered how challenged but happy I felt working on high school and university theatre productions. The excitement and fulfilment that came from working with others to create something bigger and grander than any one of us might have achieved was with me once again.

Previously these experiences and feelings had seemed so separate and unrelated to who I was that I had either forgotten or ignored them. Now as they presented themselves, I began to ask myself what meaning they held for me now.

And then I began to write, not knowing clearly, at first, just where this narrative was headed, where it was taking me. I wrote to reveal and to inquire into the patterns, rhythms and passions of my life. And as I wrote, I learned and understood myself afresh.

I told stories of growing up in a household of artists and creators: my mother a pianist, my father an inventor, my aunt a painter. I described joyful experiences of singing Latin motets in high school choirs. I recreated my university adventures in theatre production where I worked with other students to hang the lights, sew the costumes, erect the sets and act the parts. And as I thought and wrote about my current situation I recognized that while I might no longer find myself singing or working in the theatre, my greatest joys still included those same arts: supporting performers in my community and family. For several years now, I have hosted actors and musicians in my home and enjoyed feeding them and encouraging them as well as listening to them rehearse and attending their performances. It seemed that perhaps, the arts had never really left me. I felt an overwhelming sense of relief as I rediscovered and reclaimed a treasure I thought I had long lost.

As I retold and listened to these stories, I began to see how my own love of participating in the arts had transmuted to a love of supporting the participation of others, and that this delight in setting the stage for others extended from my dining room table right into my classroom.

I began to understand that my love of singing and theatrical performance was with me still and informed the ways I taught such seemingly unrelated things as geometry or European exploration. It wasn't simply that I integrated the arts when I was teaching mathematics or language or social studies. I understood that through my experiences as a chorister and a performer I had constructed a deep understanding of the power of collaboration, active participation and trust in individual intelligence to support learning. I understood that the arts informed all the ways in which I came to teaching every day, how I organized a lesson, how I set up a learning experience, how I trusted and encouraged my students to collaborate. I also saw that the ways in which I launched an inquiry and let my students take the lead were grounded in more recent experiences in the arts. I understood that I was setting the stage for my students and their learning experiences.

As I drew that narrative to conclusion, I began to see how all the disparate threads of my life wove in and out of each other. I saw how they transformed and rearranged themselves. I began to understand myself, how I teach, and how I know how to teach, in new ways. Past experience that had seemed unrelated to who I am now, I understood as integral parts of me and my teaching. I felt a sense of integrity I had not known before. All at once I felt more trusting in my own knowledge of teaching, and captivated by the process that had led me to this new sense of self.

Charting a New Course

Understanding how my own teaching was informed by my life experiences in the arts and recognizing narrative inquiry as the powerful and transformative tool that had helped me uncover this, were two critical steps that helped me refocus my interests as a graduate student, and that led me to define a research problem and a method for investigating it.

The route I followed to become a teacher was a circuitous one, despite having decided that this is what I was meant to do back at the piano in Mrs. Bull's classroom. I went to university planning to become a high school drama and English teacher, but as I approached graduation I became discouraged by the scarcity of jobs and some friends' disappointing experiences as preservice teachers. It was my own very positive experiences as an expectant mother that led me to the field of peri natal health research. Still I continued to dream that I would one day be a teacher. Later on, a chance comment by a close friend about her plan to return to university before it was "too late," woke me up and sent me scurrying to the nearest initial teacher education program.

I loved preservice teacher education, and I was particularly intrigued by theories about inquiry learning. As a teacher I found my students learned best when they were free to pursue their own questions about a topic or issue, to conduct their own research and to work with their peers to develop their understanding. I loved investigating questions with them, and finding the links to the prescribed curriculum. I had enhanced my own understanding of the theory behind inquiry through a Master's degree and came to understand it as a potent and democratic instructional strategy. By the time I entered a doctoral program I was not only using an inquiry approach in my own classroom, but I had accepted a leadership role in the school to help my teaching colleagues to do the same.

I had started this new position thinking all that I needed to do was share my knowledge and enthusiasm for inquiry with my colleagues and that they, too, would quickly adopt an inquiry practice and become co-learners with their students. Although many of my colleagues soon became engrossed with inquiry learning, there were a number who were resistant to changing their practices. I soon felt frustrated with these teachers and disappointed in myself.

The narrative research assignment helped me to begin to consider all teaching in new ways. If my own teaching practice was informed by more than what I had learned in school about educational theory, then must not that be true for other teachers? Could this growing understanding help me unravel my professional problem of trying to help teachers change their practice and integrate inquiry learning?

If this had been a health care issue, the research I would have undertaken likely would have focused on what to do with the "problem" teacher. What interventions or treatments could be found? How effective were they? However, my new appreciation of qualitative research in general and narrative inquiry in particular helped me to consider the problem from an entirely new perspective. I began by reflecting on my own experience of uncovering knowledge about teaching, and by narratively inquiring into my own particular teaching practice. This led me to consider a fresh way to investigate the problem.

Lawrence-Lightfoot (1997a) suggests that there is as much to be learned from studying what is going well as from focusing on what isn't. In my situation that meant asking: what could I learn from those teachers who were experienced and comfortable with using an inquiry approach in their classrooms? From my experience of writing autobiographically about how the arts had influenced my teaching practice, I knew the only way I could uncover any answers would be to work narratively and collaboratively with such teachers. My research proposal quickly took shape, participants came forward and I embarked on a three year investigation into how experienced inquiry-based teachers construct their role; and into the exploration of their experiences of co-learning with their students.

What I was expecting of course, was to invite each teacher to tell her stories and to uncover with her the web of life experiences that were woven into her practice of inquiry. Because this would be arts-based research, I was hoping to discover teaching metaphors and to create classroom portraits which I would present in an artful, aesthetic way. In time, all this did happen. What I did not anticipate, what I was unprepared for, was the extent of the discipline and self-examination that such a process would entail.

Obstacles on the Path

On December 22nd, I sat with one of my participants about to embark on the first interview of the study. Sitting near the window, I could see the first real snow of the season drifting gently down. I asked my participant to choose a pseudonym for the study. She chose the name I had always wanted to give a daughter should I ever have one. Such an auspicious start to my study!

Later as I listened to the tape of that first interview, I was horrified to hear myself pounce on my participant's stories, chiming in with my own connections and tales. So wrapped up was I in my reclaimed artfulness, so eager to find metaphor, meaning, and wholeness, that the new season, the snow, the name seemed fraught with significance. I was desperate to tie it all together, to make meaning of it all.

I was frustrated with myself, and embarrassed. In time I recognized that I had forgotten my role as the one who sets the scene for the others, and I saw that I was trying to take centre stage.

It took several interviews to learn to step aside and to cultivate the necessary patience to see where the stories were taking my research participant, what meaning *she* was making, and to keep my own stories to myself. It was harder work than I could have imagined.

Later when I started to construct the first narrative for the study, I found myself learning the lesson once more. Again, I inserted myself too strongly, too centrally into the narrative. "Here," I seemed to say, "look at this wonderful story *I* am telling you." Again, it took time and discipline to learn to pull back and get out of the way of the teacher from whom *I* should have been learning, and to save my interpretations and thoughts, my performance, and my analysis to myself at this stage. Keeping a personal journal to log my reactions and feelings about what I was writing helped me uncover and grapple with the challenges I faced.

From the earliest stages of planning this research and the dissertation, I had intended to include a chapter describing the school at which the study took place, the very school at which I was employed. I had spent many hours reviewing school archives, reading others' stories of the school history and culture. I had riffled through photos of the school as it had grown through the years, and had examined old report cards and outlines of curriculum. I had taken my own photos and walked through and around the building with an architect who had graduated from the school. I knew where the building materials came from and what the different structural features were called. I knew the building inside and out, and backwards and forwards through time. I envisioned this chapter as the ultimate, brilliant and beautiful portrait of the school.

I began by writing what I imagined was a lovely lyrical description of the front of the school: a grand driveway sweeping up in a great arc to the central entranceway at the base of the turreted tower. I went on to describe the school's rabbit-warren halls, rickety stairs and secret quadrangles. But I could get no further than a physical description. When I tried to write about the school's atmosphere, the culture, the traditions, I balked. I abandoned the chapter.

At first, I rationalized my resistance by thinking that the study was about teachers' knowledge and inquiry learning, not school history and architecture. But eventually I was forced to admit that their knowledge needed to be set in context and culture. As Lawrence-Lightfoot (1997b) reminded me: "We have no idea how to decipher or decode an action, a gesture, a conversation, or an exclamation unless we see it embedded in context" (p. 41).

How was I to write this chapter then? What was holding me back? I continued with my journal, writing my own stories of the school: wending my way through narrow halls, lugging projects up grand staircases, supervising countless noisy lunches, tearing up during traditional Christmas concerts, and suffering through endless staff meetings.

Heading Home

Something in the writing of these personal stories helped me recognize and come to terms with the obstacle that was holding me back. Every time I had started to write about the school, I was caught up in the "art" of the writing. I sought perfect adjectives and dazzling metaphors. Fine, perhaps, for the physical description but when it came to setting out climate and culture, a thesaurus was of little use. I was learning that this practice of narrative, arts-based research could not be solely about creating lovely, aesthetic text, but instead using the aesthetic text as both method and means for investigating and revealing. I recognized that in this practice ideas cannot be in the service of art, rather art must be an expression of ideas.

Writing my own stories of the school reminded me that all I could ever write were my own perceptions and understanding of the school. There could be no exquisite, definitive portrait. And as carefully as I might work to portray my understanding, the reader, too, would contribute his or her own. I needed to acknowledge this both to myself and to the reader. To write, at last, that the chapter was built on my focused and intentional research into the school while at the same time it was deeply rooted in my own experiences of the place, to acknowledge that I could not help but embed the chapter in the tacit and explicit understandings built over seven years of working there, liberated the chapter even as it defined its limits.

And so the portrait of the school, along with the teaching stories, classroom pictures and metaphors for practice, emerged as I learned to express what I heard and saw as clearly and honestly as I could while recognizing and admitting that it was my ears that were listening, my eyes watching and my words creating the report. It was ever a balance between confidence and scepticism about what I thought I knew.

In the end, the thesis was a mosaic of teaching stories, classroom portraits, metaphors of practice and personal teaching philosophies, framed by my own story of coming to understand inquiry learning through personal practice, and of integrating the academic and philosophic literature supporting it. The work reflected the deeply personal and entirely unique process that each teacher engaged in when she undertook to change her practice and to reconstruct her role as a co-learner and co-inquirer with her students. Through examining, interpreting, and revealing the stories of three particular teachers, the thesis showed how teachers can be encouraged and supported to integrate inquiry into their practice through a professional development process that would allow them to experiment, reflect and reconstruct their understanding of what it means to teach. And it showed all this, I hope, in an artful and aesthetic way.

Arriving Home

Recounting this story of composing and constructing a doctoral thesis has become yet another narrative inquiry. As I retell the story of my journey into narrative inquiry and arts-based research, I uncover for myself themes of tension: between the recognition of my own personal teaching theory and listening to that of others; between understanding the power and importance of understanding what one knows and understanding how that frames and informs all that we perceive, report, and analyse; and, of course, the tension between performing and supporting the performance of others.

My research began with the acknowledgement that what I knew about teaching was firmly grounded, not just in text-book theories, but in significant and powerful personal experience in the arts, and that such personal knowledge influenced my teaching in the most profound ways. The journey has now brought me to the point where I understand that the greater importance of this is not so much the identification of what I know, but the illumination of the process of how I and others may come to such knowing. By investigating our lives narratively and aesthetically, we empower ourselves, our participants and our readers, as we describe how we transform our teaching by coming to know who we are, and to understand what we are bringing to each interaction we have with our students. Seeing how all our life experiences may be embedded in even the smallest acts of teaching helps us situate and work powerfully with the knowledge we have constructed. It allows us to claim and reclaim all experiences and influences, and to re-integrate ourselves and articulate a personal philosophy of teaching that is consciously grounded in who we understand ourselves to be.

AFTERWORD: SETTING OUT AGAIN

I work now as a resource teacher helping my colleagues to integrate information and communication technologies into their inquiry practices. I find I am no longer quite so enthusiastic to share what *I* know or my thoughts about what *I* would do. I try instead to step back, to listen more closely to the voice of each teacher and remember that he or she brings a range of life experiences to a personal interpretation of what it is to teach. If I am to truly support and encourage my fellow teachers I must listen for the questions they hold about their practice and join with them as a co-inquirer into what it is we do and how we do it.

Recently, I met with the head of school to talk about the new directions my job might take now that my doctoral studies are completed. "How," she asked me, "can we get teachers to change their practice, to move away from their need to cover the content, and to engage their students in meaningful inquiry?" As I put the question into the context of my own research, I said that we would have to engage them in an inquiry of their own, into their own teaching. It seemed a satisfactory answer at the time, but not an entirely satisfying one.

The problem perhaps resides in the question. *We* do not *get* teachers to change their practice. We cannot control that performance. Yes, we can support and encourage, provide time and resources, even organize professional development that allows for experimentation, reflection and reconstruction. But in the end that may not be enough. For this is what I have come to know through my ongoing investigations of practice: As Parker Palmer would say, "We teach who we are" (1998). Therefore, when we ask teachers to change their practice we do nothing less than ask them to change who they are. The question might be better stated: How can teachers transform themselves and their practice?

We transform ourselves and our practice, when we come to understand who we are, and examine the influences that have contributed to the self we uncover. To do so we must inevitably head back and review where we have come from so that we might consider better that path that stretches before us.

The process of creating this chapter has entailed an unexpected but satisfying circling back over old terrain as I tell and retell my stories of learning through the arts, of transforming my role in the arts and working with narrative inquiry. It is terrain I thought I knew, and yet in returning to it once again, it opens up before me and I see it with fresh eyes. I understand old questions and old problems in new terms, and find new solutions and new ways of working. It is in following this recursive path that we as teachers may come to know ourselves and our practice and open up the space we need to transform both.

RAE JOHNSON

12. THE ARTFUL BODY: A NARRATIVE OF AN EMBODIED RELATIONSHIP WITH THE ARTS

I have fixed you in the soft focus of my memory
slouched out on the orange beanbag chair on a Sunday afternoon
standing in the big ugly kitchen
smelling of mildew and cumin and hashish
stirring a pot of vegan something
no one any older than you would dream of eating.

I am just twelve so your rightness is a sure thing.
I inhale tofu and patchouli and Leonard Cohen until I burst.
I drift through the edges of the house
and soak up the vibes like wine into a sponge.

A noted percussionist lies asleep on the bare boards of the back porch.
It's so much quieter here than in New York.
In the kitchen assorted members of an Irish folk group
huddle close to the phone and pour the loving in their voices
down the line in four-part harmony
to a friend just moved to Inuvik.
Remnants of a discussion on the nature of God
follow someone to the fridge to get another drink.

The late afternoon sunlight floats through the curtains
and rinses everything clean.
Everyone here has come undone
exuding smoke and hair and a mysterious relief.
You've stopped running somehow and are starting just to be.
The outsiders are safely inside at last.
Me, I am still too young to be alive.
I stand in the warmth of your shadows and
live on the air you breathe out.

I wrote this poem in my late twenties, as I reflected on my experiences growing up in the 1970's in a household often filled with artists, musicians, intellectuals and hippies. As I reflect on this poem now, I am struck by its sensory qualities – smells

M. Beattie (Author/Ed.), The Quest for Meaning: Narratives of Teaching, Learning and the Arts, 199–213.

and tastes, sounds and images – as well as its repeated references to the body in posture, gesture, and breath (Abram, 1997). I note the centrality of human relationships in the text, the presence of a variety of artistic forms, and my role as student/witness. More significantly, I am haunted by the historical and sociocultural context it describes, and by the sense of a revolutionary vision that seems to have slipped from the centre of our political consciousness.

These same elements that figured so strongly in my childhood – relationship, culture, art, and the body – continue to inform my personal life, and form the basis of my professional work. As I engage with my graduate students in somatic psychology, collaborate with research participants in examining the embodied dimensions of social injustice, or develop my "recreational" pursuits in the domestic arts, I am anchored in a commitment to cultivating what Thomas Moore (1993) might liken to his understanding of the "poetic body", and what I call here the "artful body". This concept of the artful body refers to a deep felt experience of the body in relationship to others, as expressed in or inspired by art.

This chapter offers a personal narrative of how I arrived at an understanding of the artful body, discusses how my commitment to an embodied relationship with the arts manifests in my present life, and describes how I work with the artful body as a therapist, educator, activist, and scholar. For the most part, my intended audience is educators and researchers who already include the body and/or the arts in their professional work, or who are interested in exploring the links between the personal, professional, and scholarly through narrative approaches. However, community activists and artists may also find themselves in resonance with parts of my story, and find the conclusions I have drawn useful to their own endeavours outside the bounds of a formal educational setting.

My narrative begins by tracing the roots of my concept of the artful body into my childhood, and is structured according to each artistic medium that influenced my early development. That is, I discuss the impact of my engagement with literature, music, the visual arts, and dance in sequence, before moving on to a discussion of how I have integrated, understood, and elaborated upon these experiences as an adult.

LITERATURE

The members of my family were voracious and omnivorous readers. Books of all kinds were everywhere as I was growing up on the Canadian prairie – tucked into bookcases, stacked on tables, and spilling out of nooks and crannies. There was science fiction and poetry, classic and modern fiction, philosophy textbooks and jazz magazines. My younger sister Jill and I took to reading early, cutting our teeth on cereal boxes at the breakfast table. As pre-schoolers, we would sit across from one another and take turns reading the ingredient lists from the French and English sides of the box.

From there we moved onto the thirteen-volume set of World Book Encyclopaedia's Childcraft. It proved to be a goldmine of stories and biographies on scientists, explorers, and artists. My sister and I would pore over the volumes, trading each other for the ones we hadn't read yet. The only time I was ever late for school was in first grade, when I came home for lunch and got so caught up in a story about Frank Lloyd Wright in *Childcraft,* that I lost track of the time. My father, who was the parent-in-residence on that particular day, was similarly lost in a book, and neither of us noticed that the lunch hour had slipped by until there was no time for me to run back to school and still make the bell. I remember my teacher scolding me as I slipped into my seat at ten minutes past the hour. Only later, as an adult, did I think to question her being upset with a six-year-old for reading too much.

As I progressed through public school, I began haunting the library, waiting for the particularly thick books to arrive on the shelves. In fourth grade, I tackled Margaret Mitchell's *Gone with the Wind,* by sole virtue of the fact that it was the biggest book in the library that I hadn't already read. At home, my appetite for reading continued unchecked. My parents, sister and I once spent an entire rainy summer vacation at the lake reading the *Chronicles of Narnia* series by C. S. Lewis, passing the seven slim volumes from one person to the next, pausing only briefly for food and trips to the outhouse. Another summer, my mom got us all hooked on Harlequin Romances, and we had to buy them second-hand by the shopping bag to feed our habit.

By the time I reached adolescence, I had consumed vast quantities of books. The effects of all that reading were difficult for me to assess at the time, except that I noticed that reading allowed me to be content in my own company for long periods of time, and that I had developed a capacity for stillness. I also liked the way reading a good book made me feel alive all over. I grew to love the contented body rush that signalled that I had made contact with something nurturing to my being, even if that "something" was also a little strange or intimidating. More significantly, I started to observe that my perceptions and perspectives on the world seemed to be different, broader somehow, than many of my school friends. The stories of real lives embedded in all those books provided a glimpse into the inner hearts and minds of others, deepening my capacity for empathy and underscoring the importance of relationship. Over time, these early experiences with literature also provided the multiple lenses on human experience that allowed me to cultivate the sociocultural and political focus I bring to my work today.

Fortunately, this cultivation was enriched by a family environment that was supportive of the time alone required for reading, and of thoughtful social dissent. For example, when I was thirteen, I brought home a copy of Leonard Cohen's *Flowers for Hitler*. Like most books in our house, it eventually wound up in the bathroom, where it remained for several weeks. If any other kid I knew had brought home a book of poetry filled with such rage, despair, profanity, and deeply radical philosophical thought, all parental hell would likely have broken loose and landed squarely on their heads. In my house, the Leonard Cohen fit in nicely with the Jerzy Kozinski and Lawrence Ferlinghetti already downstairs in the living room.

MUSIC

Also in the living room that year was a baby grand piano on loan from Miss Canada 1972, who had acquired it as part of her pageant prize-winnings, but who could not fit it into her small downtown apartment. The baby grand was a significant step up from the string of second-hand uprights that usually graced our family home. My parents understood that Miss Canada would eventually settle down, marry a nice man, and move into a house worthy of the piano, so we seized the moment.

We played more music on that piano than I can remember, and the imprint of the sounds we made all those years ago are impressed upon me at depths I cannot even begin to express. Jill would play old standards like *April in Paris*, and I would sing along with her – belting out chorus and verse in my finest fake operetta voice. In the summertime, the open windows carried the sound out into our little dead-end street. We were so full of our own enjoyment, so utterly sure of our right to make whatever music we wanted, that it never occurred that the neighbours would mind the noise.

I wasn't nearly as good a pianist as my younger sister, but when the house was quiet, I would plink out small melodies and write them down. Around the same time the baby grand was living at our house, I became deeply immersed in reading J.R.R. Tolkien, and decided to write a song cycle for *Lord of the Rings*. When the lyrics didn't sound the way I thought they should in English, I faked some Elvish, and wrote the lyrics in that language instead. My Elvish wasn't the linguistic accomplishment that Tolkien's was by a long shot, but the words sounded soft and clear. Neither were the songs themselves very good, but they called to my heart, which is what I understood all music should do.

I learned this understanding through immersion. I don't recall ever being taught the theory and structure of music at home, but I have countless memories of playing and listening. Some of my earliest recollections are of my parents playing old jazz standards together, long after I had gone to bed. I'd listen as the sounds wafted up to my bedroom – Mom trying to nail the tricky chord changes on Billy Strayhorn's, *Lush Life*, Dad playing alto on *Satin Doll* and *Scotch and Soda*. Sometimes they would play these furious little Spanish duets for piano and recorder, and Mom would get going so fast on the piano her fingers took on a life of their own. Other evenings, they would invite friends over to play, and the sounds resonating from the living room expanded in range and complexity. The music drifted out, up the stairs, and straight into the body and soul of a small child tucked in bed, awake and listening quietly to every note.

Dad worked for the local university radio station when I was little, and seemed to bring home new music every day. Some of the albums were clearly for children – *Peter and the Wolf, Tubby the Tuba, The Adventures of Pecos Bill* – but they were limited in number, so eventually I ventured into other musical territory. My approach was entirely trial and error; pull out an album, play some. If I liked it, I would play the rest. If I didn't like it, I'd put it back and pull out another. If I really liked it, I would play it over and over, sometimes for months. My initial choices were often guided by how appealing the album art was, and I discovered Bartok's

Concerto for Orchestra and Miles Davis' *Bitches Brew* simply because they had great covers.

Not all of the music I listened to was by my own choosing. Dad was a hard-core jazz fanatic, and played hours and hours of jazz music whenever he was at home – Stan Getz, Duke Ellington, Sarah Vaughn, Thelonious Monk, Cannonball Adderly. He actually owned a Dizzy Gillespie sweatshirt, and used to wear it around the house at lot when I was very young. I remember seeing Dizzy's face on the sweatshirt, and thinking that this black man was actually a member of our family somehow. Now I understand that he was.

What I am also just now beginning to understand is the effect of growing up in a white household where nearly all of my father's heroes were black, and where the rhythms and melodies of many peoples transcended socially-constructed barriers to reach deeply into my body. The opening phrases of Thelonious Monk's *Little Rootie Tootie,* still elicit a rush of electricity and an immediate impulse to move. So do Bach's *Brandenburg Concerto Number 5* and Ayub Ogada's *Obiero*, to name a diverse handful among the hundreds of pieces of music I have loved. I feel as though I have the music of other cultures embedded in my very cells, and the impact of that on how I relate to differences among us as human beings seems profoundly important.

FOLK ARTS

The domestic or "folk" arts were as much a natural part of growing up as music was. My mom was a school teacher who often spent the summers engaged in arts projects, and she used to let my sister and me join in at whatever level we could manage. Over the years, we experimented with batik and tie-dying and candle-making and rug-hooking and pottery and weaving and jewellery-making and papier-mâché and lots of other forms. My approach to all of these mediums was the same as my approach to music; trial and error plus creative excitement. As a child, I was an enthusiastic dabbler; by adolescence, a fearless experimenter. No form was off limits, nothing deemed too difficult or requiring more technique and discipline than I currently possessed. No art was sacred. Skim the first page of the instructions and run with it.

I also applied this approach to other creative projects – ones that might not usually be considered "art", but which equally fuelled my creativity and developing sense of self. Armed with a very basic knowledge of cooking, I tackled obscure Scandinavian cookie recipes and East Indian bread making. Supplied with some mauve cotton jersey and a pair of scissors, my father and I made me a monk's robe one Saturday morning. We accomplished this creative task by having me lie down on a length of fabric spread out on the living room floor with my arms outstretched, while my Dad took the scissors and cut around me. Two big squares for pockets, a big semi-circle for a hood, and we were set. Dad stitched the robe together on our old Singer sewing machine, and I wore it that afternoon. Instantly, I was no longer a teenaged misfit who had homework – I was a daughter of Pan, or perhaps an acolyte of Sappho. Not all of my cooking was edible, and the robe had a lopsided hem, but I was learning not to be afraid to create.

Around the same time, I took to journaling and drawing up in my room. My bedroom was a tiny space no bigger than two broom closets, but it was a haven to me as I navigated the rough waters of adolescence. I wrote poetry almost every day, and my parents allowed me to draw, paint, and inscribe my poems on the walls of my small room. I had no training, and no real materials. I remember creating a mural of faces in profile blending into a landscape of hills using nothing but some eye shadow, a felt tip marker, and various shades of shoe polish.

I made no conscious distinction between the poems I inscribed on the walls and the drawings that accompanied them. Always while I drew or wrote, I would play music, and the sound would become a seamless part of the creative process. Once when my turntable broke, I discovered that I couldn't sit still to write. My artistic forms had become so thoroughly intertwined that I found it difficult to work with just one medium at a time. The concept of *intermodality* (Knill, Neinhaus Barba, and Fuchs' 1995) in expressive arts therapy captures this experience perfectly; they argue that multiple means of expression expands the range and complexity of insight and meanings available through art. Being able to call on many art forms whenever inspiration struck gave me a freedom of creative expression that I don't think I would have cultivated had I been trained exclusively in a single discipline.

MOVEMENT AND DANCE

I learned to dance when I was four. My mom took me to the local YMCA and enrolled me in a creative movement class. Our year-end recital entailed having a bunch of us pretend we were angels while running between "clouds" that we formed on the floor with lengths of skipping rope. From that moment on, I was hooked. I took the inspiration from that class and translated it into hours and hours of "dancing" at home. My cousins and I would play Englebert Humperdinck records and take turns improvising dances to each of the songs. I would arrange the living room furniture into theatre "sets", and choreograph long sequences involving princesses dancing their way up a steep cliff of coffee tables and footstools before leaping to a tragic death upon the sea of carpet below.

As I got older, I enrolled in "real" dance classes, and sampled tap, jazz, folk, and modern dance before deciding that ballet was my form of choice. I was fortunate to have a very accomplished yet gentle woman as my first ballet teacher, and for the first time I began to see value in her disciplined approach to teaching movement. Before that, art was all about expression and vision – now it also began to be about tradition and technique.

My respect for ballet as an art form grew in direct proportion to the steepness of my learning curve. I began to realize that although a plié (bending the knee) looks like the easiest movement in the world to execute, it takes years to develop the refinement of motor control that allows a plié to serve the dancer as preparation for leaps and jumps. I began to see the depth, the nuances, and the complexity of an artistic form that previously I had considered simply as a marvellous vehicle for self-expression. Slowly, I developed the ability to move skilfully and precisely, and to expand my movement vocabulary beyond the pedestrian motions of everyday life.

The other important discovery I made in my exploration of ballet was how central my body was to my experience of art. By consciously using my body in the process of art making through dance, I began to recognize a specific state of bodily sensation as associated with artistic or creative engagement. This somatic state possessed many of the qualities that Csiksentmihalyi (1975) calls flow. Somatic is a term defined by Hanna (1970) to describe the lived experience of the body from within. Described as a whole-body sensation experienced when acting with total involvement, the flow experience tends to merge action and awareness, stimulus and response, and self and environment into a unified, connected event. It also feels utterly wonderful.

THE ARTFUL BODY

Dancing provided many opportunities for flow experiences, and I began to realize that all of my deepest and most satisfying experiences with art possessed those same qualities. Art was my catalyst into an altered state of consciousness that was more than merely blissful; it allowed me to access a deeper understanding about what it meant to be human. Through the artistic works of others, I took some of their most profoundly meaningful experiences into my body. Through my own art making, I captured the feeling of being fully alive in my body, and distilled it into an expression of my unique aliveness that I could communicate to others. Art became an existential necessity, and necessarily existential – that is, art served as the experiential means for creating the meaning and essence of my life.

My understanding of art's existential qualities might be best expressed through the following passage from Carlos Casteneda's (1987) The Power of Silence. In this book, Casteneda writes about his apprenticeship to a Mexican Indian sorcerer named don Juan Matus. Don Juan is trying to explain to Carlos that sorcerers differ from ordinary humans in that they use the idea of their own mortality as a compelling stimulus to engage with life more fully and courageously than would otherwise be possible for them. Sorcerers call this activity "stalking", and use art as one of their stalking tools:

"I have told you that there are many reasons I like poems," he said. "What I do is stalk myself with them. I deliver a jolt to myself with them. I listen, and as you read, I shut off my internal dialogue and let my inner silence gain momentum. Then the combination of the poem and the silence delivers the jolt." He explained that poets unconsciously long for the sorcerers' world. Because they are not sorcerers on the path of knowledge, longing is all they have.

> "Let us see if you can feel what I'm talking about," he said, handing me a book of poems by Jose Gorostiza. I opened it at the bookmark and he pointed to the poem he liked… "As I hear the words," don Juan said when I had finished reading, "I feel that that man is seeing the essence of things and I can see with him. I don't care what the poem is about. I care only about the

> feeling the poet's longing brings me. I borrow his longing, and with it I borrow the beauty. And marvel at the fact that he, like a true warrior, lavishes it on the recipients, the beholders, retaining for himself only his longing. This jolt, this shock of beauty, is stalking." (p. 130)

I, too, feel this shock of beauty when I engage with art. Indeed, I seek out art looking specifically for this shock, hoping that the music or the painting or the dance will send out a vibration, and that my body will allow the vibration to resonate until I remember in my bones how alive (and consequently, how mortal) I am. So at the same time that art is an expression and fulfilment of life, it is also a brush with death. Not all art lends itself to this act of stalking one's own spirit, but I've come to align myself with the kind of art that does. Living with art in this way means always living within sight of the edge of an existential abyss – to embrace art without hesitation or reservation, as though each opportunity might be our last.

MOVING ON

As the stories of my childhood suggest, my developing relationship with the arts centred on the intersection between art and embodied experience. As I grew from adolescence into early adulthood, I also became increasingly focused on the social contexts in which artistic expression is always embedded. Put another way, I came to understand art as possessing an inherent capacity to create and transform culture – indeed, to see this as one of its primary functions. More specifically, I became interested in the role of art in the creation of countercultures, as the poem at the beginning of this chapter suggests.

By linking the idea of art as an important tool in the creation of countercultures with the notion of art as an embodied experience, it is possible to examine a further set of linkages that understand the experience of "being in your body" as inherently transgressive. By this I mean not only that embodiment is always "about culture and experience insofar as these can be understood from the standpoint of bodily being-in-the-world" (Csordas, 1999, p. 143), but also that our collective cultural legacies predispose many of us to marginalize embodied experience such that we "live as though the body and its needs are repugnant … as though the body were merely a machine; as though a life that denies or even punishes the body is superior to a fully embodied life" (Johnson, 2001, p. 184).

Dance

As a young woman, I struggled to find a way to live in my body that felt like an authentic expression of who I was, despite the social constraints that discouraged me from expressing the sensual experience of "being in my body", or conversely, interpreted that expression as sexual invitation. In my early twenties, several of my female friends began to actively resist the narrow gender roles we inherited as women by collectively descending on bars and music clubs, intent on dancing with complete abandon. We danced only with each other, took up as much room as we wanted, and surrendered utterly to our bodily impulses to move. We used to call it “animus dancing”, with a sly nod to the Jungian notion of the psychological archetype in a woman that represents her male alter ego. We danced not only to embody the so-called “masculine” qualities in a woman’s psyche – including initiative, courage, and conviction – but to reclaim the social spaces typically reserved for the heterosexual courtship rituals that required us to be submissive, pretty, and objectively (rather than subjectively) sexual. Our public displays of sensual joy in movement served to disrupt a number of social conventions, and to mark a small place in our world for the authentic and artistic expression of the body. Over the years, I have found many connections to the work of others in this domain (Roth, 1999; Starhawk, 1997) and been sustained by the affirmation of our collective capacity to resist the confines of a limited view of socially-appropriate bodily expression.

Clothing

My relationship with clothing provides another example of how understanding my body as artfully transgressive translated into everyday experience. During that same period in my early twenties, I had the good luck to fall into a job as a clothing buyer and window dresser. As I became more literate about the art of fashion, and more committed to the process of reclaiming my body as a locus for art, I became increasingly attentive to the images my body conveyed about my identity within various cultural milieus. I also began to insist that these images suggest a particular quality of engagement with the felt experience of the body. I sought out clothing that elicited a visceral reaction from me, and found myself drawn to clothing lines created by other women who expressed a similar need for artistic expression through the clothes they wore. Like a talisman, my clothes became a source of personal power that oriented me toward a particular quality of felt experience – one characterized by presence, flow, and sensuality. Over the years, I have learned to use clothing as a way to shape my identity; to embody the imagination, realize the mythic and metaphoric, and to transcend the mundane. A lot to ask from a pair of pants, perhaps – but worth the trouble.

My clothing also served, and continues to serve, as socially conscious performance art. The idea that fashion is political is not new, and a growing number of artists and social theorists are making connections between clothing and social ideas (Corrigan, 1993). For example, the artist J. Morgan Puett may be best known for her clothing design, but she considers herself an interventionist who users her work to illuminate and challenge unexamined social conventions (Hubbell, 2007). I love that clothes function as powerful but subtle symbols for all kinds of complex cultural ideas, and I use mine as an act of social and political resistance; as a way to reclaim my body image from the prevailing hegemonic discourse that presses me to conform to a prescribed/proscribed set of images. For example, my clothing was, and always is, deliberately “androgynous” in a very particular way. I often wear both pants and dresses together as a way to signal to others, and also to remind myself, that I refuse the socially-dominant heterosexual matrix of gender and sexual orientation that insists there are only two mutually exclusive and appositionally-attracted genders (Butler, 1993). Every time I open my closet to get dressed, I contemplate the choices that inform the reiterative performance of my gender identity. Over the years, several of my outfits have elicited hoots of laughter and derision from gangs of passing teenage boys, and some responses have been sufficiently hostile to warrant a flutter of alarm in my stomach. While I didn't enjoy the sensation of fear this uninvited heckling produced, I appreciated the reminder that the resistance I was enacting through my body presentation was in response to a very real (and disturbing) set of social imperatives.

Poetry

The third way I experimented with embodied art as an agent of social change was to move my poetry from the private domain of my own life into a wider social context. Instead of being content to write casually-constructed passages in my journal that no one else would ever read, I began to write poems about my body that were also intended for others. The first time I submitted a poem to a poetry journal, the editor sent back a handwritten note that spoke of how personally moved she had been by my depiction of an embodied experience of domestic violence. Her response helped me to realize that my words could communicate something meaningful about the lived experience of the body, and that I could share with others the same deep sustenance that poetry offered me. Many years later, I recited a number of my poems as part of a larger performance of embodied art, and was struck with how much more potent (and terrifying) live performance of poetry can be. At the same time, I was captivated by the depth of connection between the various artists as we rehearsed and performed deeply personal work, and the impact of our collective efforts on the audience.

The Artful Body as Activism

Through these experiences of collective resistance through art, I have strengthened my understanding of my body as artful in itself, and articulated its phenomenological, linguistic, and imaginal dimensions – that is, I became more adept at accessing the felt experience of my body through art, better able to communicate that experience through language, and more skilled at creating the kind of body images that expressed something fundamental about who I am. I learned that I was an agent of personal and social change, and that my body was the locus of those transformations. From the bodies of others – through their images, voices, and movements – I absorbed knowledge and understandings about the world around me, which in turn transformed my embodied experience. Through my body, I generated new understandings and knowledge, and if I was willing to risk being fully present in my own body, the art I produced could serve as a catalyst for further transformation. As someone whose sense of personal identity often placed me outside many social norms, my capacity to be artful through my body both affirmed my status as "outsider" (Wilson, 1956) and allowed me a way to "come inside at last" (Johnson,

1997) – not to any kind of socially affirming status quo, but to a quality of engagement, aliveness, and presence in the body that was both radical and collectively relevant. In short, I understand being fully and artfully embodied as a form of political activism.

THE ARTFUL BODY IN PROFESSIONAL CONTEXTS

Because of my early experiences with art, I have chosen a professional path that allows me to continue to integrate embodied expression, psychological insight, and the articulation between self and social identities through the arts.

The Artful Body in Clinical Contexts

I have studied expressive arts therapy and movement therapy, and practiced as a somatic psychotherapist for many years. As a therapist, I was committed to helping clients learn how to listen deeply to their bodies as the precondition for creating meaningful experience, and as a way to be more fully human with one another. I often facilitated a client's capacity to follow an authentic impulse to move, generated from the felt experience of her body in relationship to others – the same impulse I learned to follow as a child in my cousin's living room.

Mary Whitehouse, a dancer, teacher, and movement therapy pioneer, understands the body as the source of our capacity to connect deeply with ourselves as well as to larger psychological, social, and spiritual contexts (1999). She and others developed a movement practice called Authentic Movement based on these insights. Over the years, I have been witness to many occasions when simply creating an opportunity for this kind of embodied movement improvisation has functioned simultaneously as education, activism, and personal transformation. While working as a dance therapist on the maximum security ward of a psychiatric hospital, I watched as a gay man engaged for the first time with his straight peers as they all danced to Prince's song, *Purple Rain.* Dancing in a public park with members of the homeless community, I witnessed a white-haired old man weeping while moving slowly to a piece of music, saying he hadn't cried since he was a young boy. I facilitated expressive arts groups for survivors of childhood sexual abuse, and was inspired by their willingness to engage with themselves and each other through drawing, movement, and music.

In my work as a therapist, I have been repeatedly reminded how crucial the relational dimension of embodiment is, and how much the ways we are with others (or fail to be) is an issue of the body and its expression. Because of the incredible social forces preventing those from subordinated groups from being fully embodied, I have focused my clinical practice on understanding how multiple social forces work through the body to bring oppression into being. Being able to use art as a "safe way in" to embodied experience has been critical to my ability to work effectively with marginalized individuals, and my own personal experiences with artistic expression through the body have provided the foundation for my professional knowledge and skills.

Teaching the Artful Body

In my current work as a professor of graduate students in somatic psychology, the idea of the artful body has extended itself to many aspects of my own teaching. As a result of the synthesis of my learning through artistic experience, I am more attentive to how my students weave artistry into their own lives. I find myself consistently impressed with the degree to which their bodies have been sources of artistic inspiration, and dismayed by the degree to which they downplay their embodied capacity for artistry. As a teacher, I am beginning to understand how something so natural to human nature as art is thwarted by an educational process and social structure that often value performance, discipline, and technique over creative expression. I also cannot help but notice the false dichotomy between professional artists and the public that consumes the products of their artistry. We elevate artists, and at the same time disown their skills and appetites in ourselves – our own capacity to write, dance, act, and sing.

In facilitating an exploration of the artful body for others, therefore, I try to replicate the essential features of the learning environment I found so helpful to me as a child. These features include an abundance of opportunity, an open-minded and experimental attitude toward the creative process, an environment richly saturated with embodied art of all kinds, confident and enthusiastic role models, and gentle encouragement to surmount some of the technical and procedural hurdles. I emphasize art's somatic dimensions – "How does this art or art-making experience make you feel in your body?" "How is your body involved with and affected by the artistic process?" I also try to remember art's existential dimensions, and not to shy away when a student brings the mystery of life and death into the process. After all, as the Irish painter Francis Bacon asserts, the job of the artist is always to deepen the mystery, and I believe the same is often (but not always) true for psychotherapists and teachers. Some topics, by simple virtue of their complexity and depth, do not lend themselves wholly to didactic explication. The embodied experience of being human is one of them.

Because of the importance I place on embodied experience, I am especially attuned to the nonverbal communication that forms a substantial part of the interaction between myself and my students. According to Marcel Danesi (1999) we have the capacity to produce nearly three-quarters of a million distinct physical signs, including different bodily postures, hand gestures, and facial expressions. Anthropologist Ray Birdwhistell (1970) claimed that about two-thirds of a message's meaning is communicated through these non-verbal clues. The importance of nonverbal communication is further demonstrated by the finding of Argyle et al. (1970) that nonverbal cues have over four times the impact of verbal ones when verbal and nonverbal cues are used together.

As an educator, I not only pay attention to the ways in which interpersonal space, gesture, and other body cues communicate implicit information about interpersonal and social relationships within the learning environment, I make these communications explicit and transparent whenever possible. For example, I frequently note aloud to students when I have used my own body to convey an idea or attitude (for example, when I model the collapsed bodily attitude of someone with depression), or when I am reading their body language to assist me in gauging their interest or level of comprehension (for example, their tendency to avoid eye contact with me when they are bored or confused). I also raise the topic of the body in relation to various diversity and equity issues, and encourage students to reflect on how their own bodies might play a part in their experience of these issues.

I also use clothing as a way to teach non-verbal communication through body art. For example, I regularly teach a graduate class on the body and diversity issues, where I ask my students to make observations about me through my clothes. I try to do this exercise very early in the term, so that my students have not yet had an opportunity to get to know me through the usual verbal exchange of inquiry and self-disclosure. Despite this, they come up with a number of inspired guesses about my gender identity, socioeconomic class, sexual orientation, personal and political values, religious affiliation, and dietary preferences. Just as they might "read" a poem or painting, students are able to connect the symbols embedded in my clothing to meaningful social, cultural, and personal ideas. More significantly, my relationship to my own body is also communicated through my clothes – "You look comfortable in your own skin", one student commented. "When I look at you, I start to breathe a little deeper".

Researching the Artful Body

My own life journey in relation to the arts shares many similarities with a heuristic research model. Echoing my own experiences of embodied art-making, heuristic research refers to a process of internal investigation through which one discovers the nature and meaning of a particular human experience, and develops methods and procedures for further investigation (Moustakas, 1990). Heuristic inquiry actively emphasizes connection and relationship with the subject matter being researched, in contrast to the relative detachment encouraged by many other research approaches. Rather than dissecting experience and leaving it in abstracted pieces, the heuristic method attempts to recreate lived experience in a process that "moves from whole to part and back to whole again" (Moustakas, 1990, p. 16).

For example, my early explorations of the arts have led me to experience art as deeply internal, always political, and inextricably connected to my sense of personal and social identity. I do not relate to art or art-making from a detached perspective – rather I engage with it in the context of intimate relationship, one in which my unique embodied presence is key. Also, my relative lack of formal instruction in many of the art forms I practice has emphasized the importance of self-discovery and an experimental, rather than prescribed, attitude toward art. My approach to artistic adventures has always been, "What will happen if I do this?", and "What can I learn about this simply through the experience of steeping myself in it?" Once I have immersed myself in an artistic experience, I attempt, over time, to extract and integrate understandings.

In describing such an embodied artistic experience, a heuristic research perspective emphasizes retaining the visibility of research participants, rather than losing them as individual persons in the process of descriptive analysis. This approach to data representation is echoed in Anderson's (2002–03) work on embodied writing in research, in which she advocates for the inclusion of the bodily experience of researchers and participants through vivid depictions that invite an embodied response in the reader. She asserts that traditional scientific and academic writing is "parched of the body's lived experience" (p. 40), and suggests that research into the lived experience of the body can only be represented through embodied writing. From the perspective of narrative inquiry, Connelly and Clandinin (1999) offer a further consideration with respect to data representation. They note that in attempting to capture the lived experiences of participants in narrative form, researchers must still attend to their own "signature," or writing style. Feminist theorist bell hooks (1994) offers a final caution with respect to writing in ways that promote the accessibility of anti-oppression theory and research. She argues that because many feminist thinkers and theorists do their work in the elite setting of the university, their work is written in highly academic language that is not easily understood by those outside academe (indeed, it could be argued that some of it is not easily understood within it either). hooks endorses a writing style that returns feminism to its grassroots by making its knowledge accessible to all people.

I have aligned my own approach to scholarly writing with these injunctions in mind. To that end, when presenting research data in my studies of embodied experience (Johnson, 2000; 2003; 2007), I privilege the first person, subjective experience of the body over other elements of writing style or content. Especially when writing narratives, much of my text is written from the inside out – letting my body's "perceptual matrix guide the words, impulse by impulse, sensation by sensation" (Anderson, 2002–03, p. 43). This does not mean my writing can be self-indulgent or meandering – it simply means that, as a writer, I need to be in my body when I write. I pay attention to the rich array of sensory and perceptual material available through embodied experience, and attune to the deeper layers of sensual, emotional, and psychological associations, memories, and undercurrents that attend such experience. Frequently, this has also meant that my writing has incorporated poetic or artistic depictions intended to illuminate the lived experience of the body. Although finding the balance between academic rigour and artistic license is never an easy task (Abbey, 2002), as a scholar committed to bringing the artful body to life, I am continually inspired by the impact this endeavour has on my own learning. Writing this chapter has been such a learning experience.

The perspectives I developed as a result of my embodied experiences with art have also informed many of the other choices I make when engaging in scholarly research. I choose research topics that speak to important social issues, and that I hope will benefit the individuals and groups connected to the research. I frequently seek out research participants whose own lives have been shaped by the arts, and by their bodily experience. Lastly, I engage in research methods that are inclusive of the body, and often draw on arts-based data collection techniques (Johnson, 1996; 2000).

CONCLUSION

In closing, what I've learned through my embodied experience in the arts is that there are important connections between art, the body, and social justice. I've learned that how I breathe, walk, dress, and move teaches an entire nonverbal curriculum to my students. If I'm going to understand the full impact of my presence as a teacher I'd better be aware of the role that my body plays in my teaching – especially given the inherent power imbalance between teacher and student. I've also come to appreciate how important it is for me to be able to communicate artfully when literal explanations don't meet my students' need to understand something as complex, profound, and frequently paradoxical as human experience. By the same token, research into embodied experience also requires an ability to understand and convey material that often eludes the hard grasp of numbers and facts, and being able to illuminate it effectively sometimes requires poetry instead of prose.

Through my own struggles to become artfully embodied in a culture that devalues both art and the body, I have come to realize that what I once understood as a personal challenge is simultaneously a form of political activism, and that I can extend the impact of this activism by consciously modelling this intention to my students and colleagues. Most importantly, I've learned that my life is deeply grounded in an artistic sensibility that calls me to feel into the places of sensation, awareness, and meaning that lie beneath the surface appearance of things and events. In my personal and professional lives, I want to integrate my embodied experiences with emergent understandings, and become more fully and artfully present – in my body, with others, and on the page.

BENJAMIN BOLDEN

13. VOICES

INTRODUCTION

I am a music educator and researcher. Very recently appointed as an Assistant Professor of Music Education at the University of Victoria, on the west coast of Canada, I am feeling exceedingly fortunate. The university position enables me to learn about something I love very much, while sharing what I learn and have learned with music educators of today and tomorrow – helping them, I hope, to go forth and carry out their life-enriching work. I am also a composer, and am eternally grateful to those musicians, from pre-school to professional, who have contributed their energy, skills, and knowledge to bring my music to life.

My particular area of research interest is teaching composing. I completed a doctoral dissertation, entitled *Teaching Composing in the Classroom: What Teachers Know*, two years ago. What follows are the stories that served as a prologue to that dissertation and also, in a manner of speaking, brought me to where I am today.

Bach and the Blues

> I began piano lessons in earnest at age twelve. There had been an attempt when I was six, but the teacher, in my estimation, was too grouchy; I did not last long. Mrs. Murphy had the best reputation around, so – despite the hefty fees – my parents signed me up and so I joined the classiest studio in our small Ontario town.
>
> My advanced age meant I was always woefully behind the others. Most of Mrs. Murphy's students began at age six or younger. Edward's lessons immediately followed mine, and Mrs. Murphy would place a stool below the piano bench so that his little legs did not have to dangle so uncomfortably far above the floor. While I put on my coat and boots to leave he would climb up on the bench, spread his chubby little fingers over the keyboard, and launch into some Beethoven sonata or other that invariably brought a delighted smile to our teacher's face, emphasized my own incompetence, and provided a gleeful sound track for my dejected departure.
>
> Every term we gave a recital. Parents and uncles and aunts and grandparents and the odd self-sacrificing grade-school teacher would crowd into folding chairs in Mrs. Murphy's piano studio. The students would wait (quietly) in the dining room until we were ushered in one by one, like lambs to the

M. Beattie(ed.), The Quest for Meaning: Narratives of Teaching, Learning and the Arts, 215–231.

slaughter, to plunk out our offering for the assembled throng (who were usually as terrified as we were).

One particular term I was to play a Bach sinfonia. I loved the piece, and after months of dedicated practicing, rigorously enforced by Mrs. Murphy's diligent tutelage, I understood it perfectly. My fingers, however, did not.

My piano technique was, and, to be honest, still is a nightmare. Bach's polyphonic musical lines, moving contrapuntally in different directions at different times, demand a rigorous physical and mental dexterity to keep them in check. My relationship with these particular polyphonic lines was still under negotiation, and on this occasion they quickly made it clear who was in charge – not me. As I sat at the piano before the captive audience, my traitorous, trembling fingers were dragged deep into an unfamiliar, atonal, and very un-Bach-like forest well past the point of no return.

I panicked. So did Mrs. Murphy. So did all the parents and uncles and aunts and grandparents and the odd grade-school teacher. I stopped playing. Everyone in the room stopped breathing. We all wished mightily we were somewhere else.

Then, magically, mysteriously, my fingers began to move. My unconscious dredged up the knowledge that the piece was in the key of A, and I tacked on a Blues cadence that Dylan, who had perfect pitch, and could play anything he heard on the radio, had taught me the week before. It fit! It was as though I had stumbled across the key to my prison cell. I pushed it into the lock, held my breath, turned the key, and . . . was free! I bolted from the room, the relieved applause ringing in my ears and reaching a rare volume in the habitually reserved ambiance of Mrs. Murphy's well-appointed studio.

Finding the Voice

I tell this story because it marks one of the first times I ever *really* expressed myself with music. I combined the muddled Bach of my formal music-lesson training with a snappy Blues cadence culled from the pick-up truck tape-deck soundtrack of my small town existence, and the cheeky result was my own voice: gloriously crying out the triumphant solution to my disastrous predicament.

Much later in life this incident was further illuminated for me by the words of composer and educator Stephen Hatfield, offered at a choral conducting workshop: "The thing to remember, ladies and gentlemen," he declaimed, in his inimitable, dramatic style, "is that there are as many different ways to be musical, as there are different ways to be beautiful." *My* way to be musical, or beautiful through music, was not by performing, but by composing.

As I analyse this experience now, I recognize the resonating feature, a theme central to my complex and cherished relationship with the arts: I was *finding my voice.* I was discovering my unique musical instrument – my means of creative self-expression. That particular piano recital stage provided me with the opportunity to fling part of myself out into the world. The captive audience was a sounding board that returned the echo, allowing me to consciously hear and recognize the joyful clamour of my own artistic self-expression.

The search to find my voice was not easy; there were serious obstacles along the way. I was primarily frustrated in my musical attempts at creative expression by my insufficient performance technique. As I sat that fateful day at Mrs. Murphy's Steinway grand I had effectively painted myself into a corner; an attentive audience waited with baited breath, and my wretched fingers gave me nothing to say. Then, suddenly, miraculously, I found another way to speak. The adversity of my situation squeezed the utterance from me as surely as a generous behind descending on a fully inflated whoopee cushion.

Becoming a Composer

> At the age of twelve my mother took me to see the film *Amadeus*, about the life of Mozart, and I realized quite forcefully what I wanted to be when I grew up. I would become a composer. I stuck with my piano lessons throughout high school. Mrs. Murphy encouraged me by supplying me with manuscript paper and listening politely to my inventions, but seemed at a loss as to what else she might do to support my desire to compose.
>
> I had been singing in church choirs since the age of eight, and along with Mrs. Murphy's piano lessons I learned, through my high school music program, to play the clarinet and saxophone. Simultaneously pursuing a less formal approach to musical development, I played keyboards in a rock/reggae band and taught myself to play guitar. Keen to expand my musical life even further, I connected with the school drama department's musical theatre productions and learned to sing in a new style.
>
> In my teens I began composing in earnest. My most successful piece was a work for a stage full of synthesizers, sequencers, drum machines, and a gigantic monolith loudspeaker (that my drama teacher found for me amongst the abandoned treasures in the school's basement bowels). I had composed a medley of Christmas carols. I also wrote a slew of pop songs that I learned to record and produce with a 4-track tape recorder.
>
> When I went to university an undergraduate degree program in music finally provided me with the opportunity to receive formal training in composition, which was a treat. I maintained my thespian interests by acting in extra-curricular theatre productions, and composing incidental music. I continued to write pop songs, and composed two pieces for children's choir, ably performed by my little sister's community chorus. My crowning achievement was a five-minute choral work, bravely supported and interpreted by my university choir.

> My postgraduate career did not have an auspicious beginning. I received resounding refusals from the Universities of Toronto, Victoria (where I am now a tenure-stream faculty member), and McGill, before I finally received late acceptance into the Master's Degree program in Music Composition at the University of British Columbia.
>
> I arrived in Vancouver at the end of August, my first time ever visiting the mythical lotus land. The day after I arrived I awoke early, not yet having adjusted to the time difference (or the different pace of life). I walked down to the ocean which was a pleasure that never failed to thrill me – (I could wake up and walk down to the *ocean*!) and was offered a boiled egg by an elderly Chinese woman collecting shellfish. I felt like a six-year-old on Christmas morning – everything was magical. I took the bus to the University of British Columbia which was at the top of a mountain, overlooking the ocean, and spent two hours trying to convince a piece of paper that I knew all there was to know about music history. Then I walked down many, many steps to Wreck Beach, which is infamous, and took off all my clothes until I was as naked as everyone else. What a place!
>
> Dr. Stephen Chatman was assigned to guide my development as a composer. In my first lesson, we fell to discussing piano playing. My teacher made an off-hand remark, which I have never forgotten . . . "As composers," he opined, "I think we are often more interested in playing music slowly, so that we can understand how the piece was put together." My mentor had no way of knowing, but his words penetrated my consciousness and exploded there like fireworks. That second person plural pronoun, that 'we,' included *me*. As far as Dr. Chatman, a real-live, professional, publishing composer, was concerned, *I* was a composer too! Up to that point I had never thought of myself as a *real* composer, and that I could be included in the category was more significant and resounding to me at that moment than any accolades I had received before or have received since.

I truly felt I had an identity – an identity that appealed to me immensely. I threw myself into the joyful work of learning to become a composer, and experienced the most exhilarating years of my life. I remember the heady moment when the university choir director asked me to compose a piece for a special performance at the new chancellor's residence. I recall the goofy camaraderie when running into Bruce, a fellow composition student, who was coming into his lesson as I was going out. We realized we were both carrying pencils behind our ears. "I think it's a composer thing," my colleague offered. From that moment forward, whenever I was in the music building, I *always* carried a pencil behind my ear! When my university choir toured Germany I was billeted with a local composer – Carsten. I was intensely impressed with my host; he taught music theory at the university, he had a room full of MIDI and audio recording equipment, listened to Renaissance music in the morning and the *Zap Mammas* at dinner, quoted Stockhausen, drank in cafés, and was, of course, German. He was probably *related* to Johann Sebastian Bach! Carsten's English was impeccable, but for some reason he stuttered when he spoke it. Our concert featured one of my compositions. Walking home afterwards, Carsten turned to me: "That piece was f-f-f-f-f—ing *good*!"

> I *am* a composer. I am not Mozart, or Beethoven, or even Richard Marsella, who wrote the banjo theme for *The Tom Green Show*. However, I have an identity, and that identity provides me with a voice – a way to express, through music, that which is uniquely me. I am a composer.

Exploring and Sharing the Voice

This narrative which describes my development as a composer, suggests the transformation of the *finding the voice* theme to one of *exploring and sharing* the voice. In describing my excited self-identification and collegial affirmation as a composer, the notion of *identity* surfaced. When I re-located to Vancouver, I embraced the new environment around me. It seemed a land of magic, and wonder, the sort of place where I might take on an attractive new identity. When the opportunity presented itself, I leaped at the offer, and happily embraced my new composer persona. When I publicly shared my compositions, the response from musical colleagues was positive, and I began to believe in my new identity. I felt successful, and *valued* for the music I was making; the voice sounded good.

I still love to sing, and I play a variety of instruments regularly. But I have become increasingly aware that performing does not offer me as rich a vehicle for self-expression; performing music composed by others does not allow me to share *my* voice. I have long been frustrated by the inability of my limited instrumental and vocal technique to recreate the music I hear in my mind. I *knew* how that Bach sinfonia of my first anecdote should sound, but my fingers were traitors. Throughout my career as a singer – from eight-year-old choirboy through teenage rock star wannabe, from earnest music theatre crooner through university art song interpreter – I *knew* the gorgeous singing I *intended*, but my instrument never quite sounded as I hoped it would. My clarinet, no matter how much I practiced, never gave up the sweet Benny Goodman-esque solos I yearned to play either, and the saxophone never really, *fully,* expressed what I had inside. As a performer, I became painfully familiar with the frustration of falling short of the communication I musically intended.

Instead, I learned to express myself musically by *composing*. I fooled around at the piano until I found notes and patterns that matched both what I wanted to say and what my fingers would allow. If there was something I wanted to express beyond my playing ability, it was not impossible; I could *write* it out for somebody else to play. When I picked up the guitar as a teenager, I was not nearly as good as my peers at imitating the latest hit song, so instead I made up my own. I wrote songs that fit my guitar playing capabilities and matched my voice and expressed what I so desperately needed to express.

During my undergraduate music degree I majored in piano until I grew tired of banging my head against the wall, trying in vain to let the music out. I switched to studying voice, and came *closer* to expressing what I wanted; but it was only when

I focused on composition that I really felt I was communicating and expressing successfully.

I distinctly recall the rehearsals of my first choral piece, as the choir soared up to the work's emotional climax. I felt something I had never felt before. The musicians around me were recreating *my* world – *my* voice was sounding throughout the hall, communicating elegantly and chillingly *exactly what I intended*! The sounds that I heard in my mind's ear were finally brought into existence, by means of black marks on a page and the good-natured willingness of my choir director and fellow singers. My own true voice was singing, a composite of forty-five glorious interpretations of my musical ideas, flung out into the concert hall – and that voice sounded *gorgeous*. *This* was aesthetic experience. I was overwhelmed, slightly nauseated by a swelling in my chest and throat, and I felt incredibly grateful to the community of musicians who had made this experience possible. They allowed me to hear *my* music, which I could not realize on my own. My need to express myself was, at last, *fulfilled*. This was my epiphany.

The applause at the end of a performance, the affirmation of my socially accepted status as a composer – the confirmation of my *identity* – is the icing on the cake. The possibility of connecting with a performer or listener, of providing the means for an emotional, aesthetic, or spiritual response is simply magical, mystical – a lucky by-product of my work which I can only treat with reverence, for I have no clear understanding. I once had an audience member stop me after a performance of one of my pieces. "Thank you so much! That was..." She struggled to find words: "I felt the presence of God." How can I understand that? I can only feel joyously flabbergasted and more than a little overwhelmed. But being able to hear the music of my mind, my own voice, no longer locked away uselessly inside me but finally free to take wing – *that* is my kind of fulfilment.

Negotiating and comprehending the terms of my relationship with music has brought me to a solid understanding: my ability to engage in the creative act of composing has enriched my life immensely; it has given me the opportunity to express myself, and to learn about myself. Composing allows me to *explore and share the music of my own voice.*

High School Music: Silencing Voices

> My high school music program offered me very little opportunity to exercise creativity or explore self-expression. I played clarinet in a performance-driven band program. I recall once taking advantage of some class downtime to teach my stand partner a duet I had composed. She played the top part, I played the bottom, and it really sounded pretty good. Ms. Drew smiled politely, and asked us to take out *Jingle Bell Rock.*

At no point during my high school music classes was I encouraged to even *attempt* a musical composition. This form of creative self-expression was simply alien to my high school music teachers – it never seemed to occur to them to encourage such an activity. As a result, I always felt a certain detachment from music class. I felt alienated. Certainly I was there, emitting sounds from the end of my clarinet or saxophone, but I was only partly there. The sounds I emitted were representative of the thoughts and ideas of Sousa, Holst, or whichever composer we happened to be playing. Their music did not work for me as a vehicle to express what *I* had to say. Those notes told the world very little about me. I wanted, and I *needed* to send out my *own* music, but in my high school music program, as a composer, *my voice was silenced.*

I found playing clarinet in the concert band a highly un-musical experience. It quickly became apparent that taking initiative with any dynamic or rhythmic nuance was pointless; my voice was drowned out by the masses. I once soundlessly played an entire concert with a broken clarinet. We were on tour, and when I unpacked my clarinet before the concert I noticed it was badly cracked. I showed the director, who said there was nothing to be done – I would just have to pretend to play. By the end of the concert I had come to a rather disturbing realization: the fact that I was not actually playing made no difference to the band's performance at all. This realization was utterly disheartening. I felt there was simply no point in playing in the band. I felt as though my contribution was meaningless and irrelevant. While the school music program continued to provide me with social opportunities and high grades, I learned to abandon any expectations of aesthetic enrichment or opportunities for meaningful artistic contributions. Not only as composer, but also as a performer, *my voice was silenced.*

One day, while in grade twelve, I arrived in the music room early, and caught the tail end of a grade thirteen music class. A student was sharing her own music – a Sting song, *Russians*, was playing on the classroom stereo. I could hardly believe it. I had never had the opportunity to share my music in class. I was very jealous. I thought it was simply marvellous that this student was permitted to bring part of herself – her own identity – into the classroom. I could hardly wait until I was in grade thirteen. Unfortunately, the following year, when I was in grade thirteen, my teacher decided to axe that aspect of his program.

I felt jealous. I felt ripped-off. During my high school music classes I was never invited to share music that I listened to. How hugely important is a teenager's personal music library? How important as a tool for discovering and sharing self-identity? How simple but wonderful to have that music legitimized and valued through a few minutes of music class air-time? Without inviting us to bring in and share our own listening choices our teachers ensured that the chasm between school music and student music (what many of us referred to as 'real' music) remained deep, wide, and unbridgeable. It was as though my music – my listening – simply did not count; it had no value in the school music context. As a listener and sharer of music, *my voice was silenced.*

To be fair, it is highly unlikely these teachers were aware that they were silencing my voice; at the time, I was not aware of it myself. I imagine their teaching choices were informed by their own understandings of what mattered in music class – an idiosyncratic amalgam of what they had experienced in their own music learning, tempered by what they had most valued and what they felt they were best at teaching, and then re-defined by the pressures of curriculum, community, administration, and colleagues. And I expect there were many in my classes for whom this program of music teaching and learning was just right. So how can a music educator provide opportunities for every voice to sing when there are so many unique voices in every class?

I do not pretend to have the answer. Howevver, I have a working hypothesis, which is that learners need to have a variety of opportunities to meaningfully express themselves through music. They need to have many diverse opportunities to play and sing, to listen and discuss, and to compose music. Learners need to believe that there are many ways to be musically beautiful, and they need a teacher who will help each individual explore and identify how she can be musically beautiful. That is how I try to let the voices sing. And this hypothesis is informed by a careful analysis of my own experiences of music teaching and learning. My experiences which are filtered by thoughtful reflection, help me to teach, and I hope, to enable others to learn.

So that is how I begin as a teacher-educator. I encourage my students who are future music teachers to tell and analyse stories of their own experiences of music teaching and learning. I encourage them to use their developing understandings of their own experiences and of those around them to shape their future practices. I encourage them to analyse the stories: to identify what was good and not so good about the music learning experiences. I invite them to compare their experiences and their perceptions of those experiences with those of their colleagues, encouraging them to realize that a music learning experience that was joyous for one student may well have been disastrous for another.

And I benefit hugely from the stories and understandings my students share with me, and use them to continue to develop my own understandings and practices as a teacher and a teacher of teachers. And that helps me to understand my own stories in new ways, and so I share more. I tell a story, for instance, about a teacher whose methods worked for me, and for many like and not so like me. I highlight in my story what it was about his teaching that helped us.

High School Drama: Encouraging Voices

> When I entered high school, as gawky and geeky in braces and fluorescent socks as any teenager could be, I was introduced to the world of theatre. Mr. Duff ran our high school drama program. He was an enabler; he went to enormous lengths to encourage and foster the creative voices of his students. Mr. Duff was quite shy, a background man, who did everything he could to ensure that students were front and centre.
>
> As a drama class project, a group of us boldly decided we would stage *The Return of the Curse of the Mommy's Revenge,* an obscure un-published musical that one of our group had seen performed at a local resort. Somehow, Duff, as we all called him, found us a copy of the script and a very loosely sketched-out vocal score. My job, as 'musical director' was to figure out how the songs were meant to sound, and come up with instrumental accompaniment. Duff built me a loft above the drama room storage space where I could spend the classes working, uninterrupted, on the music. He provided me with a

synthesizer, drum machine, and a 4-track tape recorder. Then he left me to it. I figured out musical accompaniments to go along with the vocal lines, composed original scene change music and underscoring, orchestrated everything for synthesizers and drum machine, produced a pre-recorded back-up tape for use during performances (heavily influenced by the pop music of the group, *Depeche Mode*), taught the music to the cast, and our show was a hit. That summer, Duff decided to remount the show with his own theatre company and to take it on tour to local resorts. He paid me five hundred dollars to use the back-up tape I had created.

Duff was an enigmatic teacher. He had six pairs of identical black corduroy cargo pants, and six identical white buttoned shirts. This ensemble was accessorized with thick, red suspenders. He found the outfit practical, and preferred not having to make the mundane daily decision of what to wear. Another of his oddities was his bizarre and wonderful music machine. He constructed it from a Yamaha DX7 synthesizer, a child's undersized Casio keyboard, a primitive sampler, organ foot pedals, a Leslie speaker, a drum machine, mysterious and ancient amplifiers, effects boxes, volume pedals, miles of patch cords and cables, and a slew of other gadgets and gizmos which he would add or subtract depending on (or often in spite of) the latest audio technology. This mass of bits and pieces was cobbled together with silicone and duct tape and wedged into a plywood case on wheels, complete with a fold-down padded bench for the operator. The whole thing could be folded up, packed into a trailer and transported from gig to gig. It had special handles so six of us could carry it up and down stairs.

I remember once playing my own keyboard synthesizer with him at some music night or other. "Oh no!" I exclaimed in dismay, "I forgot my amp!" "No problem," said Duff, "Give me your patch cord." And he dove into the depths of his magic machine, inserted the business end of my patch cord... somewhere, and the annoying sound of my *Roland Alpha Juno 1* filled the gymnasium.

Duff could not read music. Instead, he learned the entire score of every musical we ever performed, and there were many, by ear. I recall him sitting at his music machine in the corner of the theatre, ostensibly supervising our rehearsal but actually learning to play *Oklahoma!* by listening to the Broadway cast recording with one tinny earphone plugged into an ancient tape deck, while the choreographer put us through our paces on the stage. He approximated entire orchestral accompaniments with flailing fingers and feet, often operating the lighting board, monitoring the body microphone mixing board, and calling out missed cues at the same time. He learned the skill of shifting keys at the drop of a hat to accommodate idiosyncratic adolescent vocal ranges, and he could sweeten the sourest voice with a healthy dose of reverb and a lush bed of synthesized strings. Of course, at the time, we all took this for granted, and made fun of him for playing the occasional wrong note.

> The most beautiful part of Duff's teaching was that he did all he did solely in order to provide opportunities for his students to shine. He made us feel like professionals as we strutted out onto the stage in front of the sets he had built and into the lights he had rented, and we heard our own voices loud and clear above his careful accompaniment, spilling out into theatres and gymnasiums and cafeterias invariably packed with excited and proud family, friends, teachers, and community.

This account introduces a new theme: the *enabler-teacher*. It indicates the paramount importance and value of the kind of teaching that enables students to *find, explore, and share their voices*. In Mr. Duff's drama program, students were provided with opportunities. He often most successfully accomplished this by stepping out of the way – providing the resources and then removing himself from the picture. In my case, the result was loud and vibrant creative self-expression, which in turn made me feel valued, and fulfilled, and gave me a sense of identity.

Duff the Enabler was highly significant to the development of my personal and professional lives. On a personal level he gave me opportunities to express myself musically and to be valued for that expression, which was huge for my self-esteem and huge in making me believe my musical self was worthwhile. On a professional level, he showed me how a teacher can step to the side and support students as they find, explore, and share their own voices.

When I crossed over and became a high school teacher myself, I was a music teacher. And I made many mistakes as I did not know how to enrich my teaching with the lessons Duff had taught me. I remember jealously gazing at the endless queue of students auditioning for my school's musical theatre production, in sharp contrast to our own department's dwindling choir. My music colleague shook his head, "I don't understand why more of those students don't come out for choir". Now, with the benefit of hindsight, I understand. In choir, ironically, we rarely gave them the chance to hear their own voices.

My Own Teaching: Seeking to Encourage the Voices

I vividly remember the words of my teacher, Lee Willingham, speaking to my class of pre-service music teacher candidates. "A teacher's job is not to teach subject matter – our job is not to teach music – it's to teach *kids*. And *we* have the opportunity to teach kids through music – isn't that wonderful?" As I teach students through music, my special area of interest, of passion, of love – is in helping students explore and share their own, unique voices. What I try to do is provide opportunities for students to express themselves through music. There are many challenges with this. How do I help students overcome all the frustrating hurdles and learn the technical skills they need to realize personally satisfying and fulfilling musical utterances? How do I help them believe they are capable of using music as a meaningful vehicle for self-expression? How do I overcome the limiting pre-conceived expectations (held by my students, colleagues, administration, community, and most dangerously *myself*) of what music class should be?

One of my first teaching assignments involved helping twelve and thirteen-year-olds learn to play band instruments. There were not many triumphs that year, but I learned the necessity of celebrating small victories. Soon-Mi arrived at our school from Korea partway through the year. She spoke no English, and was small, quiet, and extremely shy. Soon-Mi wanted to play the flute, and threw herself into the task with great energy. A few weeks after she arrived, her grade eight class squawked and honked its way through a playing test. When Soon-Mi played, I almost heard the clunk of thirty-four jaws dropping. Her flute playing was gorgeous: strong, brave, expressive and clear. Most of the other students were not even aware she existed, her voice always so deeply buried beneath complex issues of culture, language, uncertainty, and fear. Through the sound of her flute, Soon-Mi communicated more about herself than we had learned in any other way.

Next, I taught music in a high school. Andrew showed early promise in my grade nine band class. He arrived from China part way through the semester, but quickly overtook the other students. He played the clarinet with a technical facility that left the rest of the section in the dust, and I could sense his increasing boredom with the course material. One day he lingered in the music room after school. Shy with his limited English, Andrew waited until the other students had cleared off before addressing me.

"Mr. Bolden…what is that?" He pointed to a poster on the wall, depicting a band of successful professionals (doctors, lawyers, etc.) proudly announcing their continued interest in music by sitting for this promotional piece of music education propaganda, instruments in hand. I did my best to explain as much.

"No…what is *that?*" Andrew indicated a bass clarinet, cradled in the arms of a smiling African American stethoscope-wearing health care professional.

We found Andrew an old, dusty bass clarinet at the back of the baritone sax cupboard, and he took to the instrument like a duck to water. It became an important part of his identity at school; he was the guy that played the jumbo-clarinet, and played it really well.

Andrew was also a wizard at matters of music theory, and keen to compose. Although composition was my own passion and favourite means of self-expression, I had only dabbled in teaching it. I was still very much a novice. My most successful composition-fostering moment took the form of loaning Andrew a bootlegged copy of music notation software. He came back with a brilliant clarinet quartet. Andrew, a recent immigrant to Canada, was hampered in matters of communication not only by his lack of English, but also by a natural disinclination to waste words. In contrast, his composition was a beautiful, dark, rich, complex, and unique expression, featuring a dazzlingly virtuosic bass clarinet cadenza. Andrew told us much more about himself by sharing this composition than he ever did by means of verbal communication.

> More recently, I instructed a first-year class of music education majors. One of their assignments involved composing a piece of music. I questioned students afterwards about their experience of the assignment, and one response sticks in my mind.
>
> Question: *What is there about your composition that makes it distinctly your own?*
>
> Rita: The rugged minor key just screams… RITA!

The account of my experiences with these students contains the now familiar themes: *finding, exploring,* and *sharing* voices. It is this part of my music teaching that I value most – helping students to express themselves through music. My role, in these instances, was as an *enabler-teacher*. Ironically, I achieved success by doing very little. I adopted the model I had observed with Mr. Duff in high school; I provided the resources and got out of the way. With Soon-Mi I provided a flute and a method book. She took them home and figured out how to play – I had virtually nothing to do with it. Similarly, with Andrew I provided a musical instrument that caught his fancy and a piece of software; the rest was up to him. With Rita I described the composition assignment parameters and offered models, then dictated a due date.

Listening for the Voices

Unfortunately, and inevitably, I have not always been successful in my fostering of student composers. Amongst my attempts, disappointments and teaching failures abound. I recall with particular frustration Karen, desperately excited to share her composer's voice. Having sought my guidance late one afternoon with a jumble of notes and ideas in hand, she left disheartened and dissatisfied with my feeble ability to guide her process. 'Brilliantly' prepared lessons in composing have often rewarded me with little more than a bevy of incomplete assignments and a class full of frustration and disinterest. I realized I needed to learn more about enabling students – about helping them to find and explore their voices. Students want to express themselves in different ways. How could I help them to develop their longed-for ways of expression?

The stories that I have shared here have greatly influenced my belief that it is immensely valuable to learn the skill of self-expression through creating. As a music educator, I try to provide my students with rich opportunities for creative music making. My experience has led me to believe that composing, often neglected in school music programs, is a particularly rich vehicle for students to explore and share their own, unique voices. Through diverse composing opportunities, students can have the chance to express themselves in many different ways. To help a student learn to compose is to acquaint that student with magnificent possibilities for personal expression.

I wish for young people to have the chance to compose; indeed, music students *deserve* this opportunity. Much of my motivation is personal – I have found composing to be deeply emotionally and aesthetically fulfilling. I desire for young people to have the opportunity to experience a similar sense of fulfilment. I know they will not all be as interested, or enjoy composing as much as I do, but I believe with all my heart that all students deserve the chance to try it out.

Composing a Piece of Research

And so I decided to learn more about teaching composing, hoping to share that knowledge with other teachers and help them to help their students to compose. I conducted and composed a piece of research – my doctoral dissertation: *Teaching Composing in the Classroom: What Teachers Know.*

My examination of the literature indicated to me that researchers in this area had rarely sought the knowledge of practicing teachers. This seemed a missed opportunity to me. I decided to learn about teaching composing by accessing the knowledge of teachers who were doing it. Accordingly, I employed a multi-site qualitative case study methodology to explore and analyze three secondary school teachers' personal understandings of their teaching-composing practices. I developed three separate case studies, each one representing the participant's personal knowledge of teaching composing. The rich knowledge revealed in each case study subsequently informed the development of a cross-case substantive-level grounded theory to explain the teaching-composing process as carried out by my participants.

Throughout the research process I drew from my understandings of narrative inquiry. Researchers working with narrative methodology collect and tell stories about people's lives (Connelly & Clandinin, 1990), because stories provide the means of communicating rich and complex data. It occurred to me that narrative, as a means of understanding and representing through stories, had immense value in seeking to share in and understand teachers' knowledge of the teaching-composing phenomenon.

Listening to Teachers' Voices

People learn from and through stories. As a principal means of collecting data I encouraged my participants to tell stories. I shared my own stories in order to trigger their stories. I focused on episodes and single events directly related to the teaching of composing, but also encouraged my participants to relate stories from beyond the classroom context. My goal was to elicit the participants' knowledge about teaching composing by tapping into whichever stories might be relevant; I collected stories about the participants' past and present experiences of music, composing, learning, and teaching both inside and outside schools.

This particular study was also designed to allow a focused period of concentrated scrutiny – a detailed glimpse into each teacher-participant's teaching-composing environment. I spent between five and eight days with each teacher in their schools and classrooms, and so gained understanding of the unique contexts of their teaching-composing practices and knowledge. I aspired to Connelly & Clandinin's (1985, 1986) use of narrative methodology to concentrate on teaching episodes and the teachers' unique knowing of classroom situations. To help me make sense of my time with the participants in their schools and classrooms I wrote my own stories – field notes describing and interpreting my observations and experiences.

Exploring Teachers' Voices

People learn not only by listening to stories, but also by creating and sharing them. In order to analyse and interpret the data I engaged in re-storying: writing field texts in a literary fashion as a means of intimately engaging with the data and so heightening my understanding of it. Narrative inquiry recognizes the value of bringing an artistic sensibility to the observation, understanding, interpretation, and representation of people and events.

Narrative methodology also guided me to learn the participant's *own understandings* of the stories told (Connelly & Clandinin, 1990). It is essential that participants have a voice in the research relationship in order to ensure their understandings are accurately represented. I shared and discussed the data I collected and my analyses of it with my participants, working always towards a shared understanding of the teacher's knowledge.

In addition, narrative methodology suggested a prominent role for my *own* knowledge of the teaching-composing phenomenon. My personal history, rich in knowledge and experience of composing, teaching, and teaching composing, was an integral element of the knowledge development the study represents. Of necessity and by design, this research was significantly informed and influenced by my own personal perspective as a learner, educator, and composer. My background provided me with a highly appropriate and discerning lens for examining the phenomena surrounding the teaching of composing in music classrooms. My knowledge helped to shed light on the data; its analysis was illuminated by my own teaching, composing, and teaching-composing experiences.

Sharing Teachers' Voices

Narrative is not only a tool for collecting and analysing data, but also a vehicle for conveying both data and analyses in a way that is rich in communicative possibilities. As a means of representing findings, I shared my re-storied field texts. As I unpacked the data I did not limit myself to an expository style of writing. The linguistic freedom allowed me to represent the participants' words, descriptions of their practices and classroom realities, and my own reflections and analyses in a text designed to engage readers and enable them to both benefit from my insight and draw their own conclusions about the data. My goal was to capture and illuminate vivid pictures of the teaching-composing phenomenon, thereby offering readers the prospect for resonant understanding – an opportunity to connect the research to their own experiences and knowledge, and to their own stories.

Musically Enhanced Research: A New Methodology

While working on my doctoral dissertation, I was also working on the development of an entirely new way of doing research, and exploring a less cautious, more experimental, and more exciting response to my developing understanding of educational research. During my doctoral studies I took two courses that were especially influential to me. Both courses made the connection between research and stories, identifying that it is possible to develop new and valuable knowledge by seeking, sharing, and analysing stories. In the first course I was encouraged to tell stories about my own experiences of teaching and learning. I was also encouraged to contact and seek stories from former educators who were important to me. The second course was a course called, *Research and Inquiry in the Arts*, where I was encouraged to reflect on the ways that my experiences with and of art influenced my understanding of the world, and introduced to arts-based research. There was much within these courses that resonated with me, particularly the notions that:

- people learn from and through stories
- people learn not only by listening to stories, but also by creating and sharing them
- art can be a vehicle for developing understandings – not only when people experience art, but also when people engage in creating art
- art can tell stories in ways that expository telling cannot – art can express the ineffable

I wondered: How could I incorporate these understandings into my own research? How could I use my artistic skills to create new knowledge? How could I wear my three hats at once – composer, teacher, and academic? Arts-based research was, and still is, a young field. As such, it seemed to me that the doors were wide open for exploring new possibilities, the challenge there to expand existing educational research paradigms. How could I meet this challenge? How could I draw from my own unique experiences, abilities, and understandings to listen to, explore, and share the voices of research participants?

Then I heard something quite remarkable on the CBC (Canadian Broadcasting Company) radio. In 1999, Toronto composer Adam Goddard won the Prix Italia for Radio Documentary. His music documentary, *The Change in Farming,* used as source material, interviews that Goddard had conducted with his grandfather, a retired Ontario farmer. Henry Haws, over ninety years old, had a rich repertoire of stories to share and considerable yarn-spinning technique. Goddard took the tales and wove them together with original electronic and acoustic music into a brilliantly illustrated narrative tapestry. Goddard set his grandfather's words within repetitive rhythmic structures, capitalizing on the old-timer's musical speaking voice to suggest the pitch and rhythm of complementary motifs. The music, thus inspired by tonal inflections and natural rhythmic cadences of the story-telling voice, seemed to evolve organically from the spoken words. Through this music Goddard was able to introduce his own voice, commenting on and audio-illustrating his grandfather's anecdotes.

When I first heard this radio broadcast, I was captivated. I wrote to the CBC, requested the cassette recording, and listened to it many times. The work resonated with me – I found the combination of storytelling and the music that grew directly from it extremely engaging. I loved the concept of Adam Goddard reverently using his own composer's voice to build a pedestal for the valued chronicles his grandfather had shared.

Although I had worked as a composer for some years, when I began studying at the University of Toronto I had very little experience composing electro-acoustic music. I seized the opportunity to enrol in a computer music course. At the other end of the music building, while exploring narrative research methodology as part of my studies in music education, I was encouraged to interview a former teacher. The recording of the interview with Mr. Duff itself was engaging to listen to, and it was a small leap to combine these two aspects of my current learning (educational research and computer composition) to produce an Adam Goddard-like 'musically illustrated interview'.

I chose a brief two-minute segment of the interview that I found particularly resonant. Mr. Duff's anecdote brilliantly captured the contrasting styles of two of his music teacher colleagues: Suds (visiting with his band from a school across town) and Stan, teaching just down the hall. The more I immersed myself in creating the musical illustration of this narrative, the more I felt connections with the training I was acquiring in my educational research classes. While grappling with qualitative research methods I was learning to recognize and pull themes from narrative accounts with the intent of rendering the themes explicit and commenting on them in reflective prose. Back in the electro-acoustic studio, narrative themes swam to the surface as I worked with the audio recording of the interview, becoming more apparent with each repeated listening. I realized the themes I had identified through repeated listening could be translated into musical themes, or motifs – motifs consisting of digitally manipulated and musically rendered audio chunks designed to capture the essence of the interviewee's words and ideas, and representative of my understanding of them. Then, instead of discussing the themes in prose, I placed them within a musical context, juxtaposing or connecting them with other themes/motifs, and weaving the musical motifs in and out of the participant's recorded words. I began to see strong potential for work of this nature within the field of educational research.

My efforts musically enhancing the interview allowed me to synthesize my educational understanding with the expression of my musical understanding. My compositional work with and around the audio recording of the interview amounted to a very thorough and particular analysis of that data; I noticed things and reached understandings of words and ideas within the interview segment that would, otherwise, have remained buried.

In my musical representation of the findings in the audio document (Bolden, 2008), I was able to suggest particular connections and ways of perceiving the data that were designed to lead listeners to unique and illuminating understandings. In this representation the participant's unique voice is not only captured, literally, but also enhanced with musical illustrations. The connections between my own author's voice and Mr. Duff's are apparent in my simultaneous musical commentary. With the musical choices I made to illustrate my participant's narrative and comment on it, I demonstrate my understanding of his words.

In the process of conducting my musically enhanced research I had cause to repeatedly hear and reflect on the words and meaning my participant shared – to listen to his voice. I developed my understanding of his words as I transformed the captured audio into a musical composition. This process served as a method of analysing the data, and a highly effective means of exploring his voice. I then communicated the understandings I gained in my musical treatment of the source material. The infinitely powerful vehicle of music was at my disposal to direct emotions, suggest connections, and invoke personal commentary. It also allowed me to amuse, entertain, and, most importantly, engage listeners in the final product which is a musical composition where the voices and understandings of both my participant and myself are shared.

CAROLE RICHARDSON

14. HEARING MY VOICE WHILE LISTENING TO THE CHOIR

Opening Measures

For someone who, early in life, wanted only to perform and never to teach, my world has been, and continues to be, rich with educational experiences. My undergraduate degree in voice performance and my subsequent artist diploma work did enable me to perform but it was, ironically, through those very experiences and my need to make music with others that I was inexorably drawn to teaching. After acknowledging this and completing undergraduate and graduate degrees in education, I continued the journey that would take me to and through choirs and ensembles, Canadian and Caribbean classrooms, and collaboration with other artists and educators to where I currently collaborate and interact with others in a teaching position with an undeniable "rightness of fit" (Goodman in Eisner, 2002, p. 75).

As an Assistant Professor of Curriculum Methods in Music at a small Northern university in Canada, I engage preservice teachers in music education and conduct many of these students in a choir that sings for the sheer joy of singing. To describe myself is challenging. My autobiographical journey has taught me that the way in which I perceive myself is often very different from the way in which others perceive me; nevertheless, I know myself as being organized in all aspects of my life and as being passionate about music; teaching it, teaching about it and being immersed in it. My husband and I, who are both university professors at Nipissing University in North Bay, Ontario, live busy, messy lives with our three wonderful and entirely unpredictable children, aged 8, 15, and 20. Daily, through laughter and tears, we interrupt each other to tell the stories which define who we have been, who we are, and who we will become.

My experience, as a woman with many of the accompanying roles (mother, wife, sister, daughter, friend), and as an artist, teacher, teacher educator, and lifelong student is that, regardless of what we name it, story is the way in which we make sense of our lives and the way in which we weave our contextual experiences into the holistic personal narrative that tells us and others who we have been, who we are and who we might become. After many years of university training in music, in education and years of teaching others, it was not until I was asked to tell my story to myself and to someone else that I was able to see and hear it as my own – to own it. It has been through autobiographical and collaborative narrative inquiry that I have ultimately reconnected with and re-conceptualized the role of music in my life, and, as with drawing (Klee, Matisse in Montgomery-Whicher,

M. Beattie (Author/Ed.), The Quest for Meaning: Narratives of Teaching, Learning and the Arts, 233–250.

2002), the very act of writing our experiences changes the way in which we see things. The journey itself and the revelations experienced as a result of the journey have enabled me to understand that I consistently experience the greatest musical and personal joy through and within collaboration with others both while performing and teaching. The realization that, for me, true musical freedom has always existed within the context of making music with others has enabled me to recognize and articulate that my teaching artistry exists in creating the context for others to experience musical joy through collaboration.

We often do not truly come to know and understand ourselves until we see and hear our voices in our printed words. In the same way that I do not grasp the essence of something until I attempt to communicate it to someone else, I cannot claim to know a song until I have sung it. What follows then, are my earliest reconnections to my story within the themes that have come to sing for me in my autobiographical narrative and the narratives of others:

- Reflecting and Reconnecting
- Reframing through Relating to Others
- Re-imagining and Rehearsing Co-created Knowledge.

Autobiographical Writing: Reflecting and Reconnecting

I am twenty-one, and I am working through the final few months of my four-year Bachelor of Music in Performance degree. During my degree, I have learned that I am supposed to sing certain songs because I look and sound like a soprano and that whether or not I enjoy singing them doesn't really matter. I have learned that I have a "passagio", (Trans: a vocal break between registers) and, that despite my best efforts, it haunts me and hampers the bel canto singing that I so desire and that is so desired. I have learned that people are eager to label me, and I have learned to suffer my insecurities in crippling silence. On this night, as I stand in the wings anticipating the opening notes of this glorious music, none of this matters. There is a full house and we will be singing excerpts from Beethoven's only opera, Fidelio. By any standard, this opera is a masterpiece of the "rescue opera" genre. We all know we are too young to sing this music; we lack the maturity and depth of voice necessary to do justice to the majesty and sincerity of the music but the opportunity to perform this repertoire is a gift that we have gladly and passionately accepted.

> I am wearing a deep pink taffeta gown, my dearest friend and fellow performer is dressed in purple, and the two men are wearing tuxedos. Though usually nervous, I am looking forward to walking across the familiar worn wooden floor of the stage into the warmth of the lights; I am acutely aware of a physical need to let my voice soar through the notes of this quartet. The orchestra tunes, the house lights go down and the four of us walk to our places at the front of the stage. The conductor looks up from the foot of the stage and smiles at us, makes eye contact with his orchestra and raises his baton. The opening notes of the orchestra drift up from the pit and invite me, as Marzelline, to begin, alone, the vocal canon of this lush quartet. I breathe, and

> sing the opening melody, "Mir ist so wunderbar…" (Trans: A wondrous feeling fills me). As I finish this phrase, another voice joins mine, and then another and another. Together we swirl and soar through the rich harmonies and, for me, time is suspended. All that matters is how I feel as I sing this extraordinary music. It is, remarkably, a physical sensation and I gladly lose myself in the magic of the moment. I hear my voice and the voices of the others but it is the pure physical joy of singing this music that transports me. This sensation transcends everything for me, and I know, that despite my insecurities, I will, for now, continue to sing because I cannot imagine life without this feeling.
> (Richardson, 2004, Unpublished 'Musical Memories' Journal)

This story of musical memory and reflection, at the same time both joyful and painful, is representative of the musical conflict that was, for many years, the silent accompaniment to my life. Even as I read these words more than twenty years after this concert, I feel tears threatening as I recall the purity of that experience. The tears surprise me and cause me to reflect on their dual origins. They are summoned by the visceral remembrance of the beauty of the moment but also because music, which had early in my life provided me with joy and recognition, had become, during my undergraduate degree, something through which to suffer and to bear. Though outwardly I projected absolute musical confidence, personally and professionally, the tension between my unspoken understanding of my musical self and the way in which others viewed me musically ran darkly beneath every aspect of my life, effectively robbing me of my authentic voice; that voice which enabled me to sing and experience music joyfully unencumbered, and to speak with a clear understanding of my musician self.

Despite this deeply felt musical conflict, I continued to study and to sing for years after this performance because such moments of pure transcendence, inevitably experienced while making music with others, had always been enough to keep me believing in myself and the music for a little longer. Even these moments, however, were not enough to carry me through the physical exhaustion and emotional wasteland of my father's death. Combined with this loss, the years of silent struggle and self-doubt overcame me and I turned my back and walked away from singing. The journey back would not begin for two years and my life altering inquiry into understanding and reconstructing myself through music would wait for more than a decade. Only then would I begin to understand that even when I thought I had abandoned music, it continued to be a powerful force in my life and informed and enriched every aspect of my personal and professional worlds.

Collaborative Narrative Inquiry: Reframing Through Relating to Others

Though my return to music as the dominant melody in my life would begin with teaching and collaborating with others, my gradual understanding and ultimate joyful acceptance of my need for musical artistry within my life was finally realized through collaborative narrative inquiry with other artists/teachers/researchers. Through the conversations, discussions, interviews, listening to and telling stories, I came to embrace the musical dissonances in my life and to welcome them as integral parts of my musical identity. I understood that through visioning and re-visioning my story and collaboratively exploring my story and the stories of others, I was constructing my authentic self; the self that transcended labels and that was located at the centre of my every action or inaction both within and without my classroom and my life. I wrote to acknowledge and make my dissonances real and explored them with others as a way of understanding and validating them. In doing so, I was transformed by a feeling of intuitive recognition as the act of collaborating to re-vision my musical story resulted in me hearing my authentic voice, and, more importantly, recognizing it as my own. My words sang for me and I embraced them as my truth.

Professional Practices: Re-imagining and Rehearsing Co-created Knowledge

As a professor of preservice music teachers, the insights gained and my subsequent self-reconceptualization as an artist/teacher/researcher have encouraged and inspired me, in my classroom, to create the context for others to engage in joyful and authentic musical experiences. In order to make music joyfully and authentically with others, to truly teach others, we must first seek to understand and then to celebrate the voice that sings in the musical life stories that we bring to our classrooms. As their voices are heard amongst and by others, students are empowered, musically and holistically, to re-vision themselves and then to rehearse these pivotal understandings in consonance during an often dissonant year of paradigm shift.

The following narrative chronicles my personal journey of inquiry into the presence and meaning of music in my life. My world changed as I journeyed into the reconceptualization of my personal music; beginning with the simple joys, moving through the cold, grey landscape of seemingly losing my musical connection and the resultant serenity and accompanying insights of finding and nurturing it (and allowing it to nurture me, and through me, others) once again. Through my own autobiographical narrative journey where I reflected to reconnect, reframed through relating to others, and re-imagined and rehearsed my new understandings, I moved from solitary dissonance to collaborative consonance within my inquiry and my life. This rediscovery and re-storying of the musical themes running throughout my life has enabled me to bring artful knowing to collaboration with my students.

Music has always been a part of my life but it is only through writing about it that I have begun to understand the ways in which music has shaped me and my relationships with others. For many years, I considered myself as an entity separate from the music that surrounded me as a singer, a teacher, a conductor or an ensemble member. Though it has long been clear to those around me that I am a 'music person', I spent many years after university resisting this musical identity because to embrace it would mean embracing my feelings of vulnerability and uncertainty with regard to my abilities as a singer.

As a vocalist who plays piano passably, (it was my minor in university), there had been many times throughout my university life and beyond, when I enjoyed playing piano far more, and practiced piano far more readily than I did my singing.

I still tend to play piano when I need to be distracted from stressful situations or when I am grappling with difficult decisions. With my background, I was expected to sing well but if I played piano well, I was congratulated. Piano wasn't affected by a cold, there were no words to be memorized, I couldn't forget pitch relationships, I didn't have to find starting pitches and I didn't have to meet the eyes of my audience. Piano seemed somehow respectable, as was the playing of other instruments and one could distance oneself from it. No piano? Ah well, can't practice, then. Singing was different. I couldn't walk away from it, or blame anything on the instrument – I was the instrument. Every pore, every breath, every vowel, consonant, body movement and facial expression was mine; indistinguishable from me and undeniably mine. Though singing is as necessary to me as breathing, there have been many times when I have fervently wished to be able to put my voice down and walk away from it. And so the song begins…

MY SONG (A DA CAPO ARIA)

Section A in the Tonic Key

Melody One: Joyful Sounds – Reflecting and Reconnecting

> I think my story starts back when, as a toddler, I wore a top hat and my older siblings encouraged me to sing, *Oh, Sweet Pea,* in front of any audience that would listen.
>
> I am singing, with the black top hat on my head, in a large, sunny kitchen, with my family seated around the kitchen table applauding. I am the youngest by many years. My brother is nine years older and my sister is eight years older. I feel special, and as always, happy to have everyone's attention. The memory makes me smile and I can still sing some of the words,
>
> "Oh Sweet Pea, come and dance with me,
> Come on, come on, come on and dance with me."
> Tommy Roe
>
> …………………… (Richardson, 2004, Unpublished 'Musical Memories' Journal)

At least that's the way I remember it. Later, at the age of five, because I read well, the church choir director asked my mother if I would like to join the choir. I did join, and sang in that choir until I graduated from high school. I still go back and sing solos with the choir at every opportunity. My children have fretted through many Easter and Christmas Eve services because I was in the choir, when they wanted to be home eating chocolate or drinking hot chocolate in front of a fire.

It was at some point during those years that I realized that singing made me happy. Friends of mine resented those Friday afternoon choir rehearsals in our large, cold church hall. I looked forward to them. Being part of a choir, practicing or performing, it didn't really matter; the joy was in the singing. My career aspirations, however, were focused more on writing and journalism and it wasn't until halfway through my first year of a Bachelor of Arts degree that I realized I wanted/needed to be immersed in music and not relegate it to hobby status. My second year of university found me in the first year of a four year Bachelor of Music in Performance degree programme.

Melody Two: The Deconstruction of Joy – Reflecting and Reconnecting

I arrived supremely confident in my ability to sing and sing well, and to succeed in this programme. I had an entire youth behind me of succeeding at everything I tried (except for functions and relations – my father was a mechanical engineer and simply couldn't understand what I didn't understand). I had taken piano lessons, (with no accompanying formal theory instruction), for years, and had been admitted to the programme on the strength of a taped audition and some entrance theory tests. My lack of formal theory instruction was rather interesting in its genesis. My brother and sister, respectively nine and eight years older than me, had both decided to quit piano lessons because they hated the theory exercises. As a result, when I took piano, my parents, older and wiser, opted to avoid formal theory and I just learned to play anything that interested me. I took lessons for years and loved every minute of it, but my lack of theory background was to haunt me throughout my music degree.

My first real moment of uncertainty at my new university came in my sight-singing and ear-training class during the first week of school. Though I had done neither of these activities previously in my life, the confidence and yes, ignorance of youth led me to believe that, as with other new experiences, my seemingly innate ability to succeed at everything I tried would carry me once again.

> When the professor played, our national anthem, *O Canada,* on the piano and asked us to write it down on a piece of music manuscript paper, I, rather smugly, wrote the words. The girl next to me looked at my paper, laughed and asked me what I was doing. (Incidentally, we have weathered much together and still share our lives through expensive visits, long distance telephone conversations and e-mails.) As I looked at her paper and realized that she was writing the notes to *O Canada* on the staff on her manuscript paper, I was initially outraged: what a ridiculous expectation! How could they possibly expect someone to be able to do that? As I looked around the classroom at the other students all confidently writing out the notes to *O Canada*, the enormity of my lack of formal music background hit me, along with the realization that, perhaps this time, my arrogance or more kindly, my self-confidence, had taken me beyond my capabilities. After class, I ran back to residence, and, sobbing, told my boyfriend that I would have to quit as, quite clearly, I could not do this. Without a music background himself, he wasn't quite clear about what I had been asked to do, or why I felt I couldn't do it, but he said all the right things, convinced me that with a lot of effort I could do it, and reminded me that I had come here to sing.
>
> (Richardson, 2004, Unpublished 'Musical Memories' Journal)

I stayed. (I also married him four years later, right after graduation and we will celebrate our 26th wedding anniversary this year). I failed that course the first year and scraped by in first year theory, but by second year, with an immense amount of work, went on to be an average student at both. Every theory class, counterpoint assignment and form and analysis submission was a triumph that fed my need to validate 'just singing' and to prove that I deserved, despite my lack of formal background, to be in the programme.

I never intended to teach, so instead of applying to a Bachelor of Music in Education degree (four year) which would also have given me a teaching license, I applied only to Bachelor of Music in Performance degree programmes (four year). I only wanted to sing, to perform, so the idea of taking education courses - even music education courses – seemed almost wasteful; time that could be spent singing and practicing would have to be spent on something other than 'pure' music.

My lack of formal music background prior to beginning my Performance degree left me unprepared for the rigorous labelling of young singers. I apparently 'looked' like a soprano and was young, nineteen years old, had a reasonably light voice and so, I 'was' a soprano. I had never taken formal voice lessons and had gained all my singing experience from singing in choirs and working with a musical director in high school. Apparently I didn't breathe properly, and my high notes, though effortless, were unsupported and unconnected. My singing, which up to this point had been a thing of great joy to me, was being deconstructed, and with it went my considerable self-confidence and my perception of myself as a singer. I realized or was informed, that I had a 'break'. That meant that I had to work very hard to make a smooth transition from one vocal register to another. My 'vocalizes' and runs were bumpy because the quality of my sound changed around the E above C2. Throughout the remaining years of my degree, I was haunted by Es. I scrutinized every piece of repertoire that I was given for Es. I circled them, I counted them, I cried over them. Though everyone else raved about Schubert lieder and how wonderful it was, I preferred Schumann because I didn't have to sing as many Es. I asked my colleagues if they had breaks, and if they didn't I resented them. I was told that my break was high for a soprano, or was low for a soprano. I was told that if I supported my sound properly then I wouldn't have to worry about it. But worry I did, and it became something that was bigger than the piano every time I entered the practice room. And so, I coped, but I began to develop this image of myself as a beautifully wrapped but empty box. I looked like a singer when I stepped onto the stage, alone, to sing, but I began to believe that I wasn't really very talented and certainly couldn't do justice to the songs I was singing. I was certain that the audience would be disappointed at the sound that emerged from the beautifully wrapped package; that I would be recognized as a fraud.

In addition to the requisite solo recitals, I sang parts in operas, opera excerpts, the vocal ensemble, the university chorus, and performed duets, trios and quartets from famous works. In retrospect, I believe that it was the joy that I continued to experience while singing with others that kept me in the programme and set the stage for continued personal and musical growth. I enjoyed every rehearsal, every performance, and, if I close my eyes, I can still remember the absolute wonder of singing the quartet from Beethoven's, *Fidelio*, with orchestral accompaniment. I thought, at the time, that I was just happier blending vocally with other singers rather than baring my vocal inadequacies to the world. Given where life has taken me, I now know that was and is not true. I have continued to sing in choirs, start new choirs, and conduct choirs, and it was/is the ensemble and choral experiences that have shaped and still inspire my classroom practice.

Melody Three: Singing as Work – Reflecting and Reconnecting

When I graduated with my Bachelor of Music in Performance, I applied for entrance into a graduate Master of Music degree programme but I wasn't accepted. I took this in stride, as I was offered advanced standing in a three year performance diploma programme, and was accepted into the studio of a well known voice teacher. This gentleman was considered by some to be somewhat of a guru, and I was certain he would be able to help me overcome my break. By this time, my break had become such a focus for me that, when asked if I was a singer, I would answer, "Yes, but I have a break." There proved, however, to be no magical solutions and he, too, felt I was a soprano, so I continued with repertoire that I really didn't enjoy and to which I couldn't commit (too many E's). When my technical singing exercises did not help me to smooth over the ever present 'passagio', he sent me to a throat specialist; perhaps my vocal chords were physically damaged. I found myself hoping that they were so it would explain my inability to solve the problem myself and, hence, vindicate me. I had many private moments where I felt it would be a huge relief if someone told me I should not pursue singing as a career. With the relatively supportive environment of a small school of music gone, and the competitive environment of a large music school very much in evidence, my self-confidence plummeted further.

My first recital was fine, but not inspired and my voice teacher agreed, under protest, to let me work on mezzo soprano repertoire for my next recital. I fell in love with the entire programme and, E's notwithstanding, began to find some enjoyment in singing again. The tessitura of the pieces was comfortable, the drama of some of the cantatas moved me, and the beauty of the song cycles left me breathless. The music sang for me and I revelled in it. My marks for my graduate recital were only slightly higher than my first, but I was beginning to realize that it didn't matter – things were slowly coming back into focus and I was singing again for the right reasons. And so, I continued to take lessons after I graduated that were still painful because I couldn't do, technically, what he wanted me to do. However, when I was alone in the practice room working on repertoire, I was again experiencing the joy of singing. My break was still there but the mezzo soprano repertoire didn't exploit it or showcase it. My teacher always said that I was an enigma because I knew exactly what he wanted me to do but couldn't seem to do it. I continued to feel that I had a huge secret, that being that I couldn't really sing the 'right' way.

My parents were my biggest fans and they supported me unquestioningly throughout my life, though; secretly, I think they both wondered how singing could be a career. Shortly after my graduate recital, my father was diagnosed with cancer for the second time – this time it was inoperable. When he died a short but excruciatingly painful year later, I quit the voice lessons that I had half heartedly continued with after graduation, began working in marketing and walked away from music for two years. My ongoing vocal struggles and his death had exhausted me, and emotionally, I had nothing left with which to sing. My world stilled and I was thankful for the quiet.

Section B in the Relative Key

Melody Four: Time to Heal – Reflecting and Reconnecting

While I was working fulltime in marketing, I began to study part time in the graduate Master of Education (M.Ed.) programme. I was still very vulnerable musically and so majored in the History and Philosophy of Women's Studies. The attraction was twofold: it interested me greatly and it had nothing to do with music. I experienced feelings of relief and of regaining balance in my life as I allowed my musical self to retreat and rest, and was able to undertake graduate work without having to prepare for a recital and spend hours in a practice room. It was during this more relaxed period in my life that I became pregnant with our first child. Feeling curiously 'at home' in the Master of Education programme, I began to feel that my marketing job was mildly interesting but, increasingly, was becoming a background to the work I was doing in my Masters programme. When I left my marketing job to have the baby, I never returned. My husband was teaching and enjoying it immensely, so after spending some time at home with our daughter, and completing my M.Ed., I decided that I really did want to teach. I applied to a Bachelor of Education (B.Ed.) programme which would qualify me to teach in Ontario. I was accepted, I successfully completed the programme, and I started teaching the following September.

Throughout this two-year musical hiatus, I remember my mother constantly questioning me as to why I wasn't 'doing anything' with my music. I found these conversations very painful and they would invariably end with me angrily and abruptly leaving the room. In retrospect, I think that I became angry because she was openly asking the question that I was constantly asking myself and couldn't honestly answer. Though I felt the absence of music during that time, I also felt the absence of stress. When I quit my voice lessons, it was as though a huge load had been lifted off my shoulders. I no longer had to pretend to be a talented singer nor did I have to conform to someone else's vision of me as a singer. I did join a prominent church choir because, physically, I still needed to hear and feel my voice soar amongst the voices of others. I also continued to play piano when I had access to one, but in both cases, I only made music on my own terms. The what, the how and the when of making music was entirely up to me and I relished the freedom; including the freedom to define myself as something other than a singer. During these years, I became a business person and pushed the publically musical part of me into a tightly locked mental box as I spent two years working trying to convince myself that that was who I was.

I believe now that my musical spirit recognized that I needed time to heal, and that those two years allowed me step back and gain some control over that part of my life. Only then could I (and I did) make a conscious decision to let music once more, play an active and positive role in my life.

Section A in the Tonic Key

Melody Five: The Hallelujah Chorus – Reframing Through Relating to Others

When I started my preservice teaching degree in the Junior/Intermediate division, I needed to have a 'teachable' subject that was to be my area of speciality. With a Music Performance degree, the most obvious one was music, and I found myself back amongst musicians and greatly enjoying the 'music' talk. We were a small but eclectic group who travelled together from class to class: drummers, singers, organists, flutists, etc. As always, it wasn't enough to be a singer and a pianist; I had to spend short painful classes working on woodwind fingerings and torturing a violin. General and vocal/choral music classes were not in vogue; everyone was also expected to be able to teach instrumental music. It was during this year that I began to rebel against this notion, and to redefine myself as a singer. I realized, consciously for the first time, that I was tired of the need, either real or imagined, to apologize for the fact that I was 'only' a singer. I had spent years of my life, some of them very painful, working to become a better singer and musician, and I wanted to bring those skills and life experiences to the classroom – not struggle to play five notes on the violin. As always, the vocalists were called upon to sing Handel's *Messiah* at Christmas, and so our happy little group of musicians was asked to join the other music teachers to sing in the lobby.

> Finding myself beside a woman I didn't know, I began to dread the high notes, knowing that she would hear my break in full force, as the Messiah is full of E's. I was suddenly very aware that I had not sung seriously for some time and as a result, had not had the pressure of singing classical repertoire or worrying about my break for a long time. Up until now, this had provided me with a great deal of relief. I found myself wondering how my voice would sound after this extended vocal 'rest'. So, as the difficult passages, fraught with Es approached, I took a deep breath - and sang through them. Just like that, my break was gone. I soared through difficult runs, enjoyed every note – and felt like a singer, for the first time in a very long time. The panic of imminent exposure as a fraud and the two years of distancing myself from my obsession had combined to form a miracle cure. The idea of supporting my sound through proper breathing clicked. The bel canto singing that I had pursued, dreamt about, agonized over and coveted suddenly became a reality. I really was a singer.
>
> (Richardson, 2004, Unpublished 'Musical Memories' Journal)

Though I have thought about this often, and have always acknowledged it as a pivotal moment, I have never, quite honestly, intellectualized it too much. Deconstruction has never worked very well for me – what if I couldn't put it back together? Interestingly, no one around me had any idea that, musically, that moment changed my life, and it remains as a cherished turning point for me. I remember my frustration in attempting to make my husband understand how my entire musical outlook had changed, and had come back into focus. In writing about it, I began to realize that this was a moment of musical resilience for me. After six years of voice lessons had robbed me of much of the joy that I had always experienced through singing, two years without the pressure of *having* to sing had set the stage for me to sing joyfully once more. I continued to sing with my church choir and have been singing and teaching music ever since. That experience in the lobby of that building changed everything for me.

Melody Six: Choir as Pedagogy – Reframing Through Relating To Others

That sounds very much like the end of a story, but it was in reality, the starting point for the first chapter of my teaching life. I was hired to teach Core subjects (Language Arts, Math, Social Studies), and Drama in a middle school. There was an Instrumental Music programme in existence in the school, so as a vocal/choral person, I didn't teach Music for the first two years. I taught Core and Drama, and as the school population increased quickly with little added funding, the Music programme underwent a series of changes, and I was asked to teach some general music in a regular classroom. With students behind desks, no piano, and only a tape recorder as a resource, my programme was not inspired or inspiring. I was overwhelmed with planning for my core class, where, although they were not officially designated English as a Second Language learners, many of my students were new to the country and were struggling with the language, with the paperwork, and with the meetings. With all this, I did not devote any time to planning a coherent music curriculum for my students. We did sing-a-longs and some work with theory and rhythm. I dreaded every class and agonized inwardly over my desultory attempt at teaching to my passion.

Outside of the classroom, but still within in the walls of the school, it was a different story. By my second year, I had organized a choir and was surprised with a great response from the students. That year, we worked on only a few songs and sang them at the board music 'gathering'. This opportunity to perform as a group provided these students with something to which to aspire, and validated and valued an experience of which they were a part. It was this choir that also confirmed that I was a 'music' person within the school and the board, and for the first time in many years; I was comfortable with that designation.

During the second year of the choir, a colleague, an accomplished singer and pianist herself, had offered to help with the choir and we quickly became a highly effective team. The choir membership grew as did the support from within the school. Our continued success prompted the principal to ask us to write a school-based curriculum for the grades 6, 7, and 8 music programme. We were able to run the entire programme as a performance based choral classroom music experience. We were provided with outstanding administrative, student and parental support and the year culminated in concerts during which every student in the school participated. Bringing the outside success with my first choir into the classroom resulted in the authentic and joyous musical experiences that had been missing from my initial attempts at teaching classroom music. It enabled me to communicate my passion for singing and to encourage students to sing together. The students learned far more about music through performing and creating than they had while I was attempting to deconstruct the various elements in order to keep them and music at their desks. I learned that my musical joy was always related, in some way, to making music with others.

Melody Seven: The Joy of Shared Magic – Reframing Through Relating to Others

Midway through our third year with the choral classroom programme, I went on maternity leave for the birth of our second child. After returning, I began three wonderful years as conductor of a choir of students who auditioned from the area schools. Initially, I had philosophical issues with regard to auditions but realized that the process was not degrading nor was it organized in such a way as to embarrass any of the students. This was, essentially, a performance-oriented choir, and students who were not accepted were advised to continue to gain choral experience through their school choirs.

I felt a little insecure at the outset as the previous conductor was highly regarded by the students and within the community. We also had different musical tastes. I loved classic choral pieces but also wanted to choose music that would enable my students to celebrate their youthful energy and exuberance. After a few rehearsals, students who couldn't adjust to my style left the choir, and the remaining students, our accompanist, and I quickly committed to each other. During the three years that I conducted this group, I consistently had wonderful students, but my third year, I had a particularly outstanding group of young people – one of those groups of students that one always remembers; and the same wonderful accompanist who was also a composer. We all chose the repertoire together and had a full house for our final concert.

> Every song was a highlight. All those bright eyes were focused on me while I conducted, and every shining face showed the emotions that they were conveying so beautifully through song. When the concert was over and the audience applauded, I was almost annoyed that they had intruded upon this final moment that I was sharing with my singers. After the concert, we all lingered to speak to family and friends and to talk about the performance. Everyone had felt the same magic that I had felt; it had been a shared experience. We had communicated with each other and with the audience.
>
> (Richardson, 2004, Unpublished 'Musical Memories' Journal)

That concert still rings for me. When I left that summer to teach in the Cayman Islands, leaving that choir was a very difficult and emotional thing for me. Those children, that performance, and many others had taught me so much about myself. What I found so gratifying and a little surprising was that, as a singer, I had done a number of solo performances but it was that choral performance for which I conducted but didn't sing that I remember the most. My idea of creating and of performing changed when I realized that I could create the context for a moment of creation, rather than be the sole performer. I found it exciting that I could find such joy in nurturing the act of musical creation in others; that the Diva in me could so joyfully work on the periphery of the glow of the spotlight. And yet, given my early experiences with music, it should not have been so surprising to me. I had sung in choirs throughout my childhood, and though I had done many solo recitals, many of my most cherished musical moments derived from singing in ensembles and being part of a group of musicians. Though I had always thought that I enjoyed these shared experiences because I was insecure as a soloist, I am now able to value that preference as a truth. I make music most readily and with the greatest joy when I make it with and amongst others.

Melody Eight: Singing as a way of Belonging – Reframing Through Relating to Others

As the teaching climate worsened in Ontario in 1997, my husband applied for and was offered a teaching job in the Caribbean. We took leaves of absence, and relocated, with our two children, to a small Caribbean island. I was offered a teaching job as soon as we arrived on the island. As there was already an itinerant Music teacher, I was offered a core teaching position, teaching everything but Music and Physical Education. I was busy adjusting and helping my family to adjust to a new life, so I did not mind this classroom musical hiatus though it did help immensely that the school day was filled with song that centred on prayer. We started the day singing praises, sang a 'grace' before lunch, a 'thanks' after lunch and often ended the day with a song or two. Though I wasn't formally teaching Music, it provided me with the opportunity to sing with my students and, despite the differences in our backgrounds, gave us a much needed common interest. As a result of the itinerant Music teacher hearing me sing, I was soon conscripted, albeit willingly, by the National Choir, and so, I found a musical community outside of school – or it found me. My feeling of belonging on the island grew as I gained a sense of welcome and belonging in the choir. Performances and practices were filled with laughter and, musically, I bloomed in the warm climate of both the island and the choir.

Melody Nine: Helping Others to Find their Voice - Reframing Through Relating to Others

After two adventure-filled years in the Caribbean, we resigned from our teaching jobs and moved to a northern community in Ontario where my husband had been offered a job as a professor at a small university. Though I was pregnant with our third child, prior to leaving Cayman, I had already been offered part- time teaching work with both the local music studio and the university, via e-mail. I accepted both and founded a small children's choir, taught Elementary Music Methods in the evenings at the university, and began my doctoral studies.

After two years of part-time teaching at the university, I was offered the position of Assistant Professor of Music Curriculum Methods for the Junior/Intermediate division in the Bachelor of Education degree programme. Though I was sceptical of my ability to truly prepare my students to teach Music with only twenty four hours of classroom time, I was confident in my ability to communicate my passion for music, and to ensure that students enjoyed the time spent in my classroom. The challenge, given the diverse musical backgrounds of my students, would be to provide a programme meaningful to everyone regardless of their skill or comfort levels. It was at this point that I recognized that, as with my earliest years of classroom teaching, for anything meaningful to happen, I would first have to create a safe environment for my students; and actively ensure that my classroom would be a place in which they would be willing to take risks. I designed my course in a way that would allow my students to experience success with small, simple musical activities, always within a group dynamic, and that I would introduce basic musical concepts to those who had no prior knowledge, while situating the activities within a context of teaching for those who had prior musical experience. Every class included singing, lots of singing. As we sang, composed, and performed together that first year, we also laughed and learned from each other. We shared our past musical experiences, positive and negative, in order to help us all understand how the actions of a single teacher could resonate throughout a student's life time. All voices were heard and validated, and students began to understand that all of their musical experiences were valued; not just the positive ones.

Though there had been instances during my teaching career when I had actively regretted my decision to do a degree in performance instead of music education. However, within the context of teaching in the preservice classroom, I discovered that the four years I had spent entirely immersed in performing, understanding the dynamics of performance, and performance practice, had been instrumental in my evolving into a teacher; both of music and of teachers. The insecurities that I saw every day in my preservice music classroom reflected those that I had experienced during my performance years; though only those very close to me had been at all aware of my self-doubt. And so I shared teaching mistakes and triumphs and emphasized that I, too, had some musical insecurities. My willingness to admit to my musical shortcomings seemed to make some students more amenable to taking musical risks of their own. Autobiographical narrative had become an authentic and effective part of my pedagogy.

Though I had vowed to myself that I would concentrate only on this new teaching experience for my first year, by the second week of September, I found myself posting an invitation throughout the university for a student choir. At the first rehearsal, I asked for volunteers for an accompanist and talked about the prerequisite for joining the choir – the willingness, but no proven ability, to sing. There were approximately 20 students at the first rehearsal, and when word spread that you 'didn't have to be able to sing' to join, there were 40 students at the next rehearsal. As always, choir rehearsals, for me, were uplifting and re-energizing. Attendance was great and when, due to timetabling glitches, I had to disband the choir after our Christmas concert, many students were saddened and dropped by my office to tell me how much they missed it. Four years later, the choir is formally part of the timetable and we sing as part of the university's graduation ceremonies. One hundred and fifty students come to choir rehearsal once a week to make music together, and I am almost physically struck by the privilege of being able to create the context for musical creation. I marvel daily at the joy I derive from these shared music experiences.

CADENZA

Finding Voice Through Singing with Others – Re-imagining and Rehearsing Co-created Knowledge

Personally, I have experienced a musical resiliency of sorts. Early in my life, I sang with joy but came to learn that I was not 'doing it right'. This knowledge almost stripped the joy from my singing forever. It was my continued happiness in making music with and amongst others that ensured that singing and music retained some magic for me. I now work to help others understand that experiencing joy in music making *is* 'doing it right'.

As a singer, I have found that voice has always had special meaning for me in the literal sense, of course, but also in other areas of my life. While writing, it has become an abiding metaphor; not only my voice, but the voices of others. I sometimes consider myself indecisive because I can hear the truth in both sides of a disagreement. I listen for, and to all of the voices I can hear. I learned, while living in a culture different than my own, to validate the reality of others. People perceive events differently, but that does not lessen the impact those events have on their lives. Such is the nature of knowledge and experience. To mediate, to educate is to hear all of the voices, recognize those realities, and introduce different perspectives from which to examine them. It is our lived experiences that bring meaning to our words; our perceptions that colour our vision of our everyday lives. Try as we might (though why would we?) we cannot change this. Our lived experience is our narrative, and our narrative, told in our own voice, defines who we are. In order to know ourselves and understand our experience, we must listen for and to our own voices.

The idea of searching for my voice in songs, books, writing, and myriad art forms has become a certainty for me - a given. It's as though I need to see a part of myself reflected, in some way, in order for something to have meaning for me. I believe that this is also true for others. I see my frustration with almost all my past voice lessons reflected in the musical anxiety I see in some of the faces of my adult students. When my voice was not being valued, I was silenced by the perceived enormity of my 'break'. When I stopped allowing others to determine whether or not my voice had value, I sang again. It is my voice - both in print and while singing - that connects me to others and helps me to reconnect them to their own voices. Through my musical experiences, I have come to understand the value of empathy, the need to support and encourage others; the need that people have in their lives for the experiences in the arts, whether or not it is acknowledged. Though my art has influenced my teaching, it is now my teaching that defines my art: I create the context for others to engage in meaningful and joyful musical experiences. I've also learned that in my classroom, I work hard to engage and relate to those who have no voice, those who choose not to sing, and those who speak little and who scurry quickly out of class. As Lawrence-Lightfoot and Hoffman Davis (1997) say when speaking of portraiture, "we pursue the silences" (p. 11). In helping others to find their voices, my own teaching and writing voice has become stronger.

Cadence: Listening for the alto Line

My understanding of the world in and through music has both inspired and enabled me to teach empathetically and to listen for the motifs which run through the lives of others. Through teaching, I have learned that no two people hear the same thing when they listen to a piece of music; that what we take from music is a reflection of what we bring to music and this is as it should be. The experiences that we bring to new experiences will influence what we take from them.

Ultimately, in my search for resonance and truth within my own story, I did not seek to right what went wrong or deconstruct what went right. I wrote as a method of discovery. I wrote to understand how silences contributed to, and illuminated both the dissonances and consonances in my story; to engage the silencers and the silenced in such a way as to welcome them as the harmony to my ongoing melody line. I sought to accept and understand my experiences and now consciously bring these understandings to my teaching, my personal life, and the collaborative inquiries undertaken with my students and colleagues. The music of my life and in my life became the metaphor through which I would finally understand the enormity of its impact on my life.

I now understand that as a result of the constant presence of my life in music, in stories as in songs, I listen for the alto line. It comes from performing with others, conducting, and learning to both hear and sing the inner parts; those parts which make a song richly beautiful with their harmony. The alto line of a story, as with a piece of music, is that which sings just below the obvious; it is the subtext and the story beneath the story. Sometimes stated, sometimes inferred, but always present, the alto line enriches our tacit knowledge most, when it is heard in balance with the melody.

The alto line in stories must sometimes be pointed out to storytellers so that they can become aware of its potential richness within their narratives. It is this collaboration that enables the story teller and the story listener to construct a duet: two voices raised in song, weaving melody and harmony into a seamless song of music in life and life in music. I have learned, through music, to 'tune in' to the alto voices of others; to that which affects them without them being fully aware of it, to point out the silences and to gently encourage them to fill those silences with their own voices.

Through the ongoing re-visioning of my personal narrative, I have come to understand that my art, though not abstract, is never entirely concrete. I can never touch it, or point it out to another and say, "There is the result of my art". It lives in the moments of music, in the echo of voices raised in song, in the aesthetic of the pure beauty physically felt when singing a note, and in the handwritten student notes such as this one that was left on my music stand,

> I just wanted to sincerely thank you for teaching us music this semester. You instilled confidence, enthusiasm and determination in all of us, beginners and the more experienced. Traditionally, Monday and Friday mornings are the hardest to pull myself out of bed but they were days I looked forward to all semester. I've never had so much fun or learned as much in a classroom as I have in yours. (Personal note from a student, 2005)

My art is embodied in authentic musical and life experiences; those things which take us beyond ourselves and enable us to be part of something bigger. My autobiographical narrative inquiry into the role of music in my life has enabled me to understand that it is through music that I am able to create the context for others to experience authentic joyful music making. In the same way, my research enables me to work collaboratively with my participants to create the research contexts for them to hear their own voices as they explore music in their lives. My art and my research, then, intersect in the creation of a context for others to make music, to inquire into their musical understanding of themselves and through doing so, to experience the journey of this collaborative transformation.

As researcher and teacher, I understand and live my identity as authentic and multifaceted, my various roles embedded within and overlapping each other, with music as the passacaglia that simultaneously grounds and links the different aspects of my story and connects me with others. In this way, the music within me permeates all aspects of my life, including all aspects of this collaborative narrative inquiry. Through acknowledging my musical strengths and weaknesses, I am able to help others do the same, both musically and personally, in such as way as to help them to take a fuller understanding of themselves to their elementary and high school classrooms.

The words we sing and speak are the melody lines but the meaning with which we imbue them and the meaning we make from them are the alto lines, rich with the understanding of our life experiences and the timbre of our souls. Through my understanding of what music has wrought in my life, for I have, indeed, been shaped by and through music, I am able to bring these musical ways of knowing to my classroom, to my research and to my art. I do not compose, and hence do not 'create' in the same way that a visual artist or a composer or choreographer would. In this sense, I truly dwell in the borderlands of creation as through interpretation and teaching, I engage my artistry as I create by re-creating. My art exists within a spiral of researcher, singer, conductor and teacher. Music is ever-present but the context within which I am creating through re-creation determines whether music is the melody, the harmony or the accompaniment. It invariably enables me, in some way, to connect to the musical self, however acknowledged or ignored, that lies in the souls of others. This is the gift that music has given me through its sometimes dormant and sometimes very active presence in my life, the ability to touch the lives of others through 'musicking', and to create the context for musical transformation through shared meaning-making in collaborative communities both inside and outside of my classroom.

As I now reflect back on the work our group undertook from the outset of our course, *Research and Inquiry in the Arts*, I recognize that it sounded the first chord in the aria that ultimately became the quest for my own voice. Having to articulate my myriad understandings of the role of music in my life and having others point out the silences amongst those understandings precipitated my exploration of the ways in which my voice had been silenced, literally and metaphorically. I wrote, and rewrote, and gradually came to know that when I articulated my experiences on paper or to someone else, I felt validated and valued. Ultimately, I was able to recognize and embrace the ways in which music had always been, for me, a different way of knowing and, through making narrative inquiry part of my pedagogical practice; I now encourage my students to do the same. The insights gained from writing the narrative, and reconnecting with my life experiences, enabled me to articulate my understandings in my own voice, written, spoken, and sung, and to celebrate that experiential knowledge as truth.

What resonates most strongly for me throughout my narrative, story, is my continuing quest for my own voice; both literally and figuratively. I searched for my own sound, for my voice, and finally heard it when I stopped listening for a solo. It was only then that I understood that it had never really been silent. My voice had always been there, singing, and during the times that I just couldn't hear it, it was soaring safely and joyfully amongst the voices of others.

AFTERWORD

- If singing makes you happy, then sing. Don't worry about how you sound.
- Spend time with people who make you laugh and avoid those who make you angry. Anger makes us defensive and laughter breaks through our defences.
- Listen for the silences. There is so much to be learned from them. Often, those who need desperately to be heard are those who don't speak.
- Don't assume that you know what someone is thinking by the look on their face. Often, they don't know they have a look on their face.
- Helping someone to find their voice will make your voice stronger but gentler.

AUTHOR BIOGRAPHIES

Mary Beattie is Professor of Education in the Department of Curriculum, Teaching and Learning at The University of Toronto/OISE. She has also been visiting professor at Stanford University in California and at the University of Iceland in Reykjavik. Professor Beattie teaches courses in narrative and arts-based research and has presented papers, workshops and keynote addresses based on her research in narrative inquiry, arts-based research, teacher education and teacher development, in Canada, the U.S, Europe and Australia.

Born and raised in the west of Ireland, Mary holds a Doctorate and a Master's degree in Education from the University of Toronto, and a Master of Arts and Bachelor of Arts from York University, Toronto. She also holds a three-year Diploma in Education from St. Paul's College in Rugby, England with a specialization in Music and English Literature. Mary has been teaching graduate and preservice students at the University of Toronto/OISE since 1989. Prior to that she taught in public school classrooms for fifteen years, in Canada, England, and Ireland.

Professor Beattie is the author of many book chapters and articles in journals such as *Curriculum Inquiry, Educational Research*, and the *Asia Pacific Journal of Teacher Education.* She is a consulting editor of the journals *Curriculum Inquiry* and *Mentoring and Tutoring*, and is a former chair of *OISE Press*. In her current research she is exploring the nature and qualities of interacting narratives in the lives of educators who have longstanding practices in the arts and in secular spiritual practices. She is the winner of a number of teaching awards, and is the author of three books:

- *Constructing Professional Knowledge in Teaching: A Narrative of Change and Development.* New York: Teachers College Press, 1995.
- *The Art of Learning to Teach; Creating Professional Narratives*. Upper Saddle River, New Jersey: Merrill/Prentice Hall, 2007/2001.
- *Narratives in the Making: Teaching and Learning at Corktown Community High School.* Toronto: University of Toronto Press, 2004.

Benjamin Bolden is an associate composer with the Canadian Music Centre, and an assistant professor of music education at the University of Victoria, in British Columbia, Canada. His research focus is teaching composing in music classrooms. Ben holds a PhD in music education from the University of Toronto; a Master of Music in composition from the University of British Columbia; a Bachelor of Education Degree from the University of Toronto/OISE, specializing in Music and Drama; and a Bachelor of Music Degree from Carleton University.

As a classroom teacher, Ben has worked with pre-school and primary children in Taiwan, with elementary and secondary students in York Region, Ontario, and in Toronto, and with undergraduate and graduate students at the universities of Toronto and Victoria. Ben's compositions have been performed by many ensembles, including the Elmer Iseler Singers, Tapestry New Opera Works, the Victoria Civic Orchestra, the University of Victoria Wind Symphony, the University of British Columbia Singers, the University of Toronto Gamelan Ensemble, the Laurier Chamber Choir, the Talisker Players, the Vancouver Cantata Singers, the Vancouver Chamber Choir, and the Oriana Singers. Ben has been awarded commissions by the Ontario Arts Council and Laidlaw Foundation. His compositions are available from Cypress Publishing.

Angélique Davies is an early childhood practitioner, currently doing studies in the field of family support and pursuing an interest in adult education. She has an undergraduate degree in Social and Cultural Anthropology from the University of Toronto, a diploma in Early Childhood Education from Mothercraft College and a Master of Education from the University of Toronto/OISE. Angélique also has an Advanced Certificate in Early Childhood Music Education from the Royal Conservatory of Music in Toronto. She is a member of the Early Childhood Music Association of Ontario and has edited their newsletter, *Music Time*, for six years. She has published various articles about music in early childhood in trade journals such as the ECE LINK and Interaction, and in a peer refereed journal, *Canadian Children*. She delivers a workshop called *Musical Links to Literacy* to early childhood practitioners throughout Toronto and the surrounding area. Her interests include cooking, reading, creative writing, knitting and playing soprano recorder. Angélique lives in Toronto with her husband Frank who is a marvellous musician.

Catherine Dowling is an Assistant Professor at Ryerson University School of Interior Design in Toronto. She graduated from the Architecture School at the University of Waterloo following a degree in Interior Design from the University of Manitoba in Winnipeg, and study at Arcosanti in Arizona. She has recently graduated with a Master of Education from the University of Toronto/OISE.

As a watercolour artist and architecture thesis student, Catherine travelled to Canada's Arctic with the Polar Continental Shelf Project. With her husband, she has travelled to several countries to study architecture, and a future trip to Japan is currently in the planning stage. Catherine's continuing studies include making pottery at Dundas Valley School for the Arts. Her teaching experience includes presenting elementary school workshops, teaching at Fanshawe College Interior Design program in London, Ontario, and at the University of Waterloo, School of Architecture, in Ontario. Her shared professional practice, Lillepold Dowling Architects, is founded on design and construction excellence, and on constantly exploring the process of making, which most recently received an Ontario Association of Architects Honourable Mention for a Painter's Studio in Dundas, Ontario. She lives in Paris, Ontario with her husband, son, calico cat, and garden.

Masayuki Hachiya is an Associate Professor in the Department of Human Development at St. Thomas University, Japan, where he teaches curriculum courses in elementary art and early childhood education. His research interests include art education for teachers and students, the role of the arts in students' lives, and the relationships between children's play and art. Masayuki received his Ph.D. from the University of Toronto/OISE. He is the co-author of the book, *The Arts Go to School*, and has written articles on the teaching of art, the arts and children, and qualitative research.

Winifred Hunsburger graduated with a doctorate in education (ED.D.) from the University of Toronto/OISE in 2008. She is currently working as a strategic program leader and teacher mentor at an independent school in Toronto, Ontario, Canada. Winnie came to teaching and narrative research following careers in childbirth education, perinatal research and freelance writing. Her narrative inquiries have helped her to weave together the apparently disparate threads of her life and to understand how her experiences in the past not only shape and inform the teacher she is today – but also to understand how the themes and patterns ever spiral through even the smallest things she does. The writing of the educational narrative for this book has reminded her of the importance and power of narrative arts-based research.

Rae Johnson, PhD, RSW, RSMT is a Professor of Somatic Psychology who draws on her background in expressive arts therapy, narrative inquiry, and somatic education to help students explore the intersecting dimensions of arts education, social justice, and embodied experience. She is currently Chair of the Somatic Psychology Department at the Santa Barbara Graduate Institute, and was previously Director of the Body Psychotherapy Program at Naropa University in Boulder, Colorado.

Rae completed her doctoral studies in education at the University of Toronto/OISE. Prior to that she undertook graduate studies in expressive arts therapy, dance movement therapy, psychology, women's studies and social work. Her published works include numerous articles for journals in somatic psychology, a book on somatic education, and several poems. Rae is a registered social worker with the Ontario College of Social Workers, and a registered somatic movement therapist with the International Somatic Movement Education and Therapy Association.

Carol Lipszyc is currently an Assistant Professor at Plattsburgh State University, SUNY, teaching English Teacher Education and Creative Writing. She earned her doctorate in education at the University of Toronto/OISE. She has taught language arts at the secondary and adult re-entry levels for both first and second language learners. Before she qualified as a teacher of English as a Second Language (ESL) at Woodsworth College, University of Toronto, Carol was a professional singer with Canadian television and radio appearances to her credit. Her ESL/Literacy Reader, *People Express*, was published by *Oxford University Press* in Canada in 1996. Select poems, prose, reviews and articles have been published in *Parchment, Midstream, English Quarterly, Canadian Woman Studies Journal, and Cambridge Press U.K. Central* to her teaching philosophy, is her focus on liberating student voices.

Melanie Markin recently graduated with her Master of Education (M.Ed.) from the Department of Curriculum, Teaching and Learning at the University of Toronto/OISE. She completed her BA/B.Ed at Brock University, and has been teaching primary level French Immersion in the Halton District School Board (HDSB) for the past ten years. Melanie also has her Canadian Dance Teachers Association qualifications, and has taught for seventeen years at Cheryle Bodrug's Burlington Dance Company where she also continues to dance herself. Melanie also works as one of the summer choreographers for Burlington Student Theatre's Performing Arts Camp. A strong believer in the importance and value of arts education, she has written and presented professional development workshops for colleagues and new teachers, and is involved in the School board's drama/dance showcase and International Dance Day celebrations. If she is not teaching at school, the studio or camp you will likely find her dancing, doing yoga, reading or spending time with her amazingly supportive friends and family.

Michelle Pereira graduated with her Bachelor of Music, in voice performance in 1996. She completed her Master of Music at the Faculty of Music, University of Toronto in 1998. She has recently completed her professional qualifications as an elementary school teacher (B.ED.) at the University of Toronto/OISE. When she isn't pursuing scholarly activities, she enjoys going for walks, doing yoga, listening to music, painting watercolours, and reading for pleasure. She lives in Toronto, Ontario with her husband. On occasion Michelle can be heard singing.

Bob Phillips holds a Master of Arts in Curriculum Studies from the University of Toronto/OISE. He is immersed in his twenty-eighth year of teaching as Head of The Arts at Harold M. Brathwaite Secondary School, Brampton. Ontario. He is also a sessional professor in the Art & Art History program, at the University of Toronto at Mississauga/Sheridan College. Bob is also a practising artist whose creative passions include printmaking, acrylic painting, and drawing, as well as theatre, film, and collecting contemporary ceramic teapots.

Bob has taught preservice and inservice elementary and secondary teachers at the University of Toronto/OISE. He has served as president and honourary president with the Ontario Society for Education through Art (OSEA) and chair of the Arts Education Council of Ontario. He has published articles in the *Journal of the Ontario Society for Education through Art* (*JOSEA*) and in OISE's *ORBIT* magazine. His current research interests include abstract art, visual culture; social justice & queer pedagogy; assessment and evaluation practices. Bob lives in Stratford, Ontario with husband, Joseph, and their cat, Dante.

Carole Richardson is an Associate Professor of Curriculum Studies in Music Education in the Faculty of Education at Nipissing University in Ontario, Canada. She earned her Ph.D., M.Ed., B.Ed. and Artist Diploma from the University of Toronto, and her B.Mus. in Performance from Acadia University in Nova Scotia. Prior to arriving at Nipissing University, Carole taught general classroom music, and conducted award winning choirs in both primary and middle schools in Ontario and the Cayman Islands. Her research focuses on the importance of arts experiences in the lives of preservice teachers and the role of autobiographical narrative inquiry in preservice education. She is a continuous advocate for and promoter of the importance of student engagement in positive and authentic musical experiences. Her publications include *Walking the Talk* (Detselig/Temeron Press, 2008), and the soon to be released *A Long Way from Home: International Experiences of First Year Teachers* (Teneo Press) both co-authored with her husband, Dr. Warnie Richardson. After many years of talking about it, Carole is finally taking guitar lessons. Making her guitar sing is a challenge which she embraces joyfully.

Carly Stasko is currently completing her Master of Arts at the University of Toronto/OISE. Her research has focused on Holistic Approaches to Media Literacy and Transformative Timeless Learning. She is a self-titled Imagitator – one who agitates imagination, and an artist, activist, educator, writer, producer, and creative healer. As founder and director of the Youth Media Literacy Project for over a decade, she has visited various High Schools, Universities and community centres across North America, leading workshops on Media Literacy, Globalization, Independent Media Production and Creative Resistance. Working with school boards and non-profits including UNESCO, Carly has played an important role in both media literacy education as well as local and global media activism.

Carly is a former producer with Canadian Broadcasting Company's Newsworld's live debate show *counterSpin,* as well as the author of journalistic articles in books, journals and magazines. She first became interested in media as a young 'zine publisher and culture jammer. She is featured in the award winning documentaries *Culturejam* by Jill Shape and *Fierce Light: When Spirit Meets Action* by Velcrow Ripper, as well as in the international best-selling book NO LOGO by Naomi Klein.

MARY BEATTIE

EPILOGUE

Teachers

My mother sang softly as she worked.
I, small and eager trailed along,
Following the tune and all the words,
The sounds and tones that made the song.

I too, sang my part with nervous voice,
A child, but given an adult's role.
Over lowered heads and silent prayers,
Into words and notes, I poured my soul.

A cold rural schoolhouse would come alive,
In poems, I learned of Arctic snow,
I could feel the wind and the bitter cold,
In his voice, in the words, in my need to know.
(M.B., 1991)

The centrality of story and the arts in education, and the importance of imagination, creativity, and inquiry is emphasized throughout these chapters. In our different voices we tell of how they have enabled us to create and re-create the stories of our lives, to transform our ways of knowing and being, and to create meaningful connections between the personal, professional and scholarly aspects of our lives. We hope that our voices provide insights into the power of story and the arts in our individual lives, and promote increased understandings of the deep connections between the arts and education at all levels.

Throughout the book, the various voices show how the three kinds of dialogue – the dialogue with the self, the dialogue with others, and the dialogue between the dialogues – provide individuals with opportunities to hear and value their own voices and those of others, and to create new narratives for their future lives. They provide the reader with opportunities to hear human minds at work, and to see from each individual's unique perspective, the contours, complexities, challenges, joys and satisfactions of their inquiries. They provide glimpses into the unique features of these learners' quests for meaning and meaning-making processes, the creation and re-creation of their ways of knowing and being, and the development of their capacities to find meaning in something greater than themselves. They show that for each person, the process of becoming a whole human being is a unique and ongoing quest that is grounded in the past, present and imagined future of that individual's life. They also show that when individuals are willing to acknowledge that they have choices, they can work to create their own destinies, and can be the authors of their own lives.

The narratives throughout the book provide a wealth of evidence that one of the primary goals of all educational practices and programmes must be that students develop their own unique voices, the commitment to listen to the voices and perspectives of others, and the desire to stay connected to the source of their creativity and to the ongoing quest for meaning in their lives. They present compelling evidence for close supportive relationships and a collaborative learning community to enable learners to bring the whole of their humanity—their unique personalities, emotions, resistances, passions, preoccupations and purposes, as well as their intellects, intuitions and imaginations—to the exploration of the stories by which they live, the reconstruction of what they know, and the creation of new stories by which to live.

In their different ways, they provide insights into the ways in which a narrative, arts-based approach to pedagogy can provide students with the kinds of learning experiences and contexts that are necessary for the making of new meanings, the continuous creation and re-creation of the self, and of being here for good. They also show how it can provide students with the kinds of experiences necessary to enabling them to learn to think narratively, to engage in narrative self-study research, and to conduct narrative, arts-based research with others. As Eisner (2002) says in his inspiring book, *The Arts and the Creation of Mind,*

> The arts are among the resources through which individuals recreate themselves. The work of art is a process that culminates in a new art form. That art form is the recreation of the individual. Recreation is a form of re-creation. The arts are the most powerful means of promoting re-creation. (p. 241)

Meanwhile, it is hoped that the voices throughout the chapters can inspire and encourage readers to picture and explore your own stories and situations, to experience your feelings and thoughts more fully, and to imagine ways to create new narratives for your own future lives. Those of us who are blessed to have a creative engagement with life in our teaching, research and writing lives have the opportunity to share it with others. We can do this when the work we do enables others to create new stories for their current and future lives where they can make their own hopes and dreams come true.

May love be ever in your heart
May joy be yours to share—
And wherever your dreams lead you,
May contentment meet you there.

Old Gaelic Blessing:

APPENDIX 1

Learning through Stories: Loving the Questions

- How does your inquiry help you to explore your experience and the stories you tell and live in your life?
- How does it help you to explore and come to greater understandings of the inner landscape of your life?
- How have the various processes of the inquiry helped you to observe the patterns, themes, and narrative unities of your life?
- How has your inquiry enabled you to explore the stories that lie beneath the surface of the stories you tell and enact in your life, to question your assumptions and interpretations, and to re-construct your understandings?
- How has the inquiry helped you to explore the nature of the critical incidents in your learning journey, (positive and negative), and to explore your significant learning experiences in both formal and informal settings?
- How has your inquiry helped you to learn from all your experiences, the negative and the positive, to understand that mistakes and wrong turns are necessary processes in the learning journey, and to use what you know to learn what you need to know?
- How have these processes of inquiry and your ongoing quest for meaning, helped you to make connections between your existing knowledge and the knowledge of the disciplines in your field of study?
- How has it helped you to make connections between your inner purposes and external actions, and to make more significant connections between the personal, professional and scholarly aspects of your life?

Learning through the Arts: Art as Experience

- How has your inquiry helped you to explore the ways in which the arts have been a source of inspiration, clarity and meaning-making in your life?
- How has it helped you to explore your significant experiences with the arts in your life, and to learn from the stories of the difficulties and disappointments as well as the triumphs and joys?
- How has it helped you to understand the distinctive ways of knowing and being that you have learned through your experiences in the arts?
- How has it helped you to understand the ways in which you can take full advantage of the skills, sensibilities and interpretive abilities you have learned through the arts, in your personal, professional and scholarly lives?

APPENDIX 1

Learning about Research: Becoming a Narrative, Arts-Based Researcher.

- How has your inquiry helped you to learn about qualitative, narrative and arts-based approaches to educational research?
- How has it helped you to understand the ways in which artistically treated forms can enable you to represent your research in ways which can illuminate the complexities of learning, and other aspects of the human condition, and can also advance human understanding?
- How has the writing and re-writing of your educational narrative helped you to respond to the criteria for quality in qualitative research, and to:
  - provide insights and interpretation that transcend the particular, and contribute to knowledge;
  - provide a reader with a sense of recognition and believability;
  - provide the details of a learning journey which acknowledges the difficulties and disappointments, as well as the joys and surprises of learning;
  - provide fresh insights into learning, unlearning and re-learning which will provoke thought and understanding;
  - present the work in an invitational way, using your distinctive voice and expressive language that has aesthetic qualities;
  - exhibit clear themes with supporting evidence, and a solid coherent, narrative structure;
  - embody the qualities of authenticity, coherence, integrity, and plausibility.
- How has the inquiry and the writing of an educational narrative helped you to design a research proposal that is qualitative, narrative and arts-based, and that is meaningful to you in the context of the personal, professional and scholarly aspects of your life?

APPENDIX 2

Research and Inquiry in the Arts

The major activities of the Research and Inquiry in the Arts course are as follows:

1. *Writing A Narrative: Doing Self-Study Research*

The narrative is a piece of self-study research in which students explore the stories they are living out in their lives, and the stories beneath those stories. Through their self-directed inquiries, they document the details of their reflections on their direct experiences with the arts and the shaping influences of these experiences on their ways of knowing and being. Students provide each other with feedback to a draft of this work in the context of a writers' workshop, and help each other by applying the criteria for an educational narrative to each others' work. I provide written feedback to each student's penultimate draft by taking on the role of co-researcher and soul friend: asking exploratory questions, seeking further information and descriptions, listening for the resonances and silences, responding to emotional hints, helping to identify themes and patterns in the text, challenging the writer to imagine other possible interpretations and other possibilities, and urging deeper reflection and making more expansive connections.

2. *Thesis Presentation: Finding The Voices That Inspire*

Students select a recently completed qualitative thesis which inspires and informs their current and future research and which will make a contribution to their colleagues' understandings of qualitative, narrative, arts-based, holistic research. This activity is focused on helping students to connect their autobiographies and their educational inquiries. Students present the research orally to the class by describing the research questions, the conceptual framework, and the methodology. They present the findings and significant contributions of the research, and a personal account of what was learned by studying and analysing the thesis in the context of their own future research.

The use of the university library and Internet allows students to access a wide range of recently completed, unpublished theses that are conceptually and methodologically innovative, creative and scholarly. They are encouraged to find one which is informative and inspirational, and which will expand their thinking. In their presentations, they are encouraged to be creative and to use artistic methods to represent the research, and to explain how the work has influenced them. Following the presentation, questions and discussions follow in an environment of collaborative inquiry and meaning-making, an openness to diverse ideas and opinions, respect for all voices, and with a focus on the co-creation of meaning.

3. Oral Presentation: Something That Inspires Me: Something I Have Made

At the beginning of the course, after introductions and short biographical histories, students are invited to bring two items to the third class of the course: one item that inspires them, and something they have made. I explain that I will make this presentation the following week and will also bring something that inspires me and something I have made. Students will then have another week to select the items they will bring to the class, and to rehearse what they will say about the sources of inspiration in their lives, and the processes of creation as they have experienced them.

4. Partner Interviews, Constructive Feedback And Writers' Workshops

Students work in partnerships to interview each other about the issues and experiences they will write about in their self-study narratives. Interviews are taped and used to provide data for the ongoing inquiries. Students also provide constructive, written and oral feedback to each others' oral presentations in the class, and to the close-to final drafts of the two written assignments of the course: the educational narrative and the qualitative research proposal.

5. Oral Presentation: Make A Museum Exhibit Of Your Life

In the middle of the course, students make a presentation to the class of a variety of artefacts that are significant to them in their ongoing inquiries, to the exploration of the role of the arts in their lives, and to the connections they are making between the personal, professional and scholarly in their lives. The goal of the exercise is to have students access their ways of knowing through the aesthetic, emotional, moral, and spiritual aspects of their being, before the intellect, as is the usual was of beginning in graduate programmes. The timing of this exercise is critical and has consequences for the extent to which students will present the deeper levels of their inquiries. It is also essential that students know that they can participate in it at whatever level they choose. As the course facilitator, I have to gauge carefully the appropriate time in the course for this activity, and have found that the results of the activity are greatly dependent on the quality of the relationships and the community that we have been able to create in the classroom.

6. Designing A Qualitative Research Proposal

The final assignment is a research proposal for a qualitative research project. The proposal will outline the research question, the conceptual framework and methodology for the research, the contribution to be made to the academic field of study and the field of professional practice. This final assignment acknowledges that students are at different places in their programmes of study, and that their proposals will be at different levels of development. A synopsis of the educational narrative written as the first assignment for the course provides an introduction to this research proposal, and serves to situate the researcher within the proposed research.

7. *Course Readings*

This list provides the core readings for the course, *Research and Inquiry in the Arts.* These readings are supplemented by other books, book chapters and articles which are included in the references at the back of the book, and by new materials as they become available. As each individual's inquiry is a unique one, the core readings provide a place to start, the references at the back of the book provide additional resources, and the provision of specific resources, support and inspiration for each individual's inquiry takes place within the collaborative relationship between the teacher and the student.

Beattie, M. (2007/2001). *The Art of learning to Teach; Creating Professional Narratives.* Upper Saddle River, NJ. Merrill Publishing Company.

Beattie, M. "Beginning with Myself: My own Story of Teaching and Learning". In, *Constructing Professional Knowledge in Teaching: A Narrative of Change and Development.* (pp1-31). New York: Teachers College Press, 1995.

Barone, T. & Eisner, E. W. "Arts-Based Educational Research". In, *Complementary Methods for Research in Education.* (2nd Edition.) Jaeger, R. M. (Ed.) American Educational Research Association, 1997.

Bullough, R. V. & Pinnegar, S. Guidelines for Quality in Autobiographical forms of Self-Study Research. *Educational Researcher,* Vol.30, No. 3, pp13-21, 2001..

Clandinin, D.J. and Connelly, F. M. (2000). *Narrative Inquiry: Experience and Story in Qualitative Research.* San Francisco: Jossey:Bass .

Clandinin, D. J. &Connelly, F. M. Personal Experience Methods. In, Sage handbook of Qualitative Research. Denzin, N.K. &Lincoln, Y. S. (pp 413-427). Thousand Oaks, CA: Sage, 1994.

Eisner, E. W. (1991). "What the Arts taught me about Education". In, *Reflections from the Heart of Educational Inquiry; Understanding Curriculum and Teaching through the Arts.* Willis, G. &Schubert, W. H. (pp.34-48). Albany, N.Y: State University of New York Press, 1991.

Eisner, E. W. (1997/1991). *The Enlightened Eye; Qualitative Inquiry and the Enhancement of Educational Practice.* New York: Merrill Publishing Company.

Eisner, E. W. "Summary and Significance". In, *Arts and the Creation of Mind,* pp. 230-241), New Haven: Yale University Press, 2002.

Greene, M. "Art and Imagination", In, *Releasing the Imagination: Essays on Education, the Arts, and Social Change.* pp.122-133. San Francisco: Jossey-Bass, 1995.

Kilbourn, B. "The Qualitative Doctoral Thesis Proposal", Teachers College Record, v.108, n4, 2004.

Heaney, S. (1995) Crediting Poetry. The Nobel Lecture, from The New Republic, Vol 215, p.9-29, New Republic Inc, 1995.

La Bosky, V. K. "The methodology of self study and its theoretical underpinnings". In J.J. Loughran, M.L. Hamilton, V.K. LaBosky and T. Russell (eds). International handbook of self-study of teaching and teacher education practices (pp.817-870). Oxford UK:Elsevier Science Ltd, 2004.

Lawrence-Lightfoot, S. "View of the Whole; Origins and Purposes". In, The Art and Science of Portraiture. Lawrence-Lightfoot, S. & Davis, J. H. pp.1-16. San Francisco: Jossey Bass, 1997.

Miller, J. (1996/1988). The holistic curriculum. Toronto: University of Toronto Press.

REFERENCES

Abbey, S. (Ed.). (2002). Ways of knowing in and through the body: Diverse perspectives on embodiment. In *Proceedings of the 4th biannual summer institute of the Canadian association for the study of women and education* (pp. 244–247). Welland, ON: Soleil Publishing.

Abram, D. (1997). *The spell of the sensuous*. New York: Vintage Books.

Anderson, N., & Anderson, E. (2003). *Emotional longevity*. New York: Viking.

Anderson, R. (2002). Embodied writing: Presencing the body in somatic research, Part I, What is embodied writing? *Somatics: Magazine/Journal of the Mind/Body Arts and Sciences, 13*(4), 40–44.

Anderson, R. (2003). Embodied writing: Presencing the body in somatic research, Part II, Research applications. *Somatics: Magazine/Journal of the Mind/Body Arts and Sciences, 14*(1), 40–44.

Argyle, M., Salter, V., Nicholson, H., Williams, M., & Burgess, P. (1970). The communication of interior and superior attitudes by verbal and nonverbal signals. *British Journal of Social and Clinical Psychology, 9*, 222–231.

Atkinson, R. (1995). *The gift of stories: Practical and spiritual applications of autobiography, life stories and personal mythmaking*. Westport, CT: Greenwood Publishing Group.

Aurelius, M. (1997). *Meditations* (W. Kaufman, Ed.). Mineola, NY: Dover.

Banner, J. M., & Cannon, H. C. (1997). *The elements of teaching*. New Haven, CT: Yale University Press.

Barone, T. (1993, Autumn). Breaking the mould: The new American student as strong poet. *Theory and Practice, 32*(4).

Barone, T. (2001). *Touching eternity: The enduring outcomes of teaching*. New York: Teachers College Press.

Barone, T., & Eisner, E. (1988). *Arts based educational research*. In R. Jaeger (Ed.), *Complementary methods for research in education* (2nd ed., pp. 75–116). Washington, DC: American Educational Research Association.

Bateson, M. C. (1989). *Composing a life*. New York: Atlantic Monthly Press.

Bawarshi, A. (2003). *Genre and the invention of the writer*. Logan, UT: Utah State University Press.

Beattie, M. (1995a). *Constructing professional knowledge in teaching: A narrative of change and development*. New York: Teachers College Press, Columbia University.

Beattie, M. (1995b). The making of a music. The construction and reconstruction of a teacher's personal practical knowledge during inquiry. *Curriculum Inquiry, 25*(2), 133–150.

Beattie, M. (1995c). New prospects for teacher education: Narrative ways of knowing, teaching and teacher education. *Educational Research, 36*(3), 53–70.

Beattie, M. (2001/2007). SSHRC research project: The construction of professional knowledge: The interaction and enactment of narrative.

Beattie, M. (2004). *Narratives in the making: Teaching and learning at Corktown community high school*. Toronto, ON: University of Toronto Press.

Beattie, M. (2007/2001). *The art of learning to teach: Creating professional narratives*. Upper Saddle River, NJ: Pearson/Merrill Prentice Hall.

Beattie, M., Dobson, D., Thornton, G., & Hegge, L. (2007). Interacting narratives: Creating and recreating the self. *The Journal of Lifelong Learning, 26*(2), 119–141.

Bersson, R. (2004). *Responding to art: Form, content, and context*. Boston: McGraw Hill.

Birdwhistell, R. L. (1970). *Kinesics and context: Essays on body motion communication*. Philadelphia: University of Pennsylvania Press.

Bloom, L. Z. (1998). *Composition studies as a creative art*. Logan, Utah: Utah State University Press.

Bolden, B. (2008). Suds and Stan: Musically enhanced research. *Journal of Creative Arts in Education*. ISSUE 01.08. Retrieved from http://www.jcae.ca/08-01/bolden.html

Bookman, B. (2007). *Autobiographical writing response: The vocal word*. Unpublished student excerpt.

Bohm, D. (1998). *On creativity*. New York: Routledge.

Bruner, J. (1986). *Actual minds: Possible worlds*. Cambridge, MA: Harvard University Press.

Buber, M. (1965). *I and thou* (R. G. Smith, Trans.). New York: Scribner's.

Bullough, R., & Pinnegar, S. (2001). Guidelines for quality in autobiographical forms of self-study research. *Educational Researcher, 30*(4), 13–21.

REFERENCES

Butler, J. (1993). *Bodies that matter: On the discursive limits of sex.* New York: Routledge.

Cameron, J. (1992). *The artist's W\way: A spiritual path to higher creativity.* Los Angeles: Jeremy P. Tarcher/Perigee.

Capps, L., & Ochs, E. (1995). *The discourse of agoraphobia.* Cambridge, MA: Harvard University Press.

Capra, F. (1996). *The web of life: A new scientific understanding of living systems.* New York: Anchor Books.

Capra, F. (2002). *The hidden connections: A science of sustainable living.* New York: Anchor Books.

Carr, D. (1986). *Time, history and narrative.* Bloomington, IN: Indiana University Press.

Carse, J. (1986). *Finite and infinite games.* New York, USA: Free Press

Carter, C. (1993). The place of story in the study of teaching and teacher education. *Educational Researcher, 22*(1), 5–12.

Carter, K., & Doyle, W. (1996). Personal narrative and life history in learning to teach. In B. Sikula & E. Guyton (Eds.), *Handbook of research on teacher education.* New York: Simon & Schuster MacMillan.

Casteneda, C. (1987). *The power of silence.* New York: Simon and Shuster.

Clandinin, D. J. (1985). Personal practical knowledge: A study of teachers' classroom images. *Curriculum Inquiry, 15*(4), 361–385.

Clandinin, D. J. (1988). *Classroom practice: Teacher images in action.* London: Falmer Press.

Clandinin, D. J., & Connelly, F. M. (1994). Personal experience methods. In N. Denzin & Y. Lincoln (Eds.), *Handbook of qualitative research.* Thousand Oaks: Sage Publications.

Clandinin, D. J., & Connelly, F. M. (2000). *Narrative inquiry: Experience and story in qualitative research.* San Francisco: Jossey-Bass.

Cobb, E. (1997). *The ecology of imagination in childhood.* New York: Columbia University Press.

Cohen, H. (2007). *Autobiographical writing response: Lion King nights.* Unpublished Student Excerpt.

Cole, A., Neilsen, L., Knowles, J. G., & Luciani, T. (Eds.). (2004). *Provoked by art: Theorizing arts-informed inquiry.* Halifax, NS: Backalong Books.

Conle, C. (2000). Thesis as narrative or what is the inquiry in narrative inquiry. *Curriculum Inquiry, 30*(2), 209.

Connelly, F. M., & Clandinin, D. J. (1984). Telling teaching stories. *Teacher Education Quarterly, 21*(2), 145–158.

Connelly, F. M., & Clandinin, D. J. (1985). Personal practical knowledge and the modes of knowing: Relevance for teaching and learning. In E. Eisner (Ed.), *Learning and teaching the ways of knowing.* (National Society for the Study of Education Yearbook). Chicago: University of Chicago Press.

Connelly, F. M., & Clandinin, D. J. (1986). On narrative method, personal philosophy, and narrative unities in the story of teaching. *Journal of Research in Science Teaching, 23*(4), 293–310.

Connelly, F. M., & Clandinin, D. J. (1990). Stories of experience and narrative inquiry. *Educational Researcher, 19*(5), 2–4.

Connelly, F. M., & Clandinin, D. J. (1991). Narrative and story in practice and research. In D. Schon (Ed.), *The reflective turn: Case studies in and on educational practice.* New York: Teachers College Press.

Connelly, F. M., & Clandinin, D. J. (Eds.). (1999). *Shaping a professional identity: Stories of educational practice.* London: Althouse Press.

Cooper, N. (2007). *Autobiographical writing response.* Finding Philologos, Unpublished Student Excerpt.

Csikszentmihalyi, M. (1975). Play and intrinsic rewards. *Journal of Humanistic Psychology, 15*(1), 15.

Csikszentmihalyi, M. (1996). *Creativity: Flow and the psychology of discovery and invention.* New York: Harper Collins.

Csordas, T. (Ed.). (1994). *Embodiment and experience: The existential ground of culture and self.* Cambridge, England: Cambridge University Press.

Davies, A. (2004). *A second chance: The role of the arts in my life.* Unpublished Paper, Ontario Institute for Studies in Education of the University of Toronto.

Davies, A. (2006). Music education for early childhood practitioners: Moving music from the margins into the child care centre. *Canadian Children, 31*(2), 21–25.

Davies, A. (2007). *From workshop to collaborative work: A case study of moving music from the margins into early childhood classrooms.* Unpublished Major Research Paper. Ontario Institute for Studies in Education of the University of Toronto.

Davies, A. (2007). Donna's lullaby. *Music Time*, *18*(3), 8.
Dawe, N. (2004). *Unpublished course paper for research and inquiry in the arts*. Ontario Institute for Studies in Education of the University of Toronto.
Dawe, N. (2004). *Emerging as a music teacher: A reflexive self-study of the development of my professional identity*. Unpublished Paper.
Dewey, J. (1902). *The child and the curriculum*. Chicago: University of Chicago Press.
Dewey, J. (1916). *Democracy in education*. New York: Macmillan.
Dewey, J. (1934). *Art as experience*. Toms River, NJ: Capricorn Books.
Dewey, J. (1938). *Experience and education*. New York: Collier Books.
Dobson, D. (2008). *Transformative teaching: Promoting transformation through literature, the arts, and Jungian psychology*. Rotterdam, The Netherlands: Sense Publishers.
Doidge, N. (2007). *The brain that changes itself*. New York: Penguin.
Eakin, P. J. (1999). *How our lives become stories: Making selves*. Ithaca, NY: Cornell University Press.
Egan, K. (1986). *Teaching as story telling*. Chicago: The University of Chicago Press.
Eisner, E. (1972). *Educating artistic vision*. New York: Macmillan.
Eisner, E. (1976). Educational connoisseurship and educational criticism: Their forms and functions in educational evaluation. *Journal of Aesthetic Education, Bicentennial Issue*, *10*(3–4), 135–150.
Eisner, E. (1985). Aesthetic modes of knowing. In E. Eisner (Ed.), *Learning and teaching the ways of knowing* (84th Yearbook of the National Society for the Study of Education; pp. 23–36). Chicago: University of Chicago Press.
Eisner, E. (1991a). *The enlightened eye: On doing qualitative research*. New York: Macmillan.
Eisner, E. (1991b). What the arts taught me about education. In G. Willis & W. H. Schubert (Eds.), *Reflections from the heart of educational inquiry: Understanding curriculum and teaching through the arts* (pp. 34–48). Albany, NY: State University of New York Press.
Eisner, E. (1991). *The enlightened eye: Qualitative inquiry and the enhancement of educational practice*. New York: Macmillan.
Eisner, E. (1997). *The enlightened eye: Qualitative inquiry and the enhancement of educational practice* (2nd ed.). New York: Merrill Publishing Company.
Eisner, E. (2002). *The arts and the creation of mind*. New Haven, CT: Yale University Press.
Eisner, E. (2005). *The arts and the creation of the mind*. New Haven, CT: Yale University Press.
Elbaz, F. (1983). *Teacher thinking: A study of practical knowledge*. London: Croom Helm.
Elliot, J. (1991). *Action research for educational change*. Milton Keynes, UK: Open University Press.
Forester, E. M. (1910). *Howard's End*. Harmondsworth, UK: Penguin Books.
Frost, R. (1964a). *The complete poems of Robert Frost*. Canada: Holt, Rinehart and Winston of Canada.
Frost, R. (1964b). *Selected letters of Robert Frost* (L. Thompson, Ed.). New York: Holt, Rinehart and Winston.
Gadamer, H. G. (1975). *Truth and method* (translation G. Barden & J. Cumming, Eds.). New York: Seabury Press
Gal, S. (1995). Language, gender, and power: An anthropological review. In K. Hall & M. Bucholtz (Eds.), *Gender articulated: Language and the socially constructed self*. New York: Routledge.
Gilligan, C. (1982). *In a different voice*. Cambridge, MA: Harvard University Press.
Goleman, D. (1995). *Emotional intelligence*. New York: Bantam Books.
Greene, M. (1995). *Releasing the imagination: Essays on education, the arts, and social change*. San Francisco: Jossey-Bass.
Grumet, M. (1987). The politics of personal knowledge. *Curriculum Inquiry*, *17*, 319–329.
Hachiya, M. (2002). *Beginning with myself: My personal journey with the arts*. Unpublished Course Paper for Research and Inquiry in the Arts, Ontario Institute for Studies in Education of the University of Toronto.
Hachiya, M. (2006). *Beyond 'wonderful': Authentic interaction in the art classroom*. Unpublished doctoral thesis, Ontario Institute for Studies in Education of the University of Toronto.
Hague, A. (2003). *Fiction, intuition and creativity*. Washington, DC: The Catholic University of America Press.
Hanna, T. (1970). *Bodies in revolt: A primer in somatic thinking*. Novato, CA: Freeperson Press.
Hardy, B. (1968). Towards a poetics of fiction: An approach through narrative. *Novel*, *2*, 5–14.
Hardy, B. (1975). *Tellers and listeners: The narrative imagination*. London: Athlone Press.
Heaney, S. (1980). *Preoccupations: Selected prose 1968–1978*. London: Faber and Faber.
Heaney, S. (1988). *The government of the tongue*. London: Faber and Faber.

Hegge, L. (2002). *The ego and the ocean: Making connections between learning and teaching through arts-based inquiry.* Unpublished Course Paper for Research and Inquiry in the Arts, Ontario Institute for Studies in Education of the University of Toronto.
Heilbrun, C. (1988). *Writing a woman's life*. New York: Ballantine.
Hillman, J. (1996). *The soul's code: In search of character and calling.* New York: Warner Books.
Hirshfield, J. (1997). *Nine gates: Entering the mind of poetry.* New York: HarperCollins.
Holstein, J., & Gubrium, J. (2000). *The self we live by: Narrative identity in a postmodern world.* New York: Oxford Books.
hooks, b. (1994). *Teaching to transgress: Education as the practice of freedom.* New York: Routledge.
Hubbell, L. (2007, Winter). The disrupting fashion of J. Morgan Puett. *Surface Design.*
Hunsburger, W. (2004). Unpublished course paper for research and inquiry in the arts. Ontario Institute for Studies in Education of the University of Toronto.
Hunt, D. (1987). *Beginning with ourselves in theory, practice, and human affairs.* Cambridge, MA: Brookline Books; Toronto, ON: Ontario Institute for Studies in Education Press.
Ignatieff, M. (2000). *The rights revolution.* Toronto, ON: Anansi.
Johnson, A. (2001). *Power, privilege and difference.* Mountain View, CA: Mayfield Publishing.
Johnson, M. (1987). *The body in the mind: The bodily basis of meaning, imagination and reason.* Chicago: University of Chicago Press.
Johnson, N. (1996). *Moving toward healing: Using somatic education with survivors of childhood sexual abuse*. Unpublished manuscript.
Johnson, R. (1996). Untitled. *Contemporary Verse II.*
Johnson, R. (1997). Pisces to Aquarius. *Contemporary Verse II.*
Johnson, R. (2000). *Elemental movement: A somatic approach to movement education.* Boca Raton, FL: Universal Publishers.
Johnson, R. (2003). Knowing in our bones: The embodied knowledge of somatic educators. *Master's Theses Abstracts International*, Publication No. AAT MQ84219.
Kafka, F. (1988). *Diaries 1910–1923.* New York: Schocken Books.
Kermode, F. (1967). *The sense of an ending: Studies in the theory of fiction.* New York and Oxford, UK: Oxford University Press.
Kilbourn, B. "The Qualitative Doctoral Thesis Proposal", Teachers College Record, v.108, n4, 2004.
King, T. (2003). *The truth about stories: A native narrative*. Toronto, ON: House of Anansi Press.
Kirshenblatt-Gimblett, B. (1995). The aesthetics of everyday life. In S. Gablik (Ed.), *Conversations before the end of time* (pp. 410–433). New York: Thames & Hudson.
Knill, P., Neinhaus Barba, H., & Fuchs, M. (1995). *Minstrels of soul: Intermodal expressive therapy.* Toronto, ON: Palmerston Press.
Lassonde, C. Galman, S.& Kosnik,C. (2009). *Self-Study Research Methodologies for Teacher Educators.* (Eds.) Rotterdam/Boston/Taipei: Sense Publishers.
La Boskey, V. K. (2004). The methodology of self-study and its theoretical underpinnings. In J. J. Loughran, M. L. Hamilton, V. K. La Boskey, & T. Russell (Eds.), *International handbook of self-study of teaching and teacher education practices* (pp. 817–870). Oxford, UK: Elsevier Science Ltd.
Lawrence-Lightfoot, S. (1997a). A view of the whole. In S. Lawrence-Lightfoot & J. Hoffman Davis (Eds.), *The art and science of portraiture*. San Francisco: Jossey-Bass.
Lawrence-Lightfoot, S. (1997b). Illumination: Framing the terrain. In S. Lawrence-Lightfoot & J. Hoffman Davis (Eds.), *The art and science of portraiture* (pp. 41–59). San Francisco: Jossey-Bass Publishers.
Lipszyc, C. (2007). *Narnia*. Unpublished Poem.
Lompart, R. (2001). *Unpublished course paper for research and inquiry in the arts.* Ontario Institute for Studies in Education of the University of Toronto
Lompart, R. (2002). *Inquiry into cavern illuminare: Personal narrative and understanding through the arts.* Unpublished Course paper for Research and Inquiry in the Arts. Ontario Institute for Studies in Education of the University of Toronto.
Loughran, J. J., Hamilton, M. L., La Boskey, V. K., & Russell, T. (Eds.). (2004). *International handbook of self-study of teaching and teacher education practices.* Dordrecht, NL: Kleuwer.
MacIntyre, A. (1984). *After virtue.* Notre Dame, IN: University of Notre Dame Press.
MacMurray, J. (1954/1961). *Persons in relation.* New York: Harper and Row.
May, W. T. (1993). Teaching as a work of art in the medium of curriculum. *Theory into practice*, *32*(4), 210–218.

McAdams, D. P. (1997). *The stories we live by: Personal myths and the making of the self.* London: Guilford Press.
McEwan, H., & Egan, K. (Eds.). (1995). *Narrative in teaching, learning, and research.* New York: Teachers College Press.
McKniff, S. (1998). *Trust the process: An artist's guide to letting go.* Boston: Shambhala.
Mechem, S. R. (1998). *Healing: A journey forward after a crisis.* In L. Rogers (Ed.), *Wish I were: Felt pathways of the self* (pp. 133–140). Madison, WI: Atwood Publishing.
Miller, J. (1994). *The contemplative practitioner: Meditation in education and the professions.* Westport, CT: Bergin and Garvey.
Miller, J. (2000). *Education and the soul: Towards a spiritual curriculum.* Albany, NY: State University of New York Press.
Miller, J. (2001). *The holistic curriculum* (revised and expanded ed.). Toronto, ON: OISE Press.
Miller, J. (2004). *Educating for wisdom and compassion.* Thousand Oaks, CA: Corwin Press.
Miller, J. (2007). *The holistic curriculum* (2nd ed.). Toronto, ON: University of Toronto Press.
Miller, R. (1990/1997). *What are schools for? Holistic education in American culture* (3rd ed.). Brandon, VT: Holistic Education Press.
Nakagawa, Y. (2000). *Education for awakening: An eastern approach to holistic education.* Brandon, VT: Foundation for Educational Renewal.
Noddings, N. (2003). *Happiness and education.* Cambridge, UK: Cambridge University Press.
Montgomery-Whicher, R. (2002). Aesthetic experiences. In M. van Manen (Ed.), *Writing in the dark: Phenomenological studies in interpretive inquiry.* Langston, ON: The Althouse Press.
Moore, T. (1992). *Care of the soul.* New York: Walker and Co.
Moore, T. (1993). *Care of the soul: A guide for cultivating depth and sacredness in everyday life.* New York: Harper Collins.
Moustakas, C. (1990). *Heuristic research.* London: Sage.
Nachmanovitch, S. (1990). *Free play: Improvisation in life and art.* New York: Tarcher/Putnam.
O'Donohue, J. (1997). *Anam Cara: Spiritual wisdom from the Celtic world.* UK: Bantam Press.
O'Donohue, J. (2003). *Divine beauty: The invisible embrace.* UK: Transworld Publishers.
Palmer, P. (1993). *To know as we are known: Education as a spiritual journey.* San Francisco: Harper.
Palmer, P. (1998). *The courage to teach: Exploring the inner landscape of a teacher's life.* San Francisco: Jossey-Bass.
Pearse, H. (1992). The lost art of pedagogy: An exploration in three parts ~ part one. *Canadian Review of Art Education, 19*(1), 60–63.
Pinar, W. (1975). Search for a method. In W. Pinar (Ed.), *Curriculum theorizing: The reconceptualists* (pp. 396–414). Berkeley, CA: McCutchan.
Pinar, W. (1980). Life history and educational experience. *The Journal of Curriculum Theorizing, 2*(2), 159–211.
Polanyi, M. (1958). *Personal knowledge: Towards a post-critical philosophy.* Chicago: The University of Chicago Press.
Polkinghorne, D. E. (1988). *Narrative knowing and the human sciences.* Albany, NY: State University of New York Press.
Read, H. (1958). *Education through art* (3rd ed.). London: Faber and Faber.
Ricoeur, P. (1984). *Time and narrative* (Vol. 1). Chicago: University of Chicago Press.
Ricoeur, P. (1985). *Time and narrative* (Vol. 2). Chicago: University of Chicago Press.
Ricoeur, P. (1988). *Time and narrative* (Vol. 3). Chicago: University of Chicago Press.
Richardson, C. (2006). *Collaborative consonance: Hearing our voices while listening to the choir. A collaborative narrative inquiry into the role of music in the lives of seven preservice teachers.* Unpublished Doctoral Thesis, Ontario Institute for Studies in Education of the University of Toronto.
Richardson, L. (2000). Writing; A method of inquiry. In N. K. Denzin & Y. Lincoln (Eds.), *Handbook of qualitative research* (2nd ed.). Thousand Oaks, CA: Sage Publications Inc.
Rilke, R. M. (1996). *The hour is striking. The book of hours.* New York: Riverhead books.
Rosen, H. (1986). The importance of story. *Language Arts, 63*(3), 226–237.
Roy, G. (1970). *Where nests the water hen.* Toronto, ON: McClelland and Stewart
Rubin, L. J. (1985). *Artistry in teaching.* New York: McGraw-Hill.
Sarason, S. B. (1999). *Teaching as a performing art.* New York: Teachers College Press.

Scholes, R., & Kellogg, R. (1966). *The nature of narrative*. New York and Oxford, UK: Oxford University Press

Schon, D. (1987). *Educating the reflective practitioner*. San Franciso: Jossey-Bass.

Shakespeare, W. (1978). *The annotated Shakespeare, Vol. 3, The Tragedies and Romances* (A. L. Rowse, Ed.). New York: Clarkson N. Potter, Inc. Publishers.

Silverstein, S. (1981). *A light in the attic*. Toronto, ON: Fitzhenry & White Ltd.

Starhawk. (1997). *Dreaming the dark: Magic, sex, and politics*. Boston: Beacon Press.

Sullivan, G. (2004). Studio art as research practice. In E. Eisner & M. Day (Eds.), *Handbook of research and policy in art education* (pp. 795814). Mahwah, NJ: Lawrence Erlbaum Associates.

Szekely, G. (1990). The teaching of art as a performance. *Art Education, 43*(3), 6–17.

Szekely, G. (1998). *The art of teaching art*. Needham Heights, MA: Simon & Schuster.

Taylor, C. (1989). *Sources of the self*. Cambridge, MA: Harvard University Press.

Taylor, C. (1992). The lost art of pedagogy: An exploration in three parts ~ part two. *Canadian Review of Art Education, 19*(1), 64–68.

Tennyson, A. (1972). *The new Oxford book of English verse* (H. Gardner, Ed.). New York and Oxford: Oxford University Press.

Tindall, B. (2005). *Mozart in the jungle: Sex, drugs and classical music*. New York: Grove Press.

Van Manaan, M. (1997). *Researching lived experience*. London, ON: The Althouse Press.

Wachowiak, F., & Clements, R. D. (2006). *Emphasis art: A qualitative art program for elementary and middle schools* (8th ed.). Boston: Pearson.

Welty, E. (2004). Listening. In L. Z. Bloom & L. Z. Smith (Eds.), *The brief Arlington reader: Canons and contexts* (pp. 48–53). New York: Bedford St. Martin's.

Whitehouse, M. (1999). The Tao of the body. In P. Pallaro (Ed.), *Authentic movement*. London and Philadelphia: Jessica Kingsley Publishers.

Wilson, C. (1957). *The outsider*. New York: Tarcher/Putnam.

Witherall, C., & Noddings, N. (1991). *Stories lives tell; Narrative and dialogue in education*. New York: Teachers College Press.

Wood, D. (1982). *Move, sing, listen, play: Preparing the young child for music*. Toronto, ON: G. V. Thompson

Wordsworth, W. (1979). *The Prelude, 1799, 1805, 1850. A Norton critical edition*. New York: W. W. Norton and Company.

Wyatt, K., & Schroeder, C. (1998). *Pocket music theory: A comprehensive and convenient source for all musicians*. Milwaukee, WI: Hall Leonard Corporation.

Yeats, W. B. (1961). *Collected poems of W.B. Yeats*. London: Macmillan & Company.

Yourcenar, M. (1974). *Memoirs of Hadrian*. UK: Redwood Burn Limited, Trowbridge & Esher.

Zukav, G. (1990). *The seat of the soul*. New York: Fireside

Zwicky, J. (1992). *Lyric philosophy*. Toronto, ON: University of Toronto Press.

Lightning Source UK Ltd.
Milton Keynes UK
UKOW06f1813080616

275905UK00014B/219/P

9 789460 910357